The Open University

AA303 Understanding Comparative History: Britain and America from 1760

Book 1   Liberal Capitalism: Political and Economic Aspects

Part 1   Political Culture: Britain and America to 1870

Part 2   Industrialization and Economic Growth to 1870

The Open University
Walton Hall
Milton Keynes
MK7 6AA

First published 1997

Edited, designed and typeset by the Open University

Printed in the United Kingdom by the Alden Press, Oxford

ISBN 0 7492 1183 0

This text is a component of the Open University course AA303 *Understanding Comparative History: Britain and America from 1760*. Details of this and other Open University courses are available from the Central Enquiry Service, The Open University, PO Box 200, Walton Hall, Milton Keynes MK7 6YZ. Tel.: 01908 653078.

1.1

Contents

Part 1 Political Culture: Britain and America to 1870

Part 2   Industrialization and Economic Growth to 1870

Part 1 Political Culture: Britain and America to 1870

1.1 The eighteenth-century Commonwealthman: ideas of state and society in Britain and the American colonies

Any comparison of ideas about the state in Britain and the American colonies must begin with the assumption that both owed much to a common heritage. But, although the thirteen colonies were settled largely by British men and women, these were people who rejected certain aspects of English society. This was even true in Virginia, which, despite its commercial origins and retention of an established church, was from the start settled by those sympathetic to the puritan wing of that church. Specific American political forms emerged. The similarity between American governmental institutions and those of England was often superficial. By the late eighteenth century the revolution crisis would force Americans to face up to the discrepancies between alien theory and native practice and to produce coherent views of society and state for themselves. While eighteenth-century Americans did not make revolutionary claims, their evolving ideas and political practices contained within them the seeds of a later revolution in state theory.

Whig and Tory theories of the state

The key concepts of English constitutional theory were developed in the seventeenth century. In both England and the colonies, innovative political thought was normally the product of tension. England's period of struggle had occurred in the previous century when ideas about the ancient constitution, mixed and limited monarchy, contract, natural rights, kingship by divine right and hereditary succession, non-resistance and passive obedience, and patriarchal authority had been formulated. In the eighteenth century the Whigs and the Tories refined their ideas to accommodate current political needs.

In the post-Restoration period (c.1660–88) after the traumas of the civil war and interregnum, the Tories were chiefly concerned to establish a strong and stable government which would preserve property and the rights of the propertied to rule. Only an absolute monarchy – that is, a monarchy in which ultimate sovereignty or power rested – could achieve this. Doctrines of divine right kingship, an indefeasible hereditary succession, non-resistance and passive obedience to the tyrannical monarch were central to this 'ideology of order'. Robert Filmer's *Patriarcha*, posthumously published in 1680, epitomized Tory ideology. The king had the authority of a father over his children. This authority over them was given him by God, and it was absolute, unlimitable and irresistible.

The moderate Tories were forced to accept the Revolution of 1688 as a *fait accompli*, but despite the severe blow which this struck at their principles, they did not embrace the Whig justification for overturning James II's monarchy. Instead, they salvaged what they could of their beliefs. They abandoned support for absolute monarchy and transferred their allegiance to the mixed monarchy of king and Parliament. The only limitation which they acknowledged to the principle of hereditary succession was that denying the succession to Catholics. The authority of the mixed monarchy was regarded as absolute: principles of non-resistance and passive obedience were retained. The success of the *de facto* kingship of William III proved to the Tories that God had ordained this change in the succession and had commanded obedience to it. William Sherlock's *The Case of Allegiance due to Sovereign Powers* (1691) put well the new Tory view that subjects owed obedience to divine authority rather than to any person who might claim the legal right to rule. It is God who creates governments. A divinely ordained government can be recognized by its ability to protect its subjects. James II's absence made him unable to offer this protection. William demonstrated his ability to do just this. Initially this theory permitted conditional acceptance of the new regime, but by 1701 most Tories found themselves able to vote for the Act of Settlement.

The Whigs denied that England had ever had an absolute monarchy. The exclusion crisis of 1679–81 (involving an attempt to exclude the Catholic Prince James of York from the succession) had produced a Whig theory that government was by consent: subjects possessed certain rights – life, liberty and property – and a government which infringed these was subject to the process of law and, in the last resort, removal. Historians have tended to assume that Whig theory rested upon John Locke's view of the contractual origins of government. His *Two Treatises of Government* (1690) sets against the Stuart (and Tory) belief in the descending power of monarchs that of power ascending to the king from the people.

Locke wrote that authority was given conditionally by the people to the king. In putting forward this important view that the authority of the king to rule rested upon the consent of the people over whom he ruled, Locke also explained that governments were designed to protect the rights of each individual to life, liberty and property. In the original state of nature, anarchy had prevailed. People combined together to form political societies and entrusted civil rulers with authority over them. These rulers were bound to respect property, to safeguard the individual against unfair arrest, trial or execution, and to ensure that murderers and thieves were punished. At the same time, the government assured to each individual liberty from domination by another, liberty to live peaceably according to common laws. Should a government not ensure these liberties, it forfeited the people's trust and they would combine to overthrow it forcibly. The Whigs certainly adopted some of Locke's views, but the details of his theory of contract were too revolutionary to be acceptable. In fact, Whigs found an appeal to the theory of the ancient constitution of England which had emerged in the course of the seventeenth century far more attractive.

According to the Whigs, historically the supreme authority in the kingdom had been the legislature. Customary and immemorial English law – the common law which contained the wisdom of successive generations – limited the actions of the legislature. Statute law, produced by the legislature, defined and clarified the principles of the common law but did not override it. Despite the appeal to history, this theory of the origin and nature of the state ahistorically assumed that the English constitution was fixed and had not evolved through the ages.

It has been demonstrated that, while the Whigs adopted the more conservative features of Locke's contract theory, they rarely appealed to it when justifying their actions, preferring to conflate the appeal to the ancient constitution with a more general belief in a vague concept of government by consent. They accepted with alacrity the view that the propertied people combined to set up a particular form of government, but shrank back from Locke's radical theory of the *pactum unionis,* in which people left the state of nature and voluntarily agreed to form a society and live under laws designed to protect their natural rights. The Whigs could not accept the idea that the people were *sovereign.* According to their understanding, the people did not set up the monarchy; rather, the monarch held his power in trust for the benefit and protection of the people. If he abused this trust he could be resisted.

In fact, the very success of the 1688 Glorious Revolution seemed to discourage further speculation about the origins and nature of government. Both Tories and Whigs were dedicated to the preservation of property and the interests of the propertied classes. The Whigs were not democrats. The Bill of Rights and the Act of Settlement were regarded as having secured the continued and extended participation of the existing ruling classes – the natural leaders – in government. Later, continental observers such as Voltaire and Montesquieu bolstered English pride in her balanced mixed constitution in which sovereignty was seen to lie not in the king alone but in king, Lords and Commons – the three social orders of monarchy, aristocracy and democracy. It was a system which ensured against corruption and arbitrary government through checks and balances. The English felt distinctive in achieving this supposed perfection of government. The euphoric atmosphere was added to by an increased commercial prosperity. This was the period in which James Thomson wrote *Rule Britannia* (1740) and *Liberty* (1735–6). In general, the American colonists shared this pride in England's constitutional achievement while becoming frustrated with its manifestations in the colonies.

The Commonwealth critique

There was a continuous minority critique of the settlement within England. During the middle of the seventeenth century a number of writers had penned significant works on the nature and functions of the state. Notable among them were James Harrington, John Milton, Andrew Marvell and Edmund Ludlow. Harrington's *Oceana* suggested devices to protect the liberties which he said the state was created to preserve. He explained that the safeguards offered to each individual must be based upon the rule of law, emphasized the importance of government by consent, and insisted upon the guarantee of certain basic rights such as freedom of religion. Harrington urged that the evils which would arise as a result of ambition and faction should be guarded against by rotation in office, by the ballot and by divisions of power between the different parts of the constitution. Most Whigs spoke of the balance of power between the different orders of society but not of a separation of functions of government; Harrington's view was distinctive and was to be shared, over a century later, by some Americans. Harrington also thought that, during a time of rapid economic change, political power must be redistributed to adjust to the redistribution of property. Milton's major contribution to the Whig canon in general and the Commonwealth tradition in particular lay in his insistence upon the right of rebellion against a tyrannical government.

In the period after the Restoration some Whigs built upon this Commonwealth tradition. Henry Neville (1640–94) followed Harrington's general line of thought but felt that there was a need for specific constitutional provision for the economic situation which Harrington had diagnosed. The balance of the economy had shifted in favour of the Commons and away from the king, who was placed in financial dependence upon the Commons and yet retained power. The king should hand over to the Commons his power to make war and peace, to control the militia, to appoint to offices and to control expenditure. Certain rights must be safeguarded by the writ of habeas corpus, by a guaranteed right to petition, by the election of MPs, by limits placed upon the length of individual parliaments and by an enforced minimal interval between parliaments. Algernon Sidney (1622–83) conflated an appeal to the ancient constitution with a belief in government by consent. He suggested that there was a need for constant change and adaptation in government. This was an argument to which later Commonwealthmen* and American leaders subscribed. Different political systems were set up to serve specific circumstances and peoples and to safeguard basic rights; experiment was necessary to find the best government. Marchamont Needham (1620–78) presented views which emphasized the role of the people themselves as defenders of their liberties. A free suffrage, a broadly based government, and the education of the people in ideas of freedom would help to ensure that they fulfilled this role and were not content to live under tyranny and oppression. Much later Thomas Jefferson (the third American president) was to display a similar faith in the ability of the sovereign people to rule in the interests of liberty.

* Women were excluded from the political debates of the period.

At a time when the majority of both Tories and Whigs conceived of the 1688 Revolution settlement as the final word in a long constitutional struggle and when the Lord Chancellor in 1766 was able to state, 'I seek for the liberty and Constitution of this kingdom no farther back than the Revolution, there I make my stand', the Commonwealth view that the constitutional experiment was a continuing one was important. Time and again they wrote that government must change to suit new circumstances. They were anything but complacent. They perceived an urgent threat to the 'perfect constitution' of England. Robert Molesworth (1656–1725) showed in his *Account of Denmark* (1693) how the Danes had lost their liberties and come under absolutist rule. The same might well happen in Britain. Parliament was seen as the guardian of the people's rights against such an eventuality, and frequent, even annual, parliaments were pleaded for by eighteenth-century Commonwealthmen. They were far from satisfied when the Septennial Act of 1716 reversed the earlier legislation regulating the interval between parliaments to three years. Moreover, it became common to demand, with Molesworth, new and more representative constituencies, the enfranchisement of new groups of men (leaseholders), and parliamentary reform which would prevent government-appointed and beholden office-holders sitting in the Commons.

Side by side with these demands developed a critique of cabinet government, of Robinocracy (i.e. rule by Robert Walpole and his clique), which was seen as exercising a new tyranny that circumvented and confounded the principle of government by consent. Some perceptive critics saw that the English government functioned harmoniously not because of the efficacy of the much applauded system of checks and balances but because the government *managed* the House of Commons. There was a virulent if ineffectual opposition to Walpole's style of government (1721–42). In a Robinocracy the sovereignty of the legislature was infringed. The argument against standing armies was a prominent feature of Commonwealth programmes to protect the liberties of the people against corrupt government.

American ideas of the state

The relationship between ideas of the state in Britain and the colonies before 1760 was a complex one. Most Americans, if they contemplated the issue at all, shared the Whig faith in the settlement. Americans were aware that they were English subjects and proud of the mixed constitution which, they assumed, protected their liberties as Englishmen. But there was also a lively political tradition in the colonies which was specific to their development. The covenanting tradition both reinforced and informed American readings of the English constitution. It made the full-blown contract theory of Locke far more attractive to radical Americans than it was to mainstream English opinion.

The germ was planted early in the history of the colonies that government therein was brought about by a covenant of the people in the people's interests. In 1620 the pilgrims who landed at Plymouth had covenanted together to form a body politic where no government existed in order to prevent anarchy:

> We do by these presents solemnly and mutually in the presence of God and one of another, covenant and combine ourselves together into a Civil Body Politic, for our better ordering and preservation and furtherance of the ends aforesaid; and by virtue hereof to enact, constitute and frame such just and equal laws, ordinances, acts, constitutions and offices, from time to time, as shall be thought most meet and convenient for the general good of the Colony, unto which we promise all due submission and obedience.

> (Quoted in Douglas, 1955)

The Plymouth tradition of covenanted government was only one of several dominant in the thirteen colonies, but it was to be of great importance when the colonists came to make their stand against George III and to justify this stance. There was an underlying sense that this was a new society with a government created by the people. When John Adams later described the settling of America in the early seventeenth century, he urged that the emigrants had set out to create in a new land a pure, free, civil and ecclesiastical government. The settlers had themselves been undefiled – America's had been a truly virgin birth:

> It was this great struggle that peopled America ... a love of
> universal liberty, and hatred, a dread, a horror, of the infernal
> confederacy of a tyrannical church and state projected, con-
> ducted, and accomplished the settlement of America.

> (Quoted in Adams, 1850–6, vol. III, p. 451)

According to this perspective, the society which Americans, in their 'state
of nature', had set up with their own consent was destined to preserve the
liberties imperilled in England herself in the seventeenth century by
Charles I and Laud, by Charles II and James II, and in the eighteenth
century by George III and his ministers. The writings of the Commonwealthman Daniel Neal on the Puritans provided the colonists with a
historical overview entirely congenial to a belief in America's mission to
preserve liberty. As Voltaire said, the colonies were better able to defend
liberty because life there was so much more simple and pure than in
England. The basis of government was much wider, and militia armies
ensured the defence of society – not the subjugation of individuals.

Underneath this calm confidence in America's freedom mission ran
a swell of discontent. Eighteenth-century Americans were for the most
part unaware of the majority British view of their place under the constitution. They believed that the government of the individual colonies
replicated that of England. The growth of bicameral (two-chamber) legislative bodies in most colonies made comparisons inevitable. The legislature in some sense represented the community and legislated for it. With
this comparison went disillusionment because the colonies wanted their
assemblies to behave like and be treated as Parliament. Political reality
was frustrating. In the colonies the executive (governor) was legally
stronger but politically weaker than the English executive. The Crown so
bound the colonial governors and lieutenant governors with detailed
instructions that the latter were unable to compromise politically with the
representative assemblies with whom they had to work. Executive intran-
sigence provided no basis for harmonious relations. At the same time, the
governors exercised little patronage and therefore could do little to
manage the assemblies, which were ridden with factions. The executive
appeared both ineffectual and irksome. The power of the executive,
delegated by the king of England, was at odds with the conception of the
assemblyman, who was the attorney of his constituents, bound by their
instructions and responsible for pursuing their precise, local interests. In
many of the colonies the political picture was that of a struggle between
'legally overgreat but politically weak executive and assertive, implacable
democracy' (Bailyn, 1968). In reality, the perfectly balanced British constitution did not seem to have brought stability to colonial government.

As we have indicated, Americans shared many assumptions with the
Commonwealthmen. Radical Americans had become accustomed to
analysing the British political situation through the eyes of the minority
Commonwealth opposition. They shared a common vocabulary and a
common pattern of thought. They saw the political world as a continuing
struggle between power and liberty. They read *Cato's Letters* (which
charged the ministers of the Crown with swooping down upon power,
armed with techniques of corruption) only eight months after they were
first published in England. They read James Burgh's *Britain's
Remembrancer* (printed three times in the colonies before 1760), which

castigated the evils of British political life. They took in the message of Henry Bolingbroke's *The Craftsman*, which attacked Robert Walpole's system of government with potent irony. As a result, the radical American colonists shared a view (itself atypical in England) that there was a conspiracy at work against English liberty. They doubted that sufficient safeguards had been provided after 1688 against arbitrary rule. Some extra protection was needed. The remedy which they eventually proposed – a written constitution – was more dramatic than that suggested by the Commonwealthmen, although the Jeffersonian belief in the people as guardians of their own liberties certainly echoed the views of some Commonwealthmen.

At first the ministers of the Crown were suspected of complicity: the *New England Courant* of 17–24 June 1723 saw them using the governors to do their dirty work in the colonies, while keeping the king in ignorance. Some were already worried that the English settlement of liberties had not been extended fully to the colonies, which remained unprotected against arbitrary power. For the most part, however, colonists were happy to accept the theory that if only the oppressed appealed to the monarch, the patriot king would realize the validity of their grievances and save them, while punishing his ministers. This position was tenable because, prior to the mid-century, Tory and Whig theorists had given little thought to the nature of the bond between the colonies and the mother country.

American fears about British intentions were strengthened by intervention in colonial affairs. For example, in 1759 the Crown disallowed a Pennsylvania law which granted life tenure to judges (a feature of the judiciary in Britain). The Stamp Act and the Townshend Acts, which taxed colonial trade, represented a further unwelcome tightening of British control and a reminder that the British believed the English Parliament was sovereign in the thirteen colonies. To make matters worse, the spectre of a standing army became a reality when two regiments of British troops arrived in Boston in October 1768. The precarious *détente* achieved by the withdrawal of the Townshend Acts and of the troops was destroyed finally by the Boston Tea Party* of December 1773 and the coercive legislation of Parliament which followed upon it. Thus it was that Thomas Jefferson in *A Summary View ...* (1774) was able to level against Britain the charge that it had deliberately attempted to enslave the colonies, to bring them under arbitrary government and total dominion.

Dynamic of liberty

During the troubles which followed the Stamp Act of 1765, colonial leaders began to look to British theorists – particularly of the Commonwealth school – to discover arguments pertaining to the relationship between England and her colonies. Some of the Commonwealthmen were deeply concerned about the position of conquered or settled countries within the English constitution, principally with reference to Scotland and Ireland. Was government within the empire rooted in any kind of consent? John Trenchard devoted the 106th of *Cato's Letters* to the question of the colonies. He spoke of the undoubted economic advantage to England of colonial products but argued that this exploitative relationship could not be maintained for ever. The colonists could not be expected 'to continue their subjection to another only because their

* Boston's Sons of Liberty (see Essay 1.2) mounted a raid disguised as Mohawk Indians on tea-carrying ships, throwing the cargo in the harbour. It was provoked by the British government's attempt to assert Parliament's right to tax colonies and curb illegal tea smuggling with the Dutch.

grandfathers were acquainted'. When these political children of England grew to adulthood, they would (as Locke had argued) have the right to reject the authority of the father. When the colonies no longer had need of England's protection, they would seek independence. Only if mutual interests were served by the close relationship would the colonists agree to maintain it. Here in a nutshell was the rationale of government to which the colonists would later subscribe. Government should be in the people's interests. When the people were economically and militarily viable, they could resist a government which was unable or unwilling to protect them. William Molyneux' *Case of Ireland* (1698) was to provide ready ammunition for the anti-colonial and anti-mercantilist interests of the eighteenth century. Molyneux spoke out against British attempts to override the acts of the Irish courts. His contemporary, William King (1650–1729), urged that government must be by consent and bemoaned the exclusion of the Irish from full civil participation in Ireland's affairs. He dubbed the unfortunate act of George I declaring Ireland to be dependent upon England 'an enslaving act'. Other British theorists concentrated upon Scotland. Andrew Fletcher coupled his traditional Commonwealth programme with a suggestion that a federal system be introduced to include the kingdoms of England and Scotland. Francis Hutcheson (1694–1746) urged that the prosperity of the whole was the criterion of good government, and that any people had the right to resist once it was clear the actions of government were inimical to the good of all parts or one part.

The radical colonists found much in this literature to appeal to them. Within the general framework of a federal relationship between the mother country and the colonies, they were able to enlarge on their own conviction that the colonies had internal sovereignty. Hutcheson's discussion of the federal relationship was printed practically verbatim in *The Massachusetts Spy* of 13 February 1772. Trenchard's opinions were well known. During the 1760s the framework of colonial thought was imperial: the request was for greater autonomy within the empire. This request found support in minority English opinion, but it was an issue which did not interest the mainstream of English thought. The questions of consent and direct representation raised alarm in British political circles.

The pressure of events and the Commonwealth framework of their thought led many Americans to consider issues which were not at the forefront of most English minds and to develop new concepts. Like the Commonwealthmen they moved from the specific to the general application. The Americans often began with the minority Commonwealth position and then moved to a more fully developed, articulate and original concept. The colonists arrived at a definition of both liberty and natural rights which government was set up to protect and also of the means with which this protection could be achieved and guaranteed. When the British and the colonists spoke of the constitution in the early 1760s, they meant that arrangement of institutions, laws and customs – and the principles which informed them – which made up the English system of government. The colonists admittedly laid more emphasis from the beginning upon the 'fundamental laws and rules of the constitution which ought not to be infringed' than did the British, but basically both shared the traditional view. The English maintained this position while the Americans moved on.

Gradually Americans attempted to define the fundamentals of the constitution. By 1768 Samuel Adams was declaring that 'the constitution is fixed; it is from thence that the supreme legislative as well as the supreme executive derives its authority'. While the Tories maintained that authority was given to a particular form of government (the mixed monarchy in the English case) and the Whigs thought that governmental authority was a trust exercised by the king in Parliament in the interests of the people, the new American view was that authority for a government to rule rested in the constitution which declared the fundamental and unencroachable liberties of the people. In order to prevent encroachments on fundamental rights, the legislature had to be prohibited from altering the constitution. A constitution had to mark out the boundaries of government. In England there was no such device: there the legislature could accomplish anything because no one parliament could bind another. The new thinking was expanded in Obadiah Hulme's *An Historical Essay on the English Constitution* (London, 1771), which saw a constitution as a 'painting for eternity' that arose out of an agreement of the people, and the *Genuine Principles of the Anglo-Saxon or English Constitution* (Pennsylvania, 1776), which stressed that the constitution must be written down if it were to achieve permanence and that any amendments must receive majority consent. Such views remained foreign to British thinking.

But common to both British and American thought was the fear of government expressed in the arguments favouring a written constitution. Thomas Paine's sentiments as expressed in *Common Sense* (1776) summed up not only the thinking behind the initial constitution but also the feelings of Englishmen:

> Some writers have so confounded society with government, as to leave little or no distinction between them; whereas they are not only different, but have different origins. Society is produced by our wants, and government by our wickedness; the former promotes our happiness positively by uniting our affections, the latter negatively by restraining our vices. The one encourages intercourse, the other creates distinctions. The first is a patron, the last a punisher.
>
> Society in every state is a blessing, but government even in its best state is but a necessary evil; in its worst state an intolerable one; for when we suffer, or are exposed to the same miseries by a government, which we might expect in a country without government, our calamity is heightened by reflecting that we furnish the means by which we suffer ...

(Paine, 1980 edn, p. 65)

Leaving aside the egalitarian strain of Paine's argument and his assumption that the good people are the source of governmental authority, we are left with an excellent definition of the negative function of government. It is set up only to preserve the liberties of the people. It is a restraining force.

In drawing up a defence of liberty and natural rights, the colonists were forced to attend to the issue of sovereignty. In England it was believed to lie in the king, Lords and Commons in aggregate. The colonists moved towards restricting parliamentary sovereignty and thus, by definition, denying it because sovereignty is ultimate power. Parliament, some said, had power to control matters which were external to the individual colonies, while the colonies themselves were sovereign in internal matters. John Dickinson saw Parliament as having the right to regulate imperial commerce but not to tax the colonies. His work assumed a distinction between an empire (in which different component parts might have various relationships with the Crown) and a unitary nation. Some colonists experimented with the idea that the king was a federal monarch who derived his authority to rule in different ways. Calvin's case (1608) provided a useful precedent for the view that subjects of the king were not necessarily subjects of the English mixed government. Effectively, radical colonists were pushed into denying parliamentary sovereignty even before they claimed independence.

This denial had its roots in the colonial assumption that power ascended from the people and that this relationship did not exist between the English Parliament and the American people, whom it did not represent. Although MPs in the medieval English Parliament had been regarded as direct attorneys of the people, there had been a movement towards a conception of virtual rather than actual representation in the House of Commons. When Edmund Burke addressed his Bristol electors in 1774, he declared that Parliament was not 'a congress of ambassadors from different and hostile interests, which interests each must maintain, as an agent and advocate, against other agents and advocates; but Parliament is a deliberate assembly of one nation, with one interest, that of the whole, where, not local purposes, not local prejudices ought to guide, but the general good, resulting from general reason of the whole'. The colonial tradition of attorneyship was, however, much more recent and vital. Residential qualifications for representatives were enforced; delegates were bound closely to their constituencies by detailed instructions. Virtual representation held no sway in American political life before the Revolution. James Otis put it well in 1765 when he said that the British might 'as well prove that the British House of Commons in fact represented all the people of the globe as those in America', as he argued against the theory that, while the Americans had no seats in the English Parliament, they were yet represented by it.

Thomas Paine's concept of 'the design and end of government' well illustrates the radical conviction that government must represent directly the interests of the people; it displays the similarity between Paine's views and Locke's twin compacts – the *pactum unionis* (which created civil society) and the *pactum subjectionis* (which created a specific form of government). Paine wrote in *Common Sense*:

> Thus necessity, like a gravitating power, would soon form our newly arrived emigrants into society, the reciprocal blessings of which would supersede and render the obligations of law and government unnecessary while they remained perfectly just to each other; but as nothing but heaven is impregnable to vice, it will unavoidably happen, that in proportion as they surmount the first difficulties of emigration, which bound them together in a common cause, they will begin to relax in their duty and attachment to each other; and this remissness will point out the necessity of establishing some form of government to supply the defect of moral virtue.

With an increase in population it would prove inconvenient for decisions to be made directly by all members of a colony:

> This will point out the convenience of their consenting to leave the legislative part to be managed by a select number chosen from the whole body, who are supposed to have the same concerns at stake which those have who appointed them, and who will act in the same manner as the whole body would act were they present.

> (Paine, 1980 edn, pp. 66–7)

The question of the continuing role of the people in the government of society took on added importance after independence. Thomas Jefferson, convinced as he was that the Constitution should protect the 'rights of man' and that the bounds of government should remain inviolate, insisted that the people themselves should legislate for the living. The original US Constitution had set out the boundaries of government jurisdiction, but it had said little about the way in which that jurisdiction should be exercised. It had said what government must *not* do, not what governments must do. The only specification had been that the form of government must be republican or representative of the majority will. 'Each generation is as independent of the one preceding as that was of all which had gone before. It has then, like them, a right to choose for itself the form of government it believes most promotive of its own happiness.' Opportunities for changing the Constitution should be provided every twenty years or so because 'the earth belongs in usufruct to the living; that the dead have neither power nor rights over it ... No society can make a perpetual constitution, or even a perpetual law' (quoted in Lipscomb and Bergh, 1903).

Jefferson's belief in the continuing role of majority consent in American political life and in the need for each generation to experiment with forms of government and with laws which suited its needs, coupled with a commitment to the rights of man, had much in common with the Commonwealth view that governments should differ according to circumstances, saving that the purpose of government was the same in every case and that experiment was not only acceptable but desirable and necessary. But this view was not shared by all American leaders. Conservatives such as John Adams insisted that majority consent had been necessary in setting up the original contract but there was no place for repeated pacts – the majority of the future was bound by that of the past in the form of the Constitution. Jefferson's insistence that the people, if educated for liberty, would prove the best guardians of liberty (itself reminiscent of the views of Commonwealthmen) meant nothing to the conservatives, who feared attacks on property as a result of 'mobocracy'. While Jefferson's concept of popular sovereignty was repulsive to most British thinkers, his position was far less remote from the British than was that of Adams in one important respect – that one generation cannot bind another.

Did the Americans move towards democracy? It seems clear that the context of their thought was the traditional English belief that those with a stake in the community and economic freedom of action had the right to be asked for their consent and their opinions. Paine's plea in the 1775 *Pennsylvania Magazine* for women's civil rights was atypical. Effectively in the colonies far more adult white males owned sufficient freehold land to meet the qualification for the franchise (40 shilling freehold) than was the case in Britain – largely because land was much more plentiful and cheap. Nevertheless, between 80 and 90 per cent of the population was disenfranchised in immediate post-revolutionary America. Black slaves, freed blacks, indentured white servants, women and white male adolescents (who were required to do militia service but not allowed to vote) were excluded from political rights. The colonists, like the British, acted within the existing framework – only the independent were allowed to constitute the people. Many of the more radical colonists did share with the Commonwealthmen a demand for a wider suffrage and especially for the enfranchisement of leaseholders. But the Constitution as drawn up in 1787 made no provision for the enfranchisement of the expanding urban proletariat. While colonists often saw the contradiction between their own fight for liberty and natural rights (which included the demand that no man have dominion over another) and the subjection in which they kept black slaves, civil rights and freedom for slaves remained contentious. If the colonists denied that the English Parliament could 'virtually represent' their interests, they clung to the idea that a section of the American population could and should 'virtually represent' the whole. And part of the leadership of the new nation wished to restrict the future participation of the democratic element in government. Adams moved dangerously close to substituting the sovereignty of the Constitution, based on an initial *pactum subjectionis,* for the sovereignty of the people. Such conservative elements shared much with the English Tories and Whigs – that the legislature was sovereign in the English case, that the Constitution was sovereign in Adams's view.

Subjects or citizens?

Independence brought the ex-colonists face to face with the question – who was an American citizen? In England people were born into subjection – native-born Englishmen were as if children of the monarch. The bond of allegiance between the subject and the monarch was inalienable, as Filmer had argued in the seventeenth century. On the other hand, Lockean ideas specifically denied that the bond was natural or unbreachable. As we have suggested, Locke's full theory of contract with its logical concomitant – popular sovereignty – was not generally accepted in Britain, and eighteenth-century British thinkers did not radically modify their positions on subjection or citizenship to accommodate the central ambiguity caused by Locke's contribution. But the colonies moved towards denying the personal and dissoluble nature of the individual's relationship with the monarch. Colonial governments had always been anxious to increase their populations and had encouraged immigration by promising the privileges which pertained to natural-born subjects. Naturalization came to be regarded implicitly as a form of contract between an individual and a community. The alien chose the community and promised to abide by its rules; the community offered protection and liberties in exchange for this allegiance and service. This concept was not fully articulated until the time of the Revolution when it was extended to include the relationship between the natural-born subject and the state. Unlike England there were no gradations of subjection – either one was a citizen or one was an alien. Parliament and the king held to the belief that subjectship could be conferred only by a free grace from the sovereign. In practice the English Parliament had relented in 1740 by permitting the colonies to issue naturalization grants without recourse to itself. When in 1773 George III banned local naturalization acts, this was seen as an attack upon the belief that citizenship arose out of a contractual relationship between community and individual and not out of a natural relationship between monarch and subject. Subjectship was a concept peculiar to 'descending power' views of government; citizenship, on the other hand, pertained to contractual theories or 'ascending power' analyses of the origins of government.

In the debate over citizenship the relationship between Britain and her colonies was itself given further definition. The Declaratory Act of 18 March 1766 set out the English view that the colonies were the children of the British state and their inhabitants the children of the British king. The king had the authority of a father, natural and uncontestable, over these subjects. America, it was said, had always accepted this relationship by acknowledging the sovereignty of Parliament in conferring citizenship. The doctrine of discovery was used to show how emigrants had taken with them applicable English laws and statutes to the colonies, had continued to claim the birthright benefits of common law, and had tacitly admitted that they were bound by acts of Parliament thereafter which specified applicability to the colonies.

Initially the colonists often accepted the doctrine of discovery and consequent subordination to the British Parliament. This was, however, always regarded as a limited subordination, and, in practice, parliamentary intervention in colonial affairs had been minimal. In the 1760s and 1770s the colonists put forward the view that there were certain rights contained in 'subjectship', as defined by the common law, which Parliament could not infringe; that allegiance to the English government was owed in return for satisfactory protection; and that Parliament's authority in the colonies depended upon consent. But the concept of a remote and unrepresentative Parliament legislating for the colonies became problematic. Benjamin Franklin suggested that the American position was analagous to that of the Scots under James I (who united the English and Scottish crowns in 1603 after the death of Queen Elizabeth I) – their allegiance was to the monarch's person and not to the institutions of the English government. This again led to a denial of the British idea that the empire was a unitary state.

The separation of the community of allegiance from the political community was important during the Revolution. It was not the king in the English Parliament but the king in all his parliaments who had sovereignty in the Americas. Such views led to proposals for representational imperial parliaments to settle issues of common concern within the empire. Joseph Galloway made such a proposal to the First Continental Congress in 1774. At this point many colonists continued to believe that the patriot king would use his prerogative to restrain his English Parliament from encroaching on other jurisdictions. Both Benjamin Franklin and Thomas Jefferson laid emphasis upon the correct use of the royal prerogative. Yet there came a point when the colonists had to face the question – what were they to do if the king encroached upon American rights? The answer lay in the idea that government was based upon a contract between government and people and that the bond of allegiance was sealed by protection. It was a *quid pro quo* relationship. The colonists were able to see George III as responsible for breaking this tie – he withdrew his protection by infringing their rights, and therefore they withdrew their allegiance and declared their independence. By 1776 the Americans had taken the decisive step of denying the inalienable nature of allegiance. New colonial constitutions were adopted which repudiated allegiance to the English king and often specified reciprocity as the basis for allegiance to the state.

There was dissent from this view. During the war the leaders felt justified in suppressing dissent in order to win the war. Afterwards there seemed to be a contradiction between the need to protect the government against the efforts of the disaffected to restore British rule and the fact that coercion undermined the declared American belief that legitimate government rested upon consent. The doctrine of the right of election emerged as the answer. In a revolution each individual would choose the side which his conscience approved. This choice had to be made within a certain time and was binding. British citizens in America who maintained their allegiance to the Crown after 1783 were treated as alien enemies. Continued residence in America implied compliance and made the individual subject to the community's sanctions. Pushed to its logical conclusion, the doctrine stated that allegiance was volitional – an individual could contract in and out of a community. The pressure of events had pushed the Americans into developing a theory of citizenship and allegiance which was alien to British thought.

Conclusion

In comparing American and British ideas about the state, one becomes aware that the two meet in the writings of the Commonwealthmen. That the colonists and the Commonwealthmen shared many of the same opinions is indisputable, but whether the Commonwealthmen actually influenced the actions of the colonists is a moot point. Certainly the colonists read and quoted from Commonwealth works – Trenchard, Molesworth, Hutcheson, Sidney were commonly consulted and cited as authorities. The radical opposition perspective on English governmental activity was important to the colonists as they argued that it was the king of England and not themselves who had breached the contract between people and government. But it may well be true that such writers were quoted because their views coincided with radical colonial preconceptions. Commonwealth arguments were cited in defence of the move to separate church and state and inaugurate religious freedom, but *de facto* established churches were weak in the American colonies where they existed and dissent was widely tolerated. Similarly, the colonists sympathized with Commonwealth demands for a wider franchise largely because the English suffrage was much narrower than in the colonies. Ideas of contractual government and of active and direct representation were already entrenched in colonial society, with its covenanting tradition and its tighter control of legislative action. Clearly the indebtedness of the Americans to the Commonwealthmen is a complex issue and is not proven.

The points of contact between the radical groups in the two countries were notable, especially before the Revolution crisis. Both groups argued that the authority of government lay in consent; that government was set up to protect the natural rights of individuals; that the English system of mixed government was imperfect because it did not adequately protect these rights against the corrupt and evasive tactics of ministerial tyranny; and that reforms were necessary to provide such safeguards. Commonwealthmen and colonists denied the right of conquest. But as the crisis progressed, the Americans moved ever closer to a commitment to Lockean contract theory from which even a theorist such as Algernon Sidney had shrunk. The ancient constitution to which Commonwealthmen had repeatedly appealed was seen as inadequate protection by the colonists, who replaced it with the concept of a written constitution which would enshrine the fundamentals and principles of government and set the bounds of government jurisdiction. Concepts of direct representation and popular sovereignty were explored more fully. A theory of citizenship – a volitional relationship between state and individual – replaced the idea of 'subjectship' prevalent in Britain, which even the Commonwealth had not overturned.

Americans drew upon existing English political ideas. Above all, they adopted the perspective of a minority element in English political thought which kept alive the ideas of some of the great seventeenth-century theorists and expanded upon them in the context of specific aspects of eighteenth-century politics. But during the course of the century the colonists were made to ask questions about the relationship between the individual and the state which seemed largely irrelevant to the English mind. It was on this ground that the colonists parted company with the Commonwealth canon. The problems which the colonists tackled in their fight for sovereignty in fact absorbed the interest of only a minority within an already atypical segment of English thought. The posture of Whig and Tory theorists was defensive: rejection of the principles which the colonists set out was regarded as a sufficient response. If the British did anything new, it was to make explicit already implicit assumptions about the authority of the king in Parliament and the permissibility of an exploitative relationship between a mother country and its subject peoples, and to reveal the fragility of even Whig commitment to the theory of the contractual foundations of government and the necessity of consent. By the close of the century the American was the citizen of a state, the Englishman the subject of a king.

References and further reading

Adams, C.F. (ed.) (1850–6) *The Works of John Adams*, Boston, Mass., Little, Brown.

Bailyn, Bernard (ed.) (1965) *Pamphlets of the American Revolution, 1750–1776*, Cambridge, Mass., Harvard University Press.

Bailyn, Bernard (1968) *The Origins of American Politics*, New York, Alfred A. Knopf.

Commager, Henry Steele (1944) *Majority Rule and Minority Rights*, Oxford University Press.

Dickinson, H.T. (1979) *Liberty and Property: Political Ideology in Eighteenth-Century Britain*, Methuen.

Douglas, David (ed.) (1955) *English Historical Documents, Volume IX, American Colonial Documents to 1776*, Eyre and Spottiswoode.

Kettner, James H. (1978) *The Development of American Citizenship, 1608–1870*, Chapel Hill, University of North Carolina Press.

Lipscomb, A.E. and Bergh, A.E. (eds) (1903) *The Writings of Thomas Jefferson*, Washington, DC.

Norton, Mary Beth (1974) *The British-Americans: The Loyalist Exiles in England, 1774–1789*, Constable.

Paine, Thomas (1980 edn) *Common Sense*, Penguin (first published 1776).

Robbins, Caroline (1959) *The Eighteenth-century Commonwealthman*, Cambridge, Mass., Harvard University Press.

1.2   'Sons of Liberty' and 'Friends of Freedom': popular politics in America and Britain, 1760–1800

During the 1760s Britain and her colonies were racked with popular disorder, and on both sides of the Atlantic this disorder was given a new political edge. In the colonies, orchestrated by the Sons of Liberty, it reached a climax in the demand for independence. In Britain the movement gained its impetus from John Wilkes during the 1770s, but other elements provided the spur in subsequent decades. It is in Britain's Friends of Freedom – Wilkites, Jacobins and others – that historians have detected both the genesis of parliamentary reform and the beginnings of British working-class consciousness. Together these movements represent a novel historical phenomenon: popular secular democracy, a decisive break not just in ideas but in modes of political action.

The crowd in America and Britain

Many foreign travellers to eighteenth-century England commented on the degree of individual and political freedom which they found among the lower orders of society. 'When one sees here how the lowliest carter shows an interest in public affairs,' wrote the Prussian Carl Philip Moritz, 'how the smallest children enter into the spirit of the nation; how everyone feels himself to be a man and an Englishman – as good as his King and his King's minister – it brings to mind thoughts very different from those we know when we watch the soldiers drilling in Berlin' (Moritz, 1965, p. 56). Moritz's comments are fairly typical, but most of these comments refer to the plebeian classes in London, and London was exceptional in many respects.

At the end of the eighteenth century, with a population of close on one million, London was the largest city in Europe. It teemed with clubs of different kinds; there were occupational clubs, lottery clubs and simply convivial clubs. Among these were gatherings at which political issues were formally debated. Lawyers, clerks, parish schoolmasters, petty tradesmen and artisans rubbed shoulders at these meetings. A correspondent of the *Gentleman's Magazine* visited the Robin Hood Club in 1754 and was 'surprised to find such amazing erudition', particularly when 'a shoemaker harangued him five minutes upon the excellency of the tenets maintained by Lord Bolingbroke' (quoted in Hans, 1951, pp. 168–71). But while there is more evidence for London, it would seem that such clubs were not a unique feature of the metropolis. Recent research has found similar debating societies and a lively attitude to politics among Birmingham artisans. How far such attitudes spread into rural areas is impossible to assess, but it would be wrong to write off the rural community simply as deferential or subservient, particularly given the way in which certain festive gatherings (the fifth of November, the annual fair, Shrovetide football matches, May Day, Plough Monday) could serve as a cover for a direct expression of hostility to gentry and persons in authority.

Similar attitudes are detectable among the population of Britain's thirteen colonies. Indeed the lack of deference and the independence of artisans and journeymen were probably more pronounced since the hierarchical structure of the colonies was only a poor imitation of that in Britain. In Virginia it was possible to find magnates living in the style of British gentlemen, but particularly in New England artisans energetically exerted their right to participate in the town meetings which dated back to the seventeenth-century origins of the northern colonies.

In 1747 the governor of Massachusetts expressed his concern about the unruly nature of Boston as follows:

> ... the principal cause of the mobbish turn in this town is in its Constitution; by which the management of it is devolved upon the populace assembled in their town meetings; where ... the meanest inhabitants who by their constant attendance there are generally in the majority and outvote the gentlemen, merchants, substantial traders and all the better part of the inhabitants to whom it is irksome to attend.

> (Quoted in Hofstadter, 1971, p. 142)

The most typical form of mass united action by eighteenth-century plebeians in both Britain and her colonies, however, was not participation in debating clubs or town meetings but crowd action. Some of this sprang out of boisterous popular recreation and traditional festivals. Yet many other disorders had clearly definable aims which the evocative words 'mob' and 'riot' tend to obscure.

The most common form of popular disorder in eighteenth-century Britain was the food riot. When bread (and bread was very much the staff of life), meat or dairy produce rose above what the crowd considered to be a fair price, then shopkeepers and stallholders found themselves the victims of crowd action as goods were taken by force and distributed for the 'fair' price. This 'fair' price was not taken as an excuse for theft or for paying less than was usual in years of plenty.

Sometimes crowds prevented the removal of grain when they believed that there was a shortage, or the threat of a shortage, in their neighbourhood. Millers and farmers suspected of sharp practice or hoarding corn had their property destroyed; their grain might be strewn along the roadway or in rivers and canals, no matter how severe the shortage. Similar notions of 'fairness' and 'justice' can be found in other forms of popular disorder: riots directed against new toll gates or enclosures, or against ballots for the militia or recruiting parties for the army and navy.

There were food riots, anti-press-gang riots, attacks on customs men and so forth in the thirteen colonies. There were also significant land riots. During the 1740s New Englanders spreading down into New York province found much of the rich land on the Connecticut and Massachusetts borders untouched and, save on the terms of a few great landowners, untouchable. The New Englanders squatted on the land and rioted to preserve their 'right' to do so. Occasionally the line between riot and rebellion in colonial America was a fine one when small farmers and frontiersmen believed that their rights and interests were being ignored by the complacent tidewater gentry (a term used to describe those wealthy gentlemen, generally landowners, living on the settled land by the coast, far from the frontier). In 1764 several hundred men from the Pennsylvania frontier marched on Philadelphia, protesting that insufficient action was being taken against marauding Indians. Between 1764 and 1771 the frontier 'Regulators'* of North Carolina campaigned against corrupt local officials and the exorbitant fees of lawyers. In 1771 the governor of the colony felt compelled to use the militia against them.

Groups of frontier settlers opposed to what they saw as the tyranny of the aristocratic tidewater politicians.

E.P. Thompson has argued that it is possible to detect a 'legitimizing notion' in almost every crowd action in eighteenth-century England – men and women (and women were especially prominent in food riots) rioted to have food at a price which they could afford, to glean for corn and kindling, to preserve their young men from the recruiting sergeant or press-gang (Thompson, 1991, ch. 4). Similar notions are detectable in American riots. Moreover this disorder could be regarded with a benevolent or paternalist eye. In 1737 Lord Granville told the House of Lords that 'the People seldom or never assemble in any riotous or tumultuous manner, unless they are oppressed, or at least imagine they are oppressed' (quoted in Rudé, 1964, p. 7). Ten years later it was inferred that from the numbers involved in New Jersey land riots 'they are wronged and oppressed, or else they would never *rebell agt. the Laws*'. In 1768 a correspondent of the *New York Journal* observed that 'tho' innocent Persons may sometimes suffer in popular Tumults, yet the general Resentment of the People is principally directed according to Justice, and the greatest Delinquent feels it most' (quoted in Maier, 1973, pp. 21–2).

In the spring of 1763 Britain signed the preliminaries of the Peace of Paris which ended the Seven Years' War and confirmed her as the sole ruler of Canada and the thirteen colonies on the north Atlantic seaboard. Criticism of the treaty in Britain led to the first shouts of 'Wilkes and Liberty!', while the British government's new security in America led it to propose measures which were to bring the Sons of Liberty into being.

'Wilkes and Liberty!'

On 19 April 1763 George III opened Parliament with the traditional King's speech in which he praised the treaty. Four days later, number 45 of an opposition journal, *The North Briton*, published by John Wilkes, MP for Aylesbury, lambasted the speech. The government responded with a general warrant for the arrest of the authors, printers and publishers of the journal, but not naming any individuals as such. Wilkes was arrested and held incommunicado for several days in the Tower while his papers were ransacked. When he appeared in court, Wilkes took his stand on his rights as an Englishman; he protested also that general warrants were illegal and that as an MP he was immune from arrest. He made an emotional appeal to the variety of gentlemen, shopkeepers and craftsmen who had been attracted to attend the trial:

> My Lords, the liberty of all peers and gentlemen, and, what touches me more sensibly, that of all the middling and inferior set of people, who stand most in need of protection, is in my case this day to be finally decided upon a question of such importance as to determine at once whether English liberty shall be a reality or a shadow.

(Quoted in Rudé, 1962, pp. 26–7)

Chief Justice Pratt (a friend of the opposition leaders) accepted Wilkes's protests and discharged him. Wilkes left the court to thunderous acclamation. But the government was not prepared to let matters rest, and the parliamentary opposition disliked Wilkes's playing to the gallery and the extreme behaviour he adopted in attempting to prosecute ministers and to get search warrants for their houses. The London crowd, and crowds in Aylesbury and Dover, hailed his appearance with shouts of 'Wilkes and Liberty!' An attempt to have number 45 of *The North Briton* burned by the public hangman outside the Royal Exchange was thwarted by crowd action in December, but later that month Wilkes fled abroad not prepared to face trial for seditious libel (*The North Briton*) and obscenity (an obscene spoof on Pope's *Essay on Man* called *The Essay on Women*). He was declared an outlaw.

The Stamp Act crisis and Sons of Liberty

Wilkes was only one of the government's problems. The Seven Years' War had been the most expensive in the nation's history, leaving a considerable debt; furthermore the government estimated that the annual cost of defending the new empire would amount to over £379,000. The ministers believed that the colonists should not endanger the empire by westward expansion, which would antagonize the Indians; a royal proclamation (not a legislative Act of Parliament) was issued to prohibit such expansion in October 1763. Ministers also wanted the colonists to contribute £100,000 to imperial defence, particularly because colonists generally paid little tax in comparison with Englishmen. In 1764 the Revenue (Sugar) Act was passed, designed to raise £45,000 for colonial defence. The Act, together with the limit on westward expansion, was unpopular with the colonists, but in the following year more taxes were sought with a Stamp Act. This put a duty on newspapers, pamphlets, many legal documents, cards and dice; it was similar to legislation which had been in force in Britain since 1694. The Act provoked an outcry. Delegates from different colonial legislatures met in New York in October 1765 and sent addresses and petitions to George III and his parliament. The missives of the Stamp Act Congress were loyal, but the precedent for a congress made up of delegates from the different colonies had now been set. In addition to this constitutional form of protest, there was widespread rioting, and merchants organized non-importation associations boycotting British goods. Early in 1766 the Stamp Act was repealed. Early the following year Charles Townshend, the Chancellor of the Exchequer, introduced a new set of duties on imports of glass, lead, paints, paper and tea. Again there was an outcry and in 1770 all the new duties were repealed, except for that on tea.

The crowd actions against the Stamp Act and in support of non-importation took many traditional forms. Officials were burned in effigy, some were even tarred and feathered; the houses and property of government supporters were attacked; Stamp Offices were demolished. The legitimizing notions of the crowds are fairly evident – the government was imposing new heavy financial burdens; men could argue that they were being taxed without being consulted, as there was no direct colonial representation in Parliament. Furthermore they were being asked to pay for an army which was being stationed in the provinces for what the government called defence; since Cromwell's day, standing armies had been anathema to ideas of English liberty. The Stamp Act riots began in August 1765, but organized local resistance groups (which merged into an inter-colonial organization) did not begin to emerge until the end of that year and did not really catch on until February 1766. These groups called themselves the Sons of Liberty. The term was not new; ten years earlier Connecticut had a club to defend civil and religious freedom called the True Sons of Righteous Liberty. It had obvious connotations given the boasted 'liberty' won by Englishmen during the seventeenth century and sought by seventeenth-century colonists fleeing from religious persecution. Local Sons of Liberty established committees of correspondence to link with neighbouring groups; they organized mass meetings to spread their ideas and overawe their opponents; they used the press (and they were fortunate that several significant printers were members) to advance their campaign. Much of the formal organization disappeared after the repeal of the Stamp Act, but the ideas of the Sons of Liberty continued to be discussed in the sympathetic press, and the same men came to the fore in organizing non-importation agreements and subsequent protests. The term 'Sons of Liberty' itself continued to serve as a label for supporters to the colonists' rights.

The evidence about who comprised the Sons of Liberty varies from colony to colony. However, it appears that while there were variations, in general the membership was drawn from the respectable and well-to-do: local officials, clergymen, professional men, merchants and tradesmen. These were men with something to lose, and although prepared to join crowd action, they were often concerned about some of the activities of their street allies and protested that they would 'suppress all Riots or unlawful Assemblies' and 'assist and support the Civil Magistrates in preserving the publick Peace and good Order' (quoted in Maier, 1973, p. 97). Many of the older historians of the Sons of Liberty tended to see crowd action which went further than such propertied gentlemen would have liked largely from the perspective of those gentlemen. Thus the attack on the house of Lieutenant Governor Thomas Hutchinson in Boston ten days after the initial Stamp Act Riot is described as a descent into anarchy. So, too, are the activities of the crowds in Newport, Rhode Island, allegedly under the leadership of a young Englishman, possibly a sailor, called John Weber. Yet it is equally probable that these crowds knew what they were doing and had 'legitimizing notions' rather different from the respectable Sons of Liberty. Thomas Hutchinson had a history of unpopularity, and his house had been threatened during the 1740s. Whether Weber was a crowd 'leader' (he had only been in Newport for three or four days before the riot, which makes such an assertion problematical) or whether he became a popular hero after his arrest, when further rioting was threatened unless he was released, remains an open question. Disorders to secure the release of arrested rioters were frequent in the immediate aftermath of food riots and similar actions.

Wilkes and popular radicalism

Wilkes returned from his European exile in 1768. He stood again for Parliament, and in a particularly turbulent election campaign he was elected member for the largely urban county of Middlesex – a county in which the franchise was notably broad. His success led to celebrations in the cities of London and Westminster; the jubilant crowds demanded that householders illuminate their windows in celebration, and those who failed to comply had their windows broken. Since he was still under sentence of outlawry, Wilkes ostentatiously surrendered himself to confinement in the King's Bench Prison. Crowds gathered outside the prison daily, and an attempt by magistrates backed by guards to disperse the crowds on 10 May 1768 resulted in what became known as the Massacre of St George's Fields when the troops fired, killing eleven and wounding about a dozen people. Nor was 'Wilkes and Liberty!' confined to London. There were demonstrations and petitions on his behalf from all over the country; the provincial press, which had rarely offered political comment before the 1760s, was crammed with information about him. Gifts were showered on him from both home and abroad – including turtles from Boston's Sons of Liberty, tobacco from Maryland planters, and £1,500 from the assembly of South Carolina. Demonstrations followed his release from prison in April 1770 and his second victory in a by-election in Middlesex (after Parliament had expelled him for a second time). He plunged into City of London politics, playing a significant role in the battle between the City and the House of Commons over the publication of parliamentary debates in the press during 1771. In 1774 he was elected Lord Mayor to the usual accompaniment of 'Wilkes and Liberty!' and the smashing glass of his opponents' windows; the same year he was finally enabled to take his seat in Parliament.

Wilkes's supporters were a cross-section of society. He spoke for the artisan and shopkeeper and identified himself with them by emphasizing their political freedoms, albeit for his own ends. Wilkes gave them pride and status and re-emphasized the Englishman's rights and liberties. Wilkite demonstrations were also great fun and gave these people the opportunity to cock a snook at authority; the ritual of the Wilkite disorders contained elements of the festive gatherings at fairs and wakes. On a different level there were serious-minded political activists in the Wilkite camp. In February 1769 the Society of the Supporters of the Bill of Rights was formed; its main initial object was to pay off Wilkes's enormous debts, but it began toying also with ideas of reform. There were about 50 members, some with wealth, position and connections with City of London politics, others aspiring young men from the professional classes dissatisfied with the existing social and political order. But the society was short-lived; it failed to bring its reform programme forward quickly enough to profit from the excitement of 1768–9; it failed also to proselytize outside London. There was also a fundamental division between men who had a radical ideology and purpose – like the Reverend John Horne Tooke and John Sawbridge, a distiller and MP for Hythe – and men who, like Wilkes, were less radical in their ideology than in their methods. Wilkes would accept support from anyone and he was, it has been argued, 'one of the first, if not *the* first political entrepreneur' (Brewer, 1976, p. 198). Brewer continues:

> He made a business out of politics, especially political journalism. Of course every opposition politician, and a great many on the government's side, had set out on previous occasions to organise press campaigns, or attempt some broad-based political appeal. Wilkes had simply organised more efficiently, more

intelligently, and with a greater sensitivity to the conditions of the political market. The Wilkite movement was a large-scale enterprise, and substantial profits were to be made. Thus printers and publishers sold more copy, brewers (who usually cut their prices during a Wilkite election) sold more ale, and manufacturers developed new lines of Wilkite artifacts.

But among the more serious-minded radicals there was some resentment at Wilkes's personal popularity and, as with the Sons of Liberty, some fear of the crowd.

'No taxation without representation!'

It is a truism to say that British radicals were affected by events in the colonies. Until the early 1770s at least, most colonists insisted that they were only demanding their rights as freeborn Englishmen. They protested that they could not be taxed without their consent: 'No taxation without representation!' Ministerial apologists responded that the colonists were as much represented as the majority in Britain; in the words of Soame Jenyns, MP for Dunwich and a member of the Board of Trade and Plantations when he wrote them:

> ... every Englishman is taxed, and not one in twenty represented: copyholders, leaseholders, and all men possessed of personal property only, chuse no representatives; Manchester, Birmingham, and many more of our richest and most flourishing trading towns send no members to Parliament, consequently cannot consent by their representatives, because they chuse none to represent them; yet are they not Englishmen? or are they not taxed?

These were dangerous arguments to deploy, as radicals like those in the Society of the Supporters of the Bill of Rights began formulating demands for reform. Yet during the 1770s popular political agitation in Britain subsided; in March 1776 Wilkes himself moved for a more equal representation of the people in Parliament, but not a voice was raised in support either inside or outside the Commons and his motion was defeated without a division. While British radicals were slowly taking note of the arguments deployed by colonial pamphleteers, the colonists themselves were becoming rapidly disillusioned with Britain. As part of a deal to help the East India Company out of financial difficulties, the British government granted it a virtual American monopoly by a remission of duties on all tea sent to America. It was calculated that this would not only help the company, but also halt the colonists' profitable tea smuggling trade with the Dutch and that, once tea was cheap enough, the colonists would readily accept the tea duty and thus implicitly acknowledge Parliament's right to tax them. But the government had miscalculated. Boston's Sons of Liberty mounted their Mohawk Indian raid on tea-carrying ships in December 1773; the following April tea landed secretly in New York was found and similarly thrown in the sea. An outraged Parliament replied with four Coercive Acts (also known in the colonies as the 'Intolerable Acts') which were designed to bring Massachusetts, and Boston particularly, under tight government supervision. The colonists replied in turn by summoning the Continental Congress.

The 55 delegates to the Congress which met in September 1774 were almost equally divided between moderates still loyal to the idea of the union with Britain, and more radical individuals who were beginning to base their claims on more abstract natural rights of men and the laws of nature. The lack of any significant support for their cause in Britain led these men to look to themselves for their own salvation, especially after the British general election of November 1774 in which the opposition failed to make any gains. As Joseph Warren, one of the Massachusetts Sons of Liberty, put it in April 1775: 'If America is an humble instrument of the salvation of Britain, it will give us the sincerest joy; but, if Britain must lose her liberty, she must lose it alone' (quoted in Maier, 1973, p. 265). Once armed conflict began in April 1775, more and more were led to the conclusion that independence was the only answer, a conclusion which was given its sharpest focus in a pamphlet written by Tom Paine, a recent English immigrant to the colonies, published in January 1776 and called *Common Sense.*

The Sons of Liberty came down on the side of independence, yet the colonists did not present a united front during the war. A large number declared themselves for the Crown, sometimes purely from conviction but sometimes as much because of who was fighting on the other side. Thus when the Tidewater of the Carolinas declared support for Congress, the old 'Regulators' declared themselves Loyalists. Furthermore even though they were allies in war, the respectable, propertied Sons of Liberty did not lose their suspicion of 'the mob', and popular politics during the first two decades of the new republic was again to highlight the division.

The Gordon Riots

The largest popular disorders in Britain during the period of the American War of Independence were the Gordon Riots. The trouble began as a protest against partial measures of Roman Catholic relief in 1778 – the repeal of legislation condemning Catholics to perpetual imprisonment for keeping schools and disabling them from inheriting or purchasing land. At the call of the Protestant Association, some 60,000 people gathered in St George's Fields in Southwark on 2 June 1780 as a preliminary to presenting a petition to Parliament. The crowds were harangued by Lord George Gordon, president of the Association; they then marched on Westminster, where Gordon continued to whip them up with periodic appearances naming members of Parliament who were opposing the petition. Eventually troops had to be deployed to disperse the crowds, some of whom then moved off to attack the private chapel of the Sardinian ambassador and that attached to the Bavarian embassy. The following day rioting began in earnest. Chapels and schools were the primary targets, after which the crowds turned on gentlemen, manufacturers, merchants and publicans. The majority but not all of the victims were Catholic; however, most victims were reasonably well-to-do as the large Irish community and poor Catholics in general were ignored. The 'legitimizing notion' behind the riots was the traditional hostility towards and fear of 'popery' which, Linda Colley has argued, played a key role in the development of a British identity. Many devout Protestants in eighteenth-century England, Scotland and Wales had an apocalyptic view of history in which Britain was Israel, opposed by the forces of anti-Christ.

> In time of danger or insecurity, Catholics – like witches – became scapegoats, easy targets on which their neighbours could vent fear and anger. The slang adjective most commonly applied to Catholics was 'outlandish', and this was meant quite literally. Catholics were not just strange, they were out of bounds. They did not belong, and were therefore suspect.
>
> (Colley, 1992, p. 23)

But Protestant or not, those men of property who, in increasing numbers, had been growing suspicious of crowd action as the eighteenth century progressed, had their worst fears confirmed by the Gordon Riots. Recollection of the riots burned itself into the memory of the propertied classes for at least the next half century.

The Gordon Riots exploded in the midst of the first significant campaign for parliamentary reform in eighteenth-century Britain. The County Association Movement grew largely out of dissatisfaction with the progress of the American war, and it was above all a movement of electors. Some of the most substantial country gentlemen in England came together to demand the correction of gross abuses in public expenditure, the reduction of emoluments, the abolition of sinecures and unmerited pensions, annual parliaments and the addition of 100 county members to the Commons to strengthen the independent interest. There was a radical wing of the movement, however, drawing its membership and support from similar groups to the Society of the Supporters of the Bill of Rights; prominent among the radical element was a new grouping formed in April 1780, the Society for Constitutional Information (SCI). The SCI had a fairly small membership, and the subscription of one guinea a year or 30 guineas for life limited membership to the well-to-do. There is no record of direct contact between it and lower-class groups during the 1780s, but the society did embark on a publicity campaign to educate 'the Commonality at large' in the excellence of the British constitution before corrupt ministers had tainted it. This campaign was furthered by the publication of pamphlets and tracts which were not to be sold at more than three pence each. In general these pamphlets were reprints of the great constitutional theorists of the past, but at least one, *An Address to the People of Great Britain of all denominations, but particularly those who subsist by Honest Industry*, written by Jeremiah Batley, was addressed to the 'poor labourer and mechanic'. It argued that neither the Crown, the nobility, nor the 'bigotted clergy' were capable of saving the nation. In August 1782 the SCI urged that meetings be held involving all classes of society to discuss 'Common Rights' and to petition Parliament for reform. The meetings did not materialize; little popular support could be mustered for reform during the 1780s, and although the SCI remained in existence it transacted little business during the second half of the decade.

The impact of the French Revolution

1788 was the centenary of Britain's 'Glorious Revolution' when the Catholic James II had been turned off the throne and replaced by the Protestant William and Mary; this was the revolution which could be justified by the political thought of John Locke and which, it was argued, had confirmed both British liberty and Protestantism. Hard on the heels of the centenary celebrations came news of revolution in France. Many Britons initially welcomed this news; some maintained France was following Britain's lead of the century before; others insisted that there were no grounds for complacency and that, unless new reforms were embarked upon, French liberty would soon supersede that of Britain. The debate became more heated with the publication of Edmund Burke's *Reflections on the Revolution in France* (November 1790), highly critical of attempts to establish a government on abstract principles, and the crop of replies which this brought forth, notably Tom Paine's *The Rights of Man*, Part One of which appeared in March 1791. The SCI revived under the impetus of the centenary celebrations and events in France; furthermore it now helped to foster new societies which drew their membership from artisans, shopkeepers and craftsmen – men who hitherto had not campaigned politically on their own behalf.

Among the first of these popular societies which sprang up in the winter of 1791–2 was the Sheffield Society for Constitutional Information. It drew its rank and file membership from the independent-minded artisans of the cutlery trades, who had a tradition of organization through their trades. Vitally important also was the membership of Joseph Gales, printer of *The Sheffield Register*; this gave the society a mouthpiece from the outset. By the early summer of 1792 the Sheffield Society boasted some 2,500 members. Similar societies sprang up in Derby, Leeds, Manchester and Norwich. In London a 40-year-old Scottish shoemaker, Thomas Hardy, having borrowed and read some of the initial publications of the SCI, met together with several like-minded men from the London Corresponding Society (LCS), so-called because it proposed to communicate with other societies in England and Scotland. Clearly the LCS owed something to the club tradition of the metropolis and to the tradition of political interest and debate among artisans, but for the first time working men were organizing to make their own political demands. The LCS's subscription of one penny a week opened up membership to all but the poorest, and it has been estimated that by November 1792 there were at least 800 'committed militants' with perhaps 5–6,000 others attending meetings of the different divisions.

Britain's Friends of Freedom, from the genteel membership of the SCI and the Manchester Constitutional Society to the artisans of the LCS and the Sheffield Society, eschewed the boisterous tumults of Wilkite radicalism. They wanted a reform of Parliament involving principally a widening of the franchise to all adult males and an end to corruption and patronage. Some of the more radical elements went even further, espousing the programme of Part Two of *The Rights of Man*, which advocated a complete reorganization of the fiscal system and the provision of education, employment and social welfare. When war broke out with revolutionary France in February 1793, the popular societies called for peace and deplored Britain's participation alongside a confederation of absolutist monarchs against a free people. In the tradition of the Commonwealthman, they feared military repression and standing armies and roundly condemned the new government policy of building small cavalry barracks in industrial districts to act as a police measure. But the approach of war and war itself also gave a tremendous boost to popular conservatism. In some areas loyalist crowds, occasionally supplied with free drink, turned on the British Jacobins, and Tom Paine – outlawed from Britain for failure to appear at his trial for seditious libel – was burned in effigy. Many in the popular classes continued to be fired by good old-fashioned xenophobia, and there continued to be tremendous popular loyalty to the constitution, church and king.

Popular democratic societies also sprang up in the United States during the early 1790s. There do not appear to have been many more than 40 of them, and their membership does not appear to have reached that of societies in London and Sheffield, but their impact and the stimulus they gave to political interest were considerable. Many of the leaders of the societies of the 1790s had been involved in 'patriotic societies' twenty years before, particularly during the war when, encouraged by Congress, such societies (often little more than committees) had met and debated in courthouses and taverns and circulated news and opinions. Some of these wartime groups were notable for their democratic ideology; the military associations of Pennsylvania, made up principally of artisans and craftsmen, protested that Congress's attempts to appoint brigadier-generals over them were infringements of their democratic procedure. Daniel Shays's rebellion of 1786, when a small army of debtor farmers descended on Worcester, Massachusetts, determined to overawe the county court where debt cases were heard, had its origins in popular meetings and committees of correspondence as well as in the tradition of small frontier farmer versus large landowner. Elsewhere in the republic during the 1780s, clubs met and debated current affairs and political issues. The 'Saturday Night Club' of Danville, Kentucky, discussed the opening of the Mississippi River and capital punishment, and campaigned for a Bill of Rights after the acceptance of the Constitution; its leaders became prominent in the democratic societies of the 1790s.

A multiplicity of factors brought the societies of the 1790s into being. The example and the excitement generated by events in France helped focus concern about suggestions being made by influential gentlemen that the new republic needed a strong centralized power, perhaps even a monarchy, and an aristocracy similar to a knighthood. Veterans of the war were critical of the inequality of remuneration between the 'few' officers and the 'many' others; such veterans formed a nucleus in several societies. There were also economic concerns: the new national debt smacked of the fiscal policies of monarchies, and while much American trade remained with Britain there were those who argued that the exchange of wheat for manufactured goods was impeding the growth of native industry. The membership of the societies ranged from liberal-minded professional men – doctors, lawyers, printers – to new, poor and dissatisfied immigrants. But the majority appear to have come from poor farmers (on the frontier the clubs were notable for their opposition to land speculators and their lawyers, high rents and excise duties) and artisans who, as the historian of the clubs put it:

> … had carried the brunt of the war for freedom as common soldiers and members of the Revolutionary bodies … Now in the 1790s they were suddenly awakened to the fact that the things for which they had sacrificed and fought were slipping through their fingers …
>
> While they were not a class-conscious proletarian group in any modern sense of that phrase, they had drawn a distinction between the interests of an 'aristocratic junta' and their own.

(Link, 1942, pp. 91, 93)

The central governments in both Britain and the United States were alarmed by popular radicalism. Pitt's ministry, and gentlemen of property in general, were concerned at the popularity of Paine's ideas among the popular societies (indeed this alarmed many of the more genteel reformers) and at the sympathy for France. From the close of 1792 the British Jacobins found themselves the victims of prosecutions for sedition (there were some 200 such prosecutions during the 1790s in England, and clearly not everyone prosecuted belonged to a society) and of more private forms of victimization such as the loss of jobs, tenancies or being 'sent to Coventry'. The government had little machinery for conducting this repression; it could exhort and, in the case of prosecutions, it could advise, but much depended upon the zeal and activity of local magistrates and loyalist associations. At times local repression of the Friends of Freedom became an extension of long-standing local political feuds. At the close of 1793 and early in 1794, following the meeting of a convention of radicals in Edinburgh, five men (including two fraternal delegates from the London Corresponding Society) were sentenced to transportation. In the late spring of 1794 a rumour that the LCS was about to call another convention prompted the government to suspend the Habeas Corpus Act and arrest leaders of both the LCS and SCI. Thomas Hardy, John Horne Tooke (Wilkes's old supporter, now a leading figure in the SCI) and John Thelwall (a radical lecturer) were prosecuted for high treason. All three were acquitted, and this, together with serious food shortages and the economic dislocation caused by the war, contributed to a new upsurge of popular society membership in 1795.

At the opening of Parliament on 29 October that year angry crowds mobbed George III's coach demanding 'Peace and bread!' The government blamed the LCS for the attack, and two bills were rapidly pushed through Parliament restricting the organization of public meetings and limiting their size to 50 persons, and extending the law of treason to encompass speech and writing as well as overt acts. The popular societies declined after 1795; some of their more radical and determined members became involved in conspiracy, turned to republicanism, and forged links with Irish revolutionaries. There is considerable historical debate about the extent of this conspiratorial activity; what is noteworthy, however, is the extent to which the language of the French Revolution was used by food rioters and the authors of threatening letters complaining about food shortages in the years 1799–1801.

The American democratic societies became closely involved with Edmond Genêt, the first minister from the French republic to the United States; indeed many of the societies' opponents believed that Genêt was their prime mover. Plans were discussed with Genêt for American expansion into the Floridas, down the Mississippi and northwards into Canada. Genêt boasted to his Parisian superiors, 'I provision the Antilles, I excite the Canadians to free themselves from the yoke of England, I arm the Kentuckians' (quoted in Wright, 1965, p. 205). He was reminded, however, that he was supposed 'to treat with the *government* and not with a *portion of the people*' (quoted in Palmer, 1964, p. 529). President George Washington's administration was appalled by Genêt's behaviour. Washington himself was alarmed by the factionalism which he believed the democratic societies to be fostering; his influential secretary to the Treasury, Alexander Hamilton, was a popular target of the societies for his financial policies and 'aristocratic' attitudes, and Hamilton's long-standing antipathy to anything resembling levelling democracy made him a natural opponent of the societies. When a protest by farmers in western Pennsylvania against a new federal tax on spirits evolved into the (hardly serious) Whiskey Rebellion of 1794, Hamilton persuaded Washington that the societies and Genêt were responsible. There were at least three societies active in western Pennsylvania, but the rebellion was also firmly rooted in the tradition of western protest. Together Washington and Hamilton marched 15,000 militiamen against the rebels, who melted away before them. Four years later President Adams found himself faced with the prospect of going to war against revolutionary France, and on a wave of war hysteria with the words 'Jacobin' and 'democrat' becoming, as in Britain, synonymous with 'traitor', Congress passed three major laws. The Naturalization Act raised the residence requirement for citizenship from five to fourteen years. The Alien Act empowered the president to deport 'dangerous' aliens. Both of these laws reflected the concern about new immigrants who joined the democratic societies. The Sedition Act made it a crime to publish false or malicious writings against either the government or any of its officers. No one was ever deported under the Alien Act; about fifteen were indicted under the Sedition Act, and eleven (including Congressman Matthew Lyon and the newspaper editor Thomas Cooper, who had fled from loyalist violence and prosecution in Manchester in 1793) were convicted.

Conclusion

During the 1760s popular politics, such as it was in Britain and her thirteen colonies, was fundamentally about the same thing: the perceived 'rights of Englishmen' as transmitted from the seventeenth century and, particularly, the right to resist abuses of civil and political power. Forty years later similar elements pervaded popular politics, though the contexts in which they were conducted in the two nations had become very different. Alarm and repression were relatively short-lived in the United States. In 1800 Thomas Jefferson, a man despised by many during the 1790s as a pro-French 'Jacobin', was elected president. Under Jefferson's presidency radical and democratic agitation died down. The old friction of frontier and tidewater continued, as did the concern of gentlemen of property for crowd action, but in comparison with Britain there was a rough form of social and political equality. Some gentlemen were concerned about the passion for universal manhood suffrage which spread throughout the Union at the end of the second decade of the nineteenth century; beginning with Connecticut in 1818 and followed first by New York and Massachusetts and then others, state legislatures extended voting rights for those who paid taxes and were liable to militia service. In Britain in 1800 even a limited parliamentary reform was still over 30 years away, and the old order, opposed to Jacobinism both at home and abroad, was solidly entrenched. Popular politics and popular demonstrations continued to take traditional forms; there were anti-recruiting riots throughout the war years and food riots during the war and in the aftermath. Disorders in support of the radical baronet Sir Francis Burdett (when he campaigned for, and won, a Middlesex seat in 1802 and when he libelled the House of Commons in defence of a radical debating club in 1810) took the form of Wilkite disorders. But the new kind of political organization developed by working men in the popular societies of the 1790s also continued, reaching its climax in the Chartist agitation of the 1840s.

References

Brewer, John (1976) *Party Ideology and Popular Politics at the Accession of George III*, Cambridge University Press.

Colley, Linda (1992) *Britons: Forging the Nation 1707–1837*, New Haven, Yale University Press.

Hans, N. (1951) *New Trends in Education in the Eighteenth Century*, Routledge and Kegan Paul.

Hofstadter, Richard (1971) *America at 1750: A Social Portrait*, New York, Vintage Books.

Link, Eugene P. (1942) *Democratic-Republican Societies 1790–1800*, New York, Columbia University Press.

Maier, Pauline (1973) *From Resistance to Revolution: Colonial Radicals and the Development of American Opposition to Britain 1765–1776*, Routledge and Kegan Paul.

Moritz, C.P. (1965) *Journeys of a German in England in 1782*, trans. and ed. R. Nettel, Jonathan Cape.

Palmer, R.R. (1964) *The Age of the Democratic Revolution: A Political History of Europe and America, 1760–1800. Volume 2: The Struggle*, Princeton University Press.

Rudé, George (1962) *Wilkes and Liberty: A Social Study of 1763–1774*, Clarendon Press.

Rudé, George (1964) *The Crowd in History, 1730–1848*, New York, John Wiley.

Thompson, E.P. (1991) *Customs in Common*, Merlin Press.

Wright, Esmond (1965) *Fabric of Freedom 1763–1800*, Macmillan.

1.3   The emergence of political parties, c.1760–c.1860

In the middle of the eighteenth century political parties, in the sense of organized political groupings with a programme for political action should they achieve power, did not exist. A century later the idea of Conservative confronting Liberal in Britain and Democrat confronting Republican in the United States was largely accepted. My aim in this essay is to sketch in the stops and starts by which parties evolved. It is divided into two main sections: the first looks at the traditional pictures of parties; the second and longer section parallels the developments in the two countries.

Traditional historical pictures of party

Eighteenth-century British political history is often portrayed as a struggle between two great parties, Whig and Tory. The Whigs, it is maintained, backed the Hanoverian monarchs who had come to power in 1714; the Tories were sympathetic to the Jacobites and a Stuart restoration; consequently the Whigs monopolized power from 1714 until George III's accession in 1760. George III is portrayed as a monarch with aspirations to restore the personal power of the king; he brought Tories back into government as the 'king's friends' and used political patronage, bribery and corruption to the full. There followed several decades of constitutional conflict, when the Whigs took the side of 'Liberty' and 'the people' against growing royal power – in the case of Wilkes, for example, and during the years of the French Revolution. George III's foolish policies led to the American Revolution; his Tory ministers savagely repressed political reformers and working-class radicals. But, as in all good stories, 'Liberty' finally triumphed with the passing of the first Reform Act in 1832 by a Whig ministry. Out of the reformed Parliament emerged the two great parties of Victorian Britain: the Liberals, descendants of the old Whig party, and the Conservatives who, under first Peel and then Disraeli, managed to shed much of the reactionary nature of early nineteenth-century Toryism.

There is no such neatly rounded picture for the USA. Nevertheless historians have spoken of 'the first party system' when analysing the political tensions of the 1790s and the friction between 'Federalists' and 'Republicans'. The 'system' declined with the fortunes of the Federalists in the early nineteenth century. 'The second party system' developed with the emergence of the Democratic party and the massive popular vote for Andrew Jackson as president in 1828; this 'system' was shattered by secession and civil war in the mid-nineteenth century.

The big question with which to begin is, of course: what is a political party? The *Concise Oxford Dictionary* gives the following definition under 'party': 'Body of persons united in a cause, opinion, etc.; system of taking sides on public questions.' Now we might need to add some suggestion of bureaucratic machinery to the definition; this machinery ensures financial support, communicates policy decisions by party leaders and the responses of the rank and file, and so on. Parties are not confined to the legislative or executive department of government but spread themselves throughout the country.

The bureaucratic organization of political parties did not exist during the eighteenth century; it was beginning to exist by the middle of the nineteenth century. Yet if the bureaucratic structure associated with modern political parties did not exist, eighteenth-century politicians used the term 'party', and subsequent historians have used it too. This was partly because men within the legislatures (and their extra-mural supporters and electors) took sides on particular issues and tended to condemn their opponents as a 'party' or a 'faction' working against the common good; also some embryonic party administrative structures did emerge from time to time.

The 'Whig interpretation of history' comes from the title of a famous book by the English historian Herbert Butterfield (1900–79) which criticized a unilinear and teleological approach to the study of history that views the past through the eyes of the present.

The 'Whig interpretation'* of the development of parties in Britain with which I began this section emerged from a multiplicity of causes, not least of which was the mistake of reading nineteenth-century party struggles back into the eighteenth century. During the 1840s the papers of many of the great landed gentlemen who had opposed George III were edited and published with introductions by their descendants, who were often active in Whig/Liberal politics. The papers were often hostile to the king and the introductions tended to enlarge the bias. Moreover, as the two-party system evolved in Britain, it became easy to read the present back into the past and to envisage George III and his 'friends' attempting to cripple such a system. Thus one of Britain's leading nineteenth-century historians, Lord Acton, could write 'government by party was established in 1714, by party acting by Cabinet', but unfortunately 'about the year 1770 things had been brought back, by indirect means, nearly to the condition which the Revolution of 1688 had been designed to remedy'. In his analysis of how George III was treated by historians, Sir Herbert Butterfield described Acton's statements as 'two of the most faulty statements ever produced by Whig historiography on the subject of British politics in the eighteenth century' (Butterfield, 1969, p. 181).

Parallel histories

In Britain the principal minister was the king's minister until well into the nineteenth century. The king generally chose his principal minister from one of the great magnates or most notable parliamentarians in either the House of Lords or the House of Commons. The minister was not chosen because he had majority support in Parliament (although this could happen); it was the minister's task to create his majority after he had been chosen. This could mean giving a plum ministerial appointment to the leader of a faction within Parliament, thus bringing that faction into line behind the new government; of course, arrangements of this kind could be initiated before the king asked an individual to form a government. Creating a majority could also involve the more direct bribery of MPs by promising sinecures, public office or titles to them or their relations. When George III chose his former tutor, the Earl of Bute, as his principal minister in 1762, he was not doing anything unconstitutional. But his choice upset the magnates among whom the king's minister was traditionally picked; the fact that Bute was a Scot and a close friend of the king's mother also enabled the English populace to indulge in a bout of xenophobia and rumours of sexual scandal. Rather than reducing faction in the first decade of his reign, George saw it develop as he lurched from one minister to another.

> Each successive minister – Bute, Grenville, Rockingham, Chatham – was able in office to build up his own party and to lead it into opposition after he had left office, but the longer he remained in opposition the smaller his following grew ... Parties which were essentially personal in their nature could not survive the natural or political death of their leader.
>
> (Namier and Brook, 1964, vol. 1, p. 198)

Most historians tend now to agree that one 'political party' did emerge out of this confusion, a party in which 'the politics of place gave way to the politics of issues and conditions, of ideology and theory' (O'Gorman, 1975, p. 19). This party centred on the Marquis of Rockingham. It provided a consistent opposition to Lord North's ministry (1770–82), in particular opposing the American war; it criticized wasteful and extravagant expenditure, urging 'economical reform'; it acquired a distinct personal dislike for George III, suspecting him of building up a new system of corruption and despotism. The party took its stand on principle; its members saw themselves as the defenders of the old constitution which was now under threat. Their interpretation of the past was incorrect, but it served to cement the party together and provided the foundation for the subsequent Whig interpretation of George III.

The Marquis of Rockingham died in 1782. The nominal leadership of the party passed to the Duke of Portland, but the real leader in Parliament was the capable and colourful Charles James Fox. The party consolidated under Fox: clubs and societies were established, and there were a subscription and full-time paid staff in a central office. Rockingham's party had become the Whig party, but with the exception of two short periods in office during the early 1780s, it remained an opposition party. In December 1783 George III asked the younger William Pitt to form a ministry, and though Pitt had no party like the Whigs and no significant personal following like the attractive figure of Fox, he remained principal minister until the beginning of 1801. Indeed it was the Whig party which broke up over concern about demands for reform in Britain, attitudes to the French Revolution and the war against revolutionary France. In the summer of 1794, following several prominent defections, the Duke of Portland led half the party across the chamber to support Pitt. Portland himself became Home Secretary and continued the vigorous anti-Jacobin line of his predecessor.

Mid-eighteenth-century Americans shared the British suspicion of party and faction. This is not to say, however, that they presented a united front to the king and his ministers. There were divisions in the Continental Congress between moderates and radicals and between northern colonies with their aggressive merchant communities and the aristocratic planters of the south. The War of Independence itself was a major trauma. Thousands fought for the Crown, turning the conflict into a brothers' war; with independence many of these emigrated. It has been estimated that there were about 24 *émigrés* per thousand of the population from America during the War of Independence compared with only five *émigrés* per thousand from France during its revolution (Palmer, 1959, p. 188). Peace and independence promised an end to conflict and a degree of unity among the citizens of the new republic. The question was how strong the bonds of unity should be.

During the first years of its existence the United States had no president and no central judiciary; Congress was the supreme arbiter of interstate rivalries and also conducted foreign affairs. The Articles of Confederation, drawn up in 1777 but not ratified by all the individual states until 1781, was the agreement under which the states united. Many regarded the Articles as insufficient. In 1785, hoping to produce some compromise out of the bickering and jealousies of the states bordering the Potomac River, George Washington called a meeting of delegations from Maryland and Virginia at his home, Mount Vernon. (This was not entirely altruistic, since Washington owned land on the upper reaches of the Potomac and recognized that its value would rise considerably with improved river navigation.) A wider meeting reconvened the following year with five states sending representatives to Annapolis, where a decision was taken to attempt to give the Union of States a firmer foundation. A third assembly, at Philadelphia in May 1787, had 55 delegates with only two states unrepresented (Rhode Island and New Hampshire, whose delegates arrived too late). This federal convention produced a draft constitution. However, it was one thing to produce a constitution and quite another to get all states to ratify it. Many, especially in the larger states (notably George Clinton of New York), regarded the presidency and the centralized government proposed in the Constitution as far too similar to that which they had recently fought – the British Crown. In response to Clinton, Alexander Hamilton, who had been closely involved in the events leading up to the 1787 convention, persuaded two like-minded politicians, John Jay and James Madison, to join with him in writing a series of letters in favour of the Constitution in the New York newspapers. The 85 letters, published under the pseudonym 'Publius', were soon to be collectively known as *The Federalist Papers*.* The Federalists carried the day, just – but the next decade saw a split in their ranks which, it has been argued, heralded the beginning of political parties in the United States.

Madison became the most influential man in the House of Representatives during the First Congress (1789–91), which had the task of creating a governmental structure out of the blueprint of the Constitution. In 1790 Hamilton was appointed secretary of the Treasury in Washington's cabinet. The contrasting interpretations of Federalism by Madison and Hamilton inaugurated party conflict. Hamilton favoured strong, centralized government and believed that it was necessary to attach men of wealth and property firmly to the national government. Madison and Thomas Jefferson, the secretary of state, who rapidly eclipsed Madison as Hamilton's principal political opponent, were much more wary of the power of central government. They objected to Hamilton's *Report on National Credit* (1790), which proposed, first, to repay the full face value of government securities even though many of the initial, smaller purchasers had been forced to sell to more wealthy men at a fraction of the initial price; and, second, to assume on behalf of the federal government all the unpaid debts contracted by the individual states during the War of Independence. They protested that Hamilton's proposals in 1791 to establish a quasi-public Bank of the United States and to attempt to make the new republic economically independent by a system of bounties, subsidies and tariffs were unconstitutional. The friction led

* Hamilton wrote 51 of the letters, Madison 26 and Jay, who was taken ill during the period of the letters, 5; the remaining 3 were a joint effort by Hamilton and Madison.
Hamilton was a New York lawyer who had served in the war alongside Washington. Jay, also a New York lawyer, had drafted the constitution of New York State in 1777 and had been Secretary for Foreign Affairs under the Articles of Confederation. Madison was the son of a wealthy Virginia landowner; he had been deeply involved in the proceedings at Philadelphia in 1787, and the notes which he kept of the proceedings and the drafting of the Constitution subsequently earned him the title 'Father of the Constitution'.

Hamilton to act rather like a party leader in Congress, organizing his supporters, furnishing them with arguments and even speeches. Madison
and Jefferson responded by encouraging Philip Freneau (with the veiled
offer of a translating clerk's post in the State Department) to establish a
paper in the capital, Philadelphia. (The federal government did not
move to Washington, DC until 1800. Washington, DC was the first city
ever created to be a national capital.) Freneau's lively propaganda
savaged Hamilton, portraying him as a sympathizer with both monarchy
and aristocracy. The conflict between Federalists and Republicans, as
their opponents became known, was intensified by the debate on the
French Revolution.

During the 1790s men were readily identifiable as Federalists or
Republicans, yet there were no party organizations. Indeed the division
existed at the very centre of the federal government during the presiden-
cies of both Washington and John Adams. President Adams tended
towards Federalism, but since the Constitution did not recognize parties,
the vice-president was to be the runner-up in the presidential election;
thus Adams's deputy was Jefferson, his political opponent.* Furthermore,
besides the friction between the pro-French Republicans and the pro-
British Federalists, the latter themselves divided over whether the
undeclared naval war against revolutionary France should be extended
into an attack upon Spanish America, as Hamilton wanted, or handled as
Adams resolved towards the end of his presidency. In 1800 the Federalists
lost heavily in the congressional elections to an alliance of northern artisans and southern farmers who favoured the Jeffersonian line of peace,
keeping out of foreign quarrels. Jefferson became president, launching
the 'Virginia Dynasty' of presidents – Jefferson himself serving two terms
(1801–9), Madison (1809–17) and James Monroe (1817–25) – all of
whom subscribed to similar ideas of the loose role of federal government,
neutrality and financial economy.

On 11 July 1804 Hamilton was killed in a duel with Vice-President
Aaron Burr. The Federalists never found a leader of similar intellect and
stature to replace him. There were no Federalist presidential candidates
to oppose Madison in 1813, nor to oppose Monroe. But men were still
identifiable as Federalists; savage rioting in Baltimore in the summer of
1812 left several Federalist gentlemen and veterans of the War of
Independence dead or seriously injured. The Federalists continued to
have the powerful voice of John Marshall in the Supreme Court. But
increasingly they were identified with businessmen from the northern
states looking out for their own interests. In 1804 the Essex Junta, a
group of wealthy merchants principally directed by Senator Timothy
Pickering of Massachusetts, contemplated secession from the Union and
informed the British ambassador of their plans. They feared that
Jefferson's purchase of the vast Louisiana territory would put the northern states in a permanent minority within the Union. As the economic
side of the Anglo-French war engulfed neutral shipping, the northern
merchants again found themselves at odds with the federal government.
Jefferson attempted to keep American ships out of the war by keeping
them at home under an embargo act. The Federalist merchants of New
England proposed a convention of states to nullify the actions of the federal government – a paradox given the earlier conflict between Hamilton
and Jefferson. By the time Madison was chosen as president, the whole of

** The 12th Amendment to
the Constitution, ratified
before the presidential
election of 1804, provided
for separate balloting for
president and vice-
president.*

New England was firmly back under Federalist control. When war broke out between Britain and the United States in 1812, the New England merchants continued to trade with the enemy, and the question of secession was raised again at the Hartford Convention (15 December 1814 to 5 January 1815) attended by delegates from the state legislatures of Massachusetts, Connecticut and Rhode Island and by individuals from New Hampshire and Vermont.

But if the fortunes of the Federalists were in decline after the death of Hamilton (or perhaps *because* the Federalists were in decline), the presidents of the Virginia dynasty did not preside over a unified majority party. These presidents were chosen from a nominating convention, a 'party' caucus; but the caucus was often boycotted by a large proportion of the so-called Republicans in Congress. Similarly there was an unwillingness among the Republicans to unite behind a 'party' candidate for the post of Speaker of the House of Representatives – a crucial position since the Speaker staffed committees and designated their chairmen. James Sterling Young's work on the voting patterns of Congress in the first three decades of the nineteenth century suggests

> that legislators looked for policy guidance, as they did for companionship, to colleagues from the same locale or region, and that these intralegislative fraternal associations were influences of major significance upon the members' voting behaviour.

> (Young, 1966, p. 104)

Washington, DC remained a city in embryo throughout this period; congressmen took lodgings in boarding houses, often with colleagues from the same state or region. The block votes of boarding house groups were noted by contemporaries, so much so in fact that early Congressional Directories took to listing members of Congress by boarding house rather than in alphabetical or in state order.

Party politics in early Victorian Britain and Jacksonian America

British politics during the period of the Revolutionary and Napoleonic Wars are generally regarded as having been dominated by Toryism. Pitt never called himself a Tory, but early in the nineteenth century George Canning, one of Pitt's disciples, began using the term to describe both Pitt and his successors. The 'Tories', who comprised most governments from the 1790s through to the resignation of the Duke of Wellington as prime minister in 1830, stood for church and king and against Jacobinism in both its foreign and home-grown varieties. The Tory governments were, and have been subsequently, vilified as repressive. During the 1790s there was Pitt's 'reign of terror' against the British Jacobins; in the aftermath of the Napoleonic Wars came 'the massacre of Peterloo' and anti-radical legislation much like that of Pitt. Yet the period also saw a gradual wearing away of patronage and 'old corruption', as much the work of some of the Tory ministers as of pressure from the Whigs or from outside Parliament. During the 1820s Tory governments reformed and restructured the legal system, abolishing the death penalty for many lesser crimes; they also introduced measures encouraging free trade. Lord Liverpool's ministers were not cast in the mould of the huntin', shootin', fishin' Tory squire (though these certainly existed among the rank and file), nor did many of them have a long aristocratic pedigree; they were administrators who saw it as their right and duty to govern. Though the Tories could present a united opposition to parliamentary reform, there was serious division among them over other issues. In 1828 Viscount Goderich's ministry was brought down partly by such a split over the question of Catholic emancipation. Interestingly Goderich was keen to bring moderate Whigs into his cabinet – a sign that there were still those in powerful positions in British politics for whom party was an irrelevance.

A combination of factors held the Whigs together during the years of Tory rule. There were strong family ties and social connections centring on the homes of Whig magnates like Holland House. Personal and social links were strengthened by resentment at long exclusion from office and adherence to the ideology which had emerged under Rockingham, developed under Fox, and virtually ossified after Fox's death. They were sympathetic to moderate parliamentary reform, but in no way were they a populist party, and none of the Whig leaders during the 1810s, 1820s and 1830s had Fox's mass popularity or courted such.

Tory dominance came to an end with the agitation for parliamentary reform between 1830 and 1832. In the election following the Reform Act, Tories and their supporters were decimated. There were bitter recriminations. Some Tories were prepared to co-operate with Radicals to bring the Whig government down, but the Duke of Wellington and Sir Robert Peel, the two leaders of the party, would have nothing to do with such action. However, Wellington (backed by the more reactionary elements in the party) and Peel (the personification of administrative Toryism) were scarcely on speaking terms. Peel was vilified by the extreme Protestants who hated him for his stand on Catholic emancipation, and blamed by agriculturalists who believed that his restoration of specie payments in 1819 had been the origin of their economic problems. (In 1797 the strain on gold bullion to fight the French war had led to the Bank of England ceasing payment in specie – gold coin as opposed to paper money.) Worst of all for the ultra Tories, Peel accepted the Reform Act and argued for a reappraisal of all institutions, with reform where necessary and conservation elsewhere – hence the increasingly accepted party label of 'Conservative'.

The Whigs were little better united in spite of their victory. There was constant wrangling within the cabinet, and resignations principally over the position of the Anglican Church in Ireland. William IV still regarded ministers as his forebears had done: they were his men who, when chosen, set about getting support in Parliament. In an effort to stop the political squabbling of the early 1830s, William asked Lord Melbourne, the Whig Home Secretary, to form a coalition with Peel and Wellington. Melbourne refused. In November 1834 the king dismissed the Whigs and asked Peel to form a government. Peel agreed, and in the general election which followed he issued a manifesto to his Tamworth constituents outlining his conservative creed. The Tamworth Manifesto was much more than a personal document; it also served as the programme for the party which gathered around Peel – as such it was unprecedented in British politics. The Conservatives improved their position by some 100 seats in the election. The opposition grouping of

* The group of Irish MPs who acknowledged Daniel O'Connell as their leader. O'Connell had been active in the campaign for Catholic emancipation at the end of the 1820s and was now campaigning for a repeal of the union with Britain. As a result of the 1832 election the O'Connellites were the largest 'Irish party' at Westminster.

Whigs, Radicals and O'Connellites* promptly formed the Litchfield House Compact designed to get rid of Peel, who had no overall majority. Peel's government resigned in April 1835. In the same way that the Tamworth Manifesto can be seen as a significant step in the formation of the Victorian Conservative party, so the Litchfield House Compact 'was in fact the point of origin for the Victorian Liberal party' (Gash, 1979, p. 161). The older Whig peers were not in favour of the compact; their younger counterparts, like Lord John Russell, had fewer scruples. During the second half of the decade the Whigs/Liberals absorbed many of the Radicals (who had no acknowledged parliamentary leader and often argued as violently with each other as with other parties) and many of the O'Connellites.

There was another significant development in party organization during the 1830s with the creation of London clubs which provided social, administrative and information centres for the emergent parties. The Carlton Club was established by Tory leaders at the climax of the Reform Bill struggle in the spring of 1832. The Reform Club was set up as a counterweight to the Carlton by a determined group of Radicals and Whigs some four years later. 'What distinguished the Carlton and the Reform from the predecessors', according to Norman Gash, 'was that the earlier political clubs were social centres in which politics had gradually taken a hold, whereas the former were from the outset designed as party political organisations' (Gash, 1977, p. 393).

After the general election of 1841, for the first time in British history a government with a previous majority in the Commons (the Whig/Liberal government of Melbourne) was replaced by the former opposition party (Peel's Conservatives, still with a large sprinkling of old Tories) as a result of a victory at the polls. The evolution of a two-party system was by no means complete; infuriated by Peel's repeal of the Corn Laws, Tory agriculturalists combined with the opposition to help bring down his government in 1846 – in the subsequent election and ensuing Parliament the divisions of Whig, Liberal, Independent Radical, Peelite Conservative and Tory were once again predominant. Yet the bases of the two parties were formed, upon which Disraeli and Gladstone were able to construct a viable two-party system with the impetus derived from the 1867 Reform Act.

It has been argued that the 1830s also witnessed a new beginning to the party system in the United States. A clutch of candidates jostled to succeed Monroe in the run-up to the presidential election of 1824. Four candidates were particularly significant: William Harrison Crawford, the secretary of the Treasury, the front-runner who had considerable support in Congress until he became bedridden by a stroke in the year before the election; John Quincy Adams, the secretary of state and son of the former president; Henry Clay, the Speaker of the House; and Andrew Jackson, a man of humble parentage who had won an enormous popular following, particularly after beating the British at New Orleans in 1815 and his conduct in subsequent Indian wars. Jackson came top of the initial ballot but lacked the necessary majority. When the three top names were presented to the House of Representatives for the final choice of who should be president, Henry Clay threw his votes behind Adams and secured the presidency for the latter. (The initial ballot had given Jackson 99 votes, Adams 84, Crawford 41 and Clay 37.) When Adams then made Clay his secretary of state, Jackson's supporters protested that self-seeking politicians had made a deal to exclude the popular choice; it was out of this discontent that 'the Democracy', as the Democratic party was known under Jackson, emerged.

The architect of 'the Democracy' was Martin Van Buren, who had risen through the politics of New York State to be a senator. During the 1820s politics in New York was dominated by De Witt Clinton, the leader of the Republicans in the state. Clinton's leadership was autocratic; he saw the party as his personal following and dispensed patronage freely, sometimes to nominal Federalists at the expense of deserving Republicans. At the close of the decade a group of young politicians (including Van Buren) known as the Bucktails began a campaign to oust Clinton. Since Clinton was following the traditional pattern of party management, they had to devise a new definition of party and new standards for party members. They insisted that parties should be democratic, egalitarian and run by the membership; in the context of early nineteenth-century America with its pride in democracy and equality (whether or not the latter existed in fact) there was no way in which Clinton could counter their arguments and re-establish his authority. The historian of the Bucktails' campaign has highlighted how they succeeded in distinguishing between party and faction in both theory and practice:

> A party (such as their own) was a democratically structured, permanent organization; a faction (such as the Clintonians) was a transient, aristocratic, personal clique ... Personal factions were bad: they were aristocratic and concerned only with enriching their leader. But parties were good: they allowed all members an equal voice; gave all members an equal chance to rise to positions of leadership and to receive party nominations for important elective positions; and provided all members with an equal chance at receiving patronage, now no longer dispensed at the whim of an arbitrary leader. The degree to which the newer politicians rejected the antiparty tradition and the personal basis of politics can be seen in their extraordinary degree of attachment to their organization. They ... developed a system of political discipline that enjoined every politician, at whatever cost to himself, to preserve and perpetuate the party.

(Wallace, 1968, p. 460)

By the early 1820s the Bucktails were entrenched in the New York State legislature and executive and were denigrated by their opponents as the Albany Regency (Albany being the state capital of New York).

The Albany Regency backed Crawford in 1824, but afterwards it was clear to Van Buren that there was no potential presidential candidate in the Crawford camp. Jackson, however, maintained his enormous popular appeal, and in the four years following Adams's victory Van Buren united the different opposition groupings behind him as 'the Democracy'. In 1826 the new party won a majority in both Houses of Congress, making Jackson's victory in the 1828 presidential election a foregone conclusion. Indeed between 1828 and 1860 the machine of the Democratic party won all but two national elections. Under Jackson the party looked much like the coalition of northern artisans and southern planters who had backed

Jefferson in 1800; furthermore, as Wiltse has indicated, it looked even more like the Democratic party which was to back Wilson, Roosevelt and Truman in the twentieth century – an alliance of big city bosses, northern and western liberals and southern conservatives (Wiltse, 1965, p. 100).

There is continuing debate among historians about what Jacksonian democracy was, what the ideas of the Jacksonians were. Were they simply opportunist? The development of the spoils system under Jackson, whereby his own men were brought in to all government posts from those at the very top down to the lowliest clerks and postmasters, suggests that opportunism did play a part. Yet, at the same time, a society which believed in equality could easily accept that, since all men were equal, any man was capable of any government task. Why, therefore, should a remote, professional bureaucracy be allowed to establish itself? Of course, the administrative tasks of government at this time were relatively straightforward and in no way as complex as those of a modern industrialized society. The spoils system was rapidly adopted by politicians of other political persuasions. But besides the opportunity of employment which involvement with a party offered, there were also issues which divided parties during the 1830s: the role of the Bank of America, the removal of Indians to reservations, the disposal of public land. What appears to have been crucial in making these party issues was the advocacy of the president or of an opposition leader. Some issues, which might well have split 'the Democracy' (and its opponents), were generally accepted as non-partisan; the question of tariffs is a case in point where it seems that party leaders were prepared to let a congressman bend to pressure from his constituents rather than be expected to follow the party line. But this too, arguably, demonstrated the effectiveness of American democracy at work. Jackson became very much the leader of a party with a popular base spread throughout the country and fostered by the press, clubs and societies; his popular support encouraged and enabled him to act as a kind of people's tribune bringing his party into line behind him and even overriding opposition majorities in Congress.

The centrality of the president or presidential candidate to party, so apparent in Jacksonian America, is worth underlining as a significant contrast between party development in America and Britain. The emergent parties had many objectives, but in the United States the aspiration for the presidency unified efforts, gave a central symbolism and, through the spoils system, offered the hope of economic or social rewards for the political efforts of party supporters. British MPs could not offer such extensive rewards, and even the great party leaders of the mid-nineteenth century, Disraeli and Gladstone, did not possess the constitutional centrality of an elected president standing at the head of both the electoral and the party system.

'The Democracy' might be said to have sprung from a mixture of opportunism and an idealistic faith in the people acting as a body. It had its roots in Jefferson's ideas of democracy, though he would probably have been alarmed at the Jacksonian conviction that the people, acting as a body, could do no wrong. Jackson himself provoked violent passions both for and against. The American Whig party evolved out of the opposition to him and the fear of mass party which backed him. The Whigs attacked Jackson in the same way that Federalists had attacked Jefferson and Madison twenty years before. Yet, even if in many respects the Whigs were the party of wealth and business, they too found it necessary to court the mass of the people.

A final point worth emphasizing is the regional nature of politics in America which militated against a party structure such as was emerging in Britain during the 1830s and 1840s. Given the size of the United States, its moving frontier, and its state government structures, it was impossible for a party to be organized around a central club like the Carlton or the Reform. Communications in pre-telegraph* times took days or even weeks, and where, for instance, could such a central focus be sited? Hardly in the sparsely populated federal capital of Washington, DC, especially given the jealous way in which individual states sought to preserve their independence from federal encroachments. Hardly in one of the big cities, since its rivals would naturally object.

In 1827 Van Buren had argued:

The Morse electromagnetic telegraph system was invented in 1835.

> We must always have party distinctions, and the old ones are the best ... If the old ones are suppressed, geographical differences founded on local instincts or what is worse, prejudices between free and slave holding states will inevitably take their place.

(Quoted in Wallace, 1968, p. 490)

Thirty years later 'instincts' and 'prejudices' led to the formation of two new parties as the Democrats fudged and the Whigs disintegrated over the question of slavery. The first of these parties, the Native American Party, arose out of concern about the political power of new immigrants. From the 1830s ethno-religious groups were beginning to identify themselves according to party (something notably absent from British politics for most of the nineteenth century, not the least because the poor Irish immigrants in British cities, like the poor native inhabitants, had no vote and therefore no opportunities for organizing, or being organized within, the established political society reflected in the political parties). The key demands of the Native American Party (its members were also known as 'Know Nothings') were for the exclusion of the foreign-born from public office and the extension from five years to 25 years of the waiting period for naturalization. They were most successful in eastern states where there was an influx of immigrants and where there was a political vacuum left by the fading Whigs, but they picked up support from a variety of groups. In Massachusetts, for example, where the large number of Irish Catholic immigrants tended to support conservative Democratic politicians, the Native American Party developed out of a coalition of all kinds of Whigs and liberal Democrats. Between 1854 and 1856 the party won elections involving six governorships and 75 Congressmen, principally in the North and East. There were also 'Know Nothings' in the South, but in contrast to Massachusetts where the party tended to be liberal, in the South it attracted conservatives since the bulk of the immigrants who came into the public eye appeared opposed to slavery.

By the 1850s slavery, which had so often been pushed to one side, had become a dominant issue in American politics. Besides the hostility of abolitionists to the South's 'Peculiar Institution', there was concern in northern states that southern expansion would compel white labour – free and dignified – to compete with black slave labour – unfree and degraded. These two elements fused to form a new Republican party whose central concern was neither out-and-out abolition nor a belief in social equality for blacks, but to prevent the spread of slavery. This new party, understandably, was confined to the northern states. The Democratic party, while it still survived in the North, became increasingly tied to the slave-owners of the South.

Conclusion

By the middle of the nineteenth century both Britain and the United States had political groupings known and readily identifiable as political parties. It was a far cry from a hundred years earlier, when a 'party' was generally regarded as suspect. Yet even if both countries now had parties, and even if the 1830s was a key decade for both, the different constitutional and political contexts – the turbulence of Jacksonian America and the adjustments necessary in Britain after 1832 – had produced vastly different kinds of party.

References

Butterfield, Herbert (1969) *George III and the Historians*, revised edn, Macmillan.

Gash, Norman (1977) *Politics in the Age of Peel: A Study in the Technique of Parliamentary Representation 1830–1850*, 2nd edn, Harvester Press.

Gash, Norman (1979) *Aristocracy and People: Britain 1815–1865*, Edward Arnold.

Namier, Lewis and Brook, John (eds) (1964) *The History of Parliament: The House of Commons 1754–1790*, 3 vols, HMSO.

O'Gorman, Frank (1975) *The Rise of Party in England: The Rockingham Whigs 1760–1782*, George Allen & Unwin.

Palmer, R.R. (1959) *The Age of the Democratic Revolution: A Political History of Europe and America, 1760–1800. Volume 1: The Challenge*, Princeton University Press.

Wallace, Michael (1968) 'The New Politics and Political Innovation: Changing Concepts of Party in the United States: New York 1815–1828', *American Historical Review*, LXXIV.

Wiltse, Charles M. (1965) *The New Nation, 1800–1845*, Macmillan.

Young, James Sterling (1966) *The Washington Community 1800–1828*, New York, Harcourt Brace Jovanovich.

1.4   The suffrage and democratic government

* Latin for 'the people's voice' or public opinion.

Vox populi.* In the late eighteenth and early nineteenth centuries more people were allowed to vote in national and local elections in Britain and America than had previously been the case. Universal white male suffrage became a reality in the United States. A widened franchise was accepted in Britain. The voice of the people was heard. But was the voice of the people heeded? Were their words the determinants of government policy? Giving the vote to more people did not necessarily ensure that the government itself was acting in the interests of a commensurately wider group. The electorate might decide who governed the country, but the system had to guarantee that that government remained sensitive to popular clamour for true government by the people to prevail. Representation as well as the extension of the franchise must command our attention if we are to establish whether a demonstrably more democratic form of government had been introduced in either country by the 1850s.

Representation in Britain and America

We must come to grips with contemporary concepts of representation. In Great Britain the concept of *virtual* representation in government prevailed. By the eighteenth century there had been a marked shift from the Elizabethan conviction that the people were actually represented by Parliament to a belief in virtual representation of the people's interests. In other words, the people had given their tacit consent to live under and obey the government of their native land. Only those who had a stake in the land itself had the right to be asked directly who should govern the country and protect their interests. The interests of all were subsumed by those of the owners of property – the independent. Parliament, therefore, was seen as actually representative of property and not of the populace at large. Once elected, Parliament was sovereign. Popular influence upon the activities of members of Parliament ceased once the new Parliament was elected. Only a minority of the English governing élite believed that this situation should be changed. The Commonwealthmen, as we have seen, often urged the benefits of adult male suffrage and even those of direct democracy, operating with annual parliaments.

For America, however, the late eighteenth and early nineteenth centuries saw the triumph of the concept of direct representation of the people in government, if not of direct democracy. This development occurred in part as a result of the struggle against English rule and of the realities of property distribution in the colonies, rather than as a result of initially diverging theoretical positions on the nature of representation.

Derek Hirst, a twentieth-century historian, has indicated that the idea of the accountability of Parliament to the electorate was still alive in seventeenth-century England. In the American colonies also, while the electors generally allowed the socio-economic leaders of society the right to govern, there were occasions when government was held to account by the people.

In the colonies the property qualifications for the vote had an inclusive rather than an exclusive effect – so many people owned 40 shillings' worth of freehold land that the electorate was large. Nevertheless, the colonists still subscribed to the traditional view of property rather than people being represented. Early emigration to the New World largely involved the have-nots of the old. A general study of emigration from East Anglia in the early seventeenth century by Norman Tyack demonstrated the coincidence between emigration and slump in the local cloth trade and the relative unimportance of religious motives for emigration. Recent work on emigration from Bristol and Southampton (notably by David Galenson, David Souden and Anthony Salerno) has indicated that a high proportion of the emigrants were male, young and unmarried and drawn from either the servant class or among urban artisans. Moreover, many of the emigrants through Southampton came from already mobile communities and had existing family ties with the colonies. When in the 1640s and 1650s it became more difficult for poorer youths to gain places as apprentices, emigration appeared especially attractive. Simultaneously, it was becoming more difficult for young adults to acquire landed holdings or jobs as agricultural labourers in Wiltshire. Large numbers of indentured servants emigrated to the New World through London (80–90 per cent of the total number of indentured servants). James Horn suggests that a majority of these were migrants to London who could not find a sufficient livelihood in the capital. Most of the indentured servants were bound for the Chesapeake, which replenished its declining population in this way throughout the seventeenth century. Once a servant had fulfilled the terms of his indenture, he was a freeman, possessed of clothing, an axe and a hoe and three barrels of corn from his master and, until 1681, a warrant for 50 acres of land obtainable from the proprietor. Until the 1680s opportunities for such freedmen to become householders were good. It was not until the turn of the century that many emigrated from the Chesapeake to newer colonies in order to acquire property. If emigration to New England and the Chesapeake in the seventeenth century was largely English, that to the colonies in the eighteenth century was principally European. Although some European emigration was religious in motivation (for example, that of the Mennonites to Lancaster County, Pennsylvania), by far the predominant motive was economic. Germans and Northern Irish, who formed the bulk of the eighteenth-century emigrants, went to the colonies to find work and land.

We would do well to remember, therefore, that however different colonial society became from the society of the Old World, the colonists were nonetheless striving to duplicate the social and economic structure of the Old World in their own interests. Oscar Handlin put it well when he wrote:

> The colonists who settled at Jamestown and elsewhere along the coast after 1607 brought with them fixed conceptions of what a social order should be like. Their whole effort thereafter was devoted to recreating the forms they had known at home. Yet in practice their experience persistently led them away from the patterns they judged desirable. The American social order that finally emerged was abnormal. That is, it not only diverged from the experience of the European society from which the newcomers emigrated, but it was also contrary to their own expectations of what a social order should be.

(Handlin, 1959, p. 4)

* The colony's legislature and still the official name of the state legislature.

In the light of this statement it is important to grasp that if the vote was possessed by more adult white males in the colonies (and eventually the United States) than in Britain, this was because there were more haves than have-nots in one society than in the other and *not* because Americans accorded the same social and political weight to the have-nots as to the haves. For example, the William and Mary Charter of Massachusetts in 1691 allowed 40 shilling freeholders and £40 property holders the right to vote in the town meeting to the General Court,* those with £20 of rateable property to vote for the town meeting and to be formally admitted as inhabitants by the Selectmen. More people fulfilled these qualifications in Massachusetts than would have been the case in an equivalent community in Britain because of the amount of land available relative to population and the method of its distribution. There are those who would argue that, once land became more difficult to acquire in a given colony, the propertyless moved on to open up other lands to colonization. But there was no challenge to the basic assumption that property conferred upon a man the entitlement to vote. J.R. Pole (1966) has argued that this basis of government was so successful as a means of representing the interests of all in the Massachusetts townships of the late eighteenth and early nineteenth centuries that it commanded loyalty.

During the eighteenth century conflict between the governors and the assemblies led some factions in the colonies to emphasize the representative and accountable character of their assemblies in a way dissimilar from Britain. Massachusetts Whigs used the General Court to fight battles against the Crown's prerogative. A public gallery was built in 1766, exposing for the first time the deliberations and decisions of the court to public inspection. Speeches were henceforth actually directed at this audience in the gallery. Petitions were received to make the proceedings of the assembly fully public. But the public to which such appeals were made was that of the propertied.

We should not forget either that it was the propertied vote to which government was increasingly being made accountable when we note certain innovations in Massachusetts politics. In both 1749 and 1760 there were vociferous objections to certain names on the electoral ticket, appealing to voters to reject one who 'had lately refused to follow the instructions of his constituents'. Also, when the state House of Representatives actually circulated a draft bill (for the compensation of victims of the Stamp Act) to towns for their views, it was the views of the propertied which were sought. In the 1780 Massachusetts State Constitution, the doctrine of the direct accountability of the representatives to electoral instructions was certainly specified and seen as non-controversial, but no one denied that the electorate should be propertied.

The Stamp Act controversy sparked off an interest in controlling general policy, as opposed to individual measures affecting particular interest groups. J.R. Pole argues that it was this desire to take over government which gave irresistible force to the idea of the sovereignty of the popular will. In other words, it was the fight against foreign control of their destinies which led Americans to espouse the cause of government for the people by the people. For the moment leaders found it convenient to argue their accountability to a group of electors and to urge the support of those electors for revolutionary actions. As we have pointed out, the revolutionary leaders advocated that governments should be elected by a propertied electorate. But a number of Massachusetts political leaders were extremely wary of the concept of sovereignty even in this form. John Adams, for example, felt that any constitution must protect the government against the repeated appeal to interest groups which the suggestion of direct popular accountability implied. Members of this camp envisaged the written constitution as a protection against direct democratic rule – which they saw as leading inevitably to an unstable government. It would, therefore, be incorrect to assume that all the American revolutionary leaders spoke with the same voice on this issue of representation.

It is certainly possible to argue that in America the concept of government representing people rather than property triumphed earlier than it did in Great Britain. But the transformation often seems to have taken place for pragmatic reasons rather than because of an initial belief in democracy. In 'The eighteenth-century Commonwealthman' we have seen how American politicians were influenced by the ideas of English Commonwealthmen, which certainly advocated a more direct representation of popular interests in government. But a glance at the constitutional history of Massachusetts, for example, will indicate that it was often practical politics rather than ideology which impelled Americans towards 'democratic' declarations.

In Massachusetts in the later eighteenth century, the towns of the eastern seaboard, which were larger and more populous than the newer corporations of the interior, came to support the idea of representation based upon population rather than upon wealth or privilege, precisely because this allowed them to maintain their own influence in the face of rivalry from the countryside and other towns. Under the Massachusetts Constitution of 1780 the allocation of seats in the state legislature was based upon the population of the constituencies. A distinction was beginning to be drawn between persons and property, although it was by no means fully developed. And it should be noted that the Massachusetts Constitution made no attempt to grant representation to the inhabitants of communities which were not incorporated. They were still politically non-existent.

The development of a distinction between the representation of people and of property can be traced by way of certain responses to the creation of the Massachusetts State Constitution. Massachusetts, of course, was not the United States of America. The development of concepts of representative government took place in varying ways and at different paces in the states of the Union. Nevertheless, ideas produced in Massachusetts did not have a purely parochial importance. The theory and practice of government on the national stage owed much to the ideologies prevalent in the constituent states and particularly to those of two very different societies: the landed society of Virginia and the commercial society of Massachusetts. It is, therefore, well worth our while to explore reactions to the work of the Massachusetts Convention in the revolutionary period.

The Essex Result was a pamphlet produced by the towns of Essex County, Massachusetts which objected to the proposed state constitution of 1778. The authors of the pamphlet argued for a bicameral system of government which would represent and safeguard the *two* interests of government – property and persons. Because the state House of Representatives was to represent persons, there should be no property qualification for it; because the Senate did represent property, on the other hand, there should be a property qualification for it. The representatives, once elected, should be the people in miniature – a mirror of the people.

When the Massachusetts Convention drew up a new draft constitution in 1779, it made explicit that this distinction between property and persons was the principle underlying the new structure. Seats in the House of Representatives were apportioned on a numerical basis to represent the population. Seats in the Senate were distributed on the basis of taxes paid by the counties. The property qualification for the vote was actually raised, which gave rise to some objections, but most 'independent' men over the age of 21 had the right to vote. At any event, when the constitution was settled these stipulations were widely disregarded – all poll-paying males over the age of 21 were in practice allowed to vote. The right to further participation in government was, however, much more restricted. For example, there was a strict economic control on who might become governor.

In Massachusetts the constitution was itself drawn up by a convention of delegates which was elected on universal white male suffrage within the towns. The procedure reinforced the view that the constitution – which provided the accepted boundaries for future government activity – must arise directly from the popular will, even if control of the details of actual government did not rest with the whole people. But in characteristic Massachusetts fashion, the convention neglected the political existence of rural dwellers. The convention delegates were elected townspeople. The draft constitution was circulated in and debated by the town meetings. The importance of the older, incorporated, commercial societies in Massachusetts' political life was thus revealed.

In Virginia, a society in which land rather than commerce conferred status, the idea that delegates represented landed property interests remained dominant. Thomas Jefferson's view that the government represented the majority interests of politically equal individuals was that of a vocal minority only. The 1776 Virginia State Constitution based the suffrage qualification upon the freehold ownership of land and, in general, permitted election to the state House of Representatives to all who were qualified to vote and to the Senate to all freehold residents of 25 years or above. What was, in fact, a very wide suffrage should not delude us into thinking that the Virginians thought in terms of a democratic franchise. What we are seeing here is the representation of propertied interests and a vote granted to those with property.

Thomas Jefferson's views on the franchise were unusual in their emphasis upon active involvement in government by the people. Jefferson argued that residence and payment of taxes should form the basis of qualification for the vote and for office. However, wherever possible, he recommended facilitating participation by the people in government. His policy was one of inclusion and not exclusion. Thus he would have *given* 50 unimproved acres of land to enfranchise landless citizens. When he penned his *Notes on Virginia* he urged a strictly numerical basis for representation and the introduction of measures to counter the emerging despotism of legislative assemblies. His carefully argued views on the nature of representation were used to great advantage some years later by the Jacksonian democrats.

In Virginia itself in the late eighteenth and early nineteenth centuries there was little agitation for white manhood suffrage; in communities which sent delegates to the assemblies it was effectively present in any case. But population movements into the west of the state had led to such inequities of representation that there was considerable agitation for reapportionment of seats. The War of 1812 saw those areas without representation making unorganized and ineffective attempts to petition for reform. When, however, the 1827 elections came around, the electors extracted pledges from the new Convention to reform the basis of representation. This saw a battle between Conservatives, who wanted to base representation upon the enumeration both of the population and of slave and land ownership, and Reformers, who wanted a new assessment of the white population as the sole basis for distribution of seats. The Reformers did not argue for universal manhood suffrage. In 1830 the state suffrage in Virginia was extended to leaseholders at the same time that seats were reallocated on a strictly numerical basis. It was not until 1845 that the suffrage was given to all adult white males who were not paupers.

Both Vermont and New Hampshire had universal adult white male suffrage by the 1780s, and the same was true of Illinois, Missouri and Indiana by 1820. Other states had extremely wide franchises by the 1820s, and by 1845 property restrictions on the right to vote were all but extinct in the United States. But before we rush to conclude that the Americans had won the fight for adult manhood suffrage many years before the British, we should recall that in America there was no real campaign for a widening of the franchise. The real fight was over representation. Universal adult white male suffrage was granted as a postscript to allowing representation to new interest groups and communities. In communities which already had representation, there was often *de facto* manhood suffrage long before it was claimed as a matter of principle. It should be noted that the right to vote was *not* written into the original US Constitution or into the Bill of Rights as a fundamental human right. And the individual states set their own limitations upon the franchise for federal as well as for state elections. Positive political participation had to be won in the nineteenth century. It was won because it caught onto the coat-tails of the campaign for representation.

Parliamentary reform

In Great Britain, as well as in the United States, the campaign which had most force behind it was that for the representation of new interests and new communities. In the United States the new communities were those produced as the frontier was pushed further and further back. In Great Britain they were the rapidly growing industrial towns of the North and Midlands and the parts of London which had inadequate representation. The movement to gain representation for commercial and manufacturing interests in Britain was triumphant. The Reform Act of 1832 disfranchised 56 boroughs and redistributed their seats largely to industrial towns and to areas of London previously unrepresented. The movement towards universal manhood suffrage, however, suffered from its revolutionary associations and from the fact that representation was so easily won by the new industrial towns. There was no need for commercial and manufacturing interests to seek and maintain alliances with the radical working-class politicians who sought manhood suffrage. It was thus far less easy for the movement for an extended suffrage to harness itself strategically to the demand for direct representation than it had been in America.

Perhaps the easiest way to understand the British parliamentary reforms of the nineteenth century is through the system of deference which permeated British society and politics. The society was based upon the idea that each and every individual owed deference to another. At its simplest, this had once been seen in the feudal organization of society in which the lords held their power and land from the king, to whom they owed allegiance and deferred. Below this, the tenants held land from the lord and owed him deference. By the nineteenth century society was much more complex, but the idea that some persons or classes naturally commanded the deference of their 'inferiors' was still very much alive. Traditionally, the claim to deference was based upon the ownership of land. It was much more difficult for the British system to accommodate the idea that there were other forms of property which conferred this right than it was, for example, for a commercial society such as Boston, Massachusetts. But by the nineteenth century other claims were being lodged which were based upon wealth made through commerce and manufacture. Nevertheless, few of the ruling groups (or of those aspiring to enter them) wished to destroy the ordered system and replace it with one based upon the free expression of the individual will.

In the early years of the nineteenth century some of the country's political leadership began to seek reform of the system of representation not because they wanted to end the influence of men of property – far from it – but because they came to believe that the existing operation of the system denied the very principles of representation in which they believed. In some boroughs it was one magnate, and probably not even a very important local landowner, who returned the members of Parliament. This was a travesty of the system. For it was regarded as axiomatic that the local landowner would command the political deference of the constituents (his tenants) because they knew that he, with his own vested interests in the welfare of the community, would act in their interests. In other words, when they voted according to the landowner's wishes, they would not be acting out of fear or because they were being bought, but out of inclination in their own self-interest. Where there were several important landlords, all would exercise such influence. There would be no question of bringing in out-voters (i.e. persons who lived outside the constituency) to effect the election of a particular candidate. This smacked too much of personal ambition and too little of a sense of responsibility towards the community. A few examples of what was considered to be wrong will suffice. At Banbury, for instance, the Earl of Guildford maintained control of the election because the corporation was packed with his kinsmen and friends (who were nonresident). The citizens of Banbury, on the other hand, had no spokesman on the corporation and no vote in the election. At Nottingham in 1817 the Whig corporation actually created a large number of honorary freemen in order to control elections to both parliamentary seats.

Essentially, the cries for reform from among the ruling élite stemmed not from a new conviction that a system based upon property was wrong or that the vote should be given to more people. Rather it was convinced that the system actually in operation did not give due influence to property and instead gave it to the personal ambitions of a very few persons. Eventually attacks upon the electoral system as it stood became so frequent that reform based upon the redistribution of seats became probable. Those new groups seeking representation in Parliament were able to achieve it because members of the existing ruling élite also sought change.

Of course, not everyone believed that the society based on deference should continue. Put at its simplest, the industrial proletariat, living in abominable conditions and suffering the consequences of endemic slumps, had little faith in the 'responsible' attitudes of the governing classes. On the whole, this discontent was unorganized, and because there was little tradition of political interest among the propertyless, expressions of political unrest tended to coincide with worsened economic conditions (such as those of 1817 and 1819) and to disappear when conditions improved. There are, therefore, some problems in accepting too readily E.P. Thompson's thesis that these years witnessed the rapid transformation of the 'labouring poor' into the 'working class'.

In the minds of many, however, the worrying spectre of popular unrest was associated with the demands of the late eighteenth-century radicals for universal manhood suffrage – universal political rights. It has been suggested that, as a result of the terror of 1793–4, a whole generation of manufacturers, merchants and shopkeepers were gripped by a lasting fear of the consequences of giving the vote to the working classes. These same people were resentful of the political leadership of the country because they felt that the system denied themselves the rewards to which their hard work and material success entitled them, but as a rule they did not wish to distribute these rewards lower down the social scale. The radical programme for an extension of the franchise based upon individual rights was not, therefore, popular among these groups as long as they believed they could achieve what they wanted from the ruling élite. The success of the movement for an extension of the franchise would depend on how successful its supporters were in harnessing it effectively to the reform of representation which the middle classes did want and which the political leadership saw increasingly as inevitable.

Michael Brock (1973) has made a persuasive case for arguing that the Whigs proposed parliamentary reform in the early 1830s as a direct response to fear. Riots in the South-east, trades union activities, and continental revolutions made it seem sensible to reform Parliament in a way which would strengthen the influence of men of property and the existing aristocratic leadership, while enlisting the support of important sections of the commercial and manufacturing communities. The cabinet issued instructions to a committee to prepare a bill which would satisfy public opinion so that further innovation would not be sought, and yet which would not set the existing form of government at risk. The reforms which were accepted were very moderate, based upon the abolition of rotten boroughs, the representation of populous areas, and the enfranchisement of groups of copyholders and leaseholders (in the countryside) and householders (in the boroughs) who might be judged to be 'independent'.

The 1832 Act, then, did not introduce universal manhood suffrage. In fact, it did not introduce any new *principle* into the concept of government. In the new system as in the old, only 'independent' men might vote. What had changed was the criterion used to determine independence. The operation of government after 1832 depended upon deference just as it had before. But it was now accepted grudgingly that industrial society demanded that 'new men' be deferred to in addition to the traditional ruling élite and new interests be represented. The electorate was formed of 'propertied, deferential and independent' men, the Parliament of propertied men of influence. Even in the 1860s moderate bills proposing minor extensions of the electorate were sufficient to bring down governments – as in 1866. When the Conservatives introduced the Second Reform Bill in 1867, they did so because Disraeli wished to ensure the moderation of what he and others regarded as inevitable – further extension of the electorate and redistribution of seats. This Act did give the vote to artisans, but the electorate of Great Britain still represented less than 10 per cent of the total population.

Jacksonian democracy?

Our study has suggested that, while in practice the electorate in the United States was far broader than that in Great Britain, in both countries the theory was similar: government directly represented the interests of the propertied, who participated in government and elected governments. The propertyless were not directly represented. The wide franchise in America may have been more an accident of geography than a design. Yet Americans proclaimed their commitment to democracy. Why?

Some American politicians certainly made the idea of democratic government a matter of propaganda and/or principle. In the United States as in Great Britain, the natural leaders of society had ever feared their displacement and consequent social revolution as a concomitant of universal suffrage and a government truly responsive to the popular will. The debate mentioned in 'The eighteenth-century Commonwealthman' continued throughout the antebellum (pre-war) period. In 1776 John Adams had been enthusiastic about the 'opportunity of making an election of government' for 'When, before the present epoch, had three millions of people full power and a fair opportunity to form and establish the wisest and happiest government that human wisdom can contrive?' But with independence came revived fear of the masses and proposals such as those of Massachusetts for two-chamber governments which would preserve the interests of the 'natural' leaders as well as of the people. The views of John Adams and of his son, John Quincy Adams, were sharply contrasted with those of Thomas Jefferson, who had no fear of democratic government. According to Jefferson a democracy or republic meant 'a government by its citizens in mass, acting directly and personally, according to rules established by the majority'. He was steadfastly opposed to any idea that the courts should decide on the constitutionality of legislative acts. Jefferson argued that this task rested with the people. He felt that the courts were not necessarily more objective than the mass of the people. Moreover, there could be no checks on the judges (who, at that level, were political appointees) whereas democracy furnished its own natural checks and balances, being flexible, responsive to public needs and, of necessity, slow to act. Such principles were reiterated continually by Jacksonian democrats at a time when adult white male suffrage was a reality in much of the United States and a truly democratic government thus a possibility.

The Jacksonians laid great stress in public upon the popular basis of government. For instance, in 1838 John L. O'Sullivan wrote the following in the opening editorial of his new *Democratic Review:*

> We cannot, therefore, look with an eye of favor on any such forms of representation as, by the length of tenure of delegated power, tend to weaken that universal and unrelaxing responsibility to the vigilance of public opinion, which is the true conservative principle of our institutions ...
>
> We believe, then, in the principle of democratic republicanism, in its strongest and purest sense. We have an abiding confidence in the virtue, intelligence and full capacity for self-government, of the great mass of our people – our industrious, honest, manly, intelligent millions of freemen.

And in his farewell speech of 4 March 1837 Andrew Jackson himself expressed his belief in the wisdom of the people, whose self-interest, at the very least, would lead to balanced government.

But do such public statements really prove either that the Jacksonian Democrats were the champions of democratic reform or that, when in office, their government served the interests of a broader spectrum of the electorate than other governments? In the first half of the twentieth century it was fashionable to see Jacksonian America as the age of the 'common man' and to see Andrew Jackson as his hero. Variously, historians proposed that the core of Jacksonian democracy was to be found either in the movement of urban working men in the East or among the backwoods farmers of the western frontier. Alternatively, it was seen as the expression of the interests of entrepreneurs. In taking this line, historians were accepting the observations of Alexis de Tocqueville in the nineteenth century regarding the contrasts between the society of the New World and that of the old. America was a society of self-made men who, although born to humble families, both amassed wealth and power and lost them amazingly quickly. It was a dynamic society in flux and a society in which each man had to *earn* deference, as opposed to that of Britain where men were born to command deference. In American society the possessors of wealth had dwindling social and political influence. The masses ruled and the 'old aristocracy' opted out of politics. But there are considerable problems in accepting either de Tocqueville's characterization of American society or the assumption that under Jackson the masses actually ruled the country.

It is true that voter participation in national politics in the United States reached a high point in the early nineteenth century. The proportion of qualified voters who exercised their vote in presidential elections between 1828 and 1840 was always near the highest point reached, and this was especially true in 1840. Andrew Jackson seems demonstrably to have been swept to power by the popular vote, which responded to him as the hero of the War of 1812. But it would be rash to assume that Jacksonian policies were dictated by this same popular vote. There seems to be considerable evidence to the contrary and a strong suggestion that the high rate of voter participation in presidential elections had as much to do with the organization of mass politics by the Democrats as with warranted faith in Jackson's commitment to popular policies. In other words, while the British feared to give the people the vote, anticipating riot and even revolution, the Jacksonian Democrats, faced with a wide suffrage, saw its potential and organized the mass vote to fight their own political enemies – the Whigs.

In recent years a number of historians have studied aspects of the age of the common man to establish whether or not American society was as dynamic as Alexis de Tocqueville would have us believe and, as a corollary, whether wealth and birth had less sway there than in the Old World. Was this a society in which the interests of the self-made man reigned supreme? Edward Pessen has indicated that very few of the United States' wealthiest men came from humble backgrounds – with important and well-known exceptions such as John Jacob Astor in New York. In general, affluence was combined with high social status. Pessen maintains that the so-called era of the common man was marked by more and not less social rigidity than previous periods in American history. Similarly, Edward Willis argues that evidence of social mobility in New York was marked prior to 1815 but came to an abrupt halt thereafter. Moreover, the rich seem to have tightened their hold upon community wealth after the colonial period. Far from there being a more equal distribution of property and wealth, there was a more unequal one. The socio-economic élite continued to dominate local government, invariably holding the mayoral office and a disproportionate number of seats in council and aldermanry. Unskilled labourers and journeymen, who composed three-fifths of urban populations, were completely absent from such local government offices. Of course, it is possible that the rich were disproportionately represented and yet uninfluential, but a study of city government politics suggests that this was not the case. Even after the 1840s when the artisan/middle classes became more numerous on city councils, the policies of urban councils continued to favour the entrepreneurial and professional groups. Significantly, the traditional socio-economic élite, while now unwilling to occupy seats on councils increasingly concerned with mundane affairs, remained attracted to the position of true power in city politics – the mayoralty. It is noticeable that the budgets of councils remained small because the wealthy refused accurate assessments of wealth and consequent higher taxation. When money was spent upon the improvement of the environment – for example, to pave Boston's streets, provide lighting and sewerage – it was chiefly expended in middle class and wealthy areas. In Brooklyn a much needed sewerage system was directly blocked by the refusal of the rich to pay a new tax. When Philadelphia's council wished to economize in the 1820s, it cut its poor relief despite the recent doubling of the urban population, while launching forth into enormous expenditure upon a transport system which would serve the private commercial concerns of the well-to-do. In Boston and New York policing was sorely neglected until ethnic riots began to impinge upon the lives of the wealthy.

If local government was conducted in the interests of a traditional 'aristocracy' of wealth and property, was national government any the less so? Did the Jacksonian governments really work to promote political democracy and economic opportunity for all? Historians have concentrated above all upon the significance of the Jacksonian opposition to the banking interest in government. In his farewell address Jackson gave an excellent summary of his stated policy regarding the bank. He wanted to exclude the bank from control over the currency in order to prevent periodic depressions manipulated to serve particular interests, to prevent the rise of independent powers not responsible to the people and able to defy the government, and to prevent the rule of a monied aristocracy that could exploit the people. Jackson consistently represented the power of the incorporated bank as a constitutional issue: 'The Bank of the United States is in itself a Government which has gradually increased in strength from the day of its establishment. The question between it and the people has become one of power.'

And the bank itself played into his hands. In 1834 the bank's president, Nicholas Biddle, refused to allow a committee of Congress to investigate bank records or to examine the bank's officers. The bank in his view was independent. Jackson and other Democrats rephrased this assertion to read that the bank was independent of government – that is, popular – control. Others were tempted to rephrase the conflict as one between employer and employed. Thus Orestes Brownson of the *Boston Quarterly Review* wrote, 'The Banks represent the interest of the employer, and therefore of necessity interests adverse to those of the employed; that is, they represent the interests of the business community in opposition to the laboring community.' Whereas most Jacksonians would have found the corollary of this analysis unacceptable – an appeal to the destruction of all monopolies and all hereditary privilege – they would have lent certain support to the point that the government of the United States was not to be controlled by sectional interests.

Indeed, the Jacksonians made great play upon the old Jeffersonian point that the majority will must triumph in the federal government. Attempts to divide the nation against itself along geographical or other lines were wrong. Left to themselves, the people would rule wisely and well. And a further traditional point was reiterated continually: the best government is that which governs least. Such views led to a development of *laissez-faire* policies well-suited to a burgeoning commercial and industrial society and to the needs of enterprising frontiersmen, but in conflict with the idea that social and economic inequalities should be legislated against. One of the most notable aspects of the bank episode is the manner in which the Jacksonians were able to absorb its 'message' into a total perspective on the state of the Constitution. It became part of the Jeffersonian myth which the Jacksonians used to rally support for their claim to office. Central to this myth was the choice which Americans must now make between democratic and aristocratic government, between a government which honoured states' rights and one which created an overweening federal power, between decentralization and concentration of power, between economy and debt, between pure government and corruption.

This was the myth but the reality – the motivation behind Jacksonian policies – is far less easy to identify. In the 1930s Frederick Jackson Turner made an attempt to relate Jacksonian democracy to the traits of frontier society. Jackson's support, he claimed, came from such men, and his policies therefore reflected their desire for less government and an economic framework which encouraged the competitive spirit. Arthur Meier Schlesinger, Jr's *The Age of Jackson* repudiated this thesis, indicating that eastern ideas moulded Jacksonian policies. Jackson was directly influenced by the bullionist theories of eastern merchants. Jackson was able to carry this policy in the frontier states only on the strength of his reputation as Old Hero. Nevertheless, it had a strong appeal for the farmers of the South and the 'submerged classes' of the East. And the Jacksonians were quick to try to win the working-class vote by making it seem that the depression of the late 1820s and 1830s was due to the paper-money system alone. The historian Richard Hofstadter countered this argument, and that of Turner, with a thesis which depicted Jackson as the agent of policies designed to please the capitalists. In the 1950s Bray Hammond laid emphasis upon the impact of the new immigration upon American politics. According to him, the Jacksonian government introduced policies in tune with *laissez-faire* and the spirit of enterprise. For example, Chief Justice Taney decided against the claims of the proprietors of the old Warren Bridge on the Charles River when he favoured the demand for a new bridge. This judgement of the Supreme Court set an important precedent: when the interests of the majority were at stake, the private interests of the minority would be overruled. The rights of property should be 'sacredly guarded', but 'we must not forget that the community also have rights and that the happiness and well-being of every citizen depends upon their faithful preservation'. His decision against the old Warren Bridge monopoly left the way open for new development, providing a precedent for the building of new railroads and roads on the lines of old turnpikes. Something can be said in favour of all these interpretations, but on balance those which see the Jacksonians as most influenced by the demands of eastern commercial and manufacturing interests and by the needs of enterprising immigrants seem most persuasive.

When Jackson conducted his presidential campaign against Adams in 1828, it was based not upon a specific platform with promise of economic reform, but upon a series of attacks upon Adams's monarchist, aristocratic and bureaucratic beliefs – upon his constitutional position and the groups in society whom he was seen to represent. Jackson triumphed in that election by 647,000 votes to 508,000. When Jackson governed he acted in the interests of those who had not been the 'natural leaders' of post-revolutionary American society: the 'liberals of the small propertied type' and, more specifically, eastern manufacturers and small merchants. The support of the wider electorate was retained because the Jacksonian publicity machine managed to show these policies as part of a total approach to the American system of government, acceptable to urban and rural voters alike. The economic ideal was that of a society made up of small property owners left free to make their fortunes with a minimum of government interference. The constitutional ideal was that of a government for the people by the people, with a federal government responsive to the wishes of the people and yet deliberately non-interventionist in state affairs.

Although much work remains to be done on the actualities of politics in Jacksonian America, it seems reasonable to suggest that this was not an egalitarian society such as de Tocqueville painted. It also seems plausible to claim that the Jacksonians, while appealing to a wide electorate of small property owners in towns and countryside, in the East and on the frontier, geared their policies to serve the needs of specific sections of eastern society.

Conclusion

This is not to say that American society was *like* British society, but it does remind us of the importance of looking behind the public statements of politicians and the terminology employed within them. Louis Hartz (1955) claimed that during the early nineteenth century Americans were trying to apply European liberal ideas in a society which was highly dissimilar from that of Europe. In fact, when the American spoke of a democrat he was really identifying people who would in England have been called liberals from the small propertied classes. Jacksonian political philosophy spoke for these groups rather than for the mob. Once we grasp this point, it is possible to see the points of contact between the British and American experiences.

American historians have demonstrated the great interest shown by voters in state and national politics. While traditional wealth retained and even extended its grasp on the corridors of power, the independent voters were active in local politics and elections. In Great Britain, also, great interest was shown in politics. This is most demonstrably true of local elections, in which voters of the middle classes were involved. Polls of lower than 50 per cent were unusual in Chester County Council elections before 1918, and polls of 70–80 per cent were not unusual. But this is not to contend that the lower echelons of the urban middle classes had an important say in local government decisions. Studies of local government policies in the nineteenth century – for example, in the new spa towns and resorts – suggest that urban development and improvement was designed to benefit the well-to-do merchants and manufacturers as well as the traditional social leaders.

If we look at the national government, the impact of the newly enfranchised middle classes upon the composition of government seems no more startling. The composition of the House of Commons in the nineteenth century remained overwhelmingly upper middle class and aristocratic. Few prime ministers came from families outside high society. And modern scholarly accounts show the major parties striving to rule in the interests of an élite, making only such concessions to lower middle-class and working-class interests as were deemed absolutely necessary to secure their support. Government by the majority in the interests of the majority was still light years away.

In the political world of the late eighteenth and early nineteenth centuries in both countries, the campaign for adult male suffrage was considered as of little consequence by the leaders of political society. Their main concern was that property retained its proper influence upon government. The key issue was what constituted property in a changing society. Twentieth-century historians, influenced by current preoccupations with political equality and rights, do their understanding of the eighteenth- and nineteenth-century political scene a disservice by laying undue stress upon the campaign for universal suffrage. Political thought at the time was still preoccupied with the traditional view of government as serving the interests of property. Changing ideas about the nature of property in an increasingly commercial and industrialized society led in time to an adaptation of the old system of government in Britain. In the United States, where property was so much within the grasp of all, universal male suffrage for white adults became a *fait accompli* rather than a principle. When Jackson spoke of the role of democracy in government, he was speaking of the *direct representation of a specific type of property*, not of mass suffrage.

References and further reading

Brock, Michael (1973) *The Great Reform Act*, Hutchinson.

Duesen, Glyndon G. van (1959) *Jacksonian Era, 1828–1848*, Hamish Hamilton.

Handlin, Oscar (1959) 'The Significance of the Seventeenth Century' in James Morton Smith (ed.) *Seventeenth Century America*, New York, Norton.

Hartz, L. (1955) *The Liberal Tradition in America*, New York, Random House.

Pole, J.R. (1966) *Political Representation in England and the Origins of the American Republic*, Macmillan.

Rozwenc, E.C. (ed.) (1963) *The Meaning of Jacksonian Democracy*, Boston, Heath.

Rozwenc, E.C. (ed.) (1964) *Ideology and Power in the Age of Jackson*, New York, Anchor Books.

Tate, T.W. and Ammerman, D.L. (eds) (1979) *The Chesapeake in the Seventeenth Century*, Chapel Hill, University of North Carolina Press.

1.5   The individual and the law

> To speak this as plainly as I can. As the laws of the land are the
> measures of our active obedience, so are also the same laws
> the measure of our submission. And as we are not bound to
> obey but where the laws and constitution require our obe-
> dience, so neither are we bound to submit but as the laws and
> constitution do require our submission.

(John Sharp, Archbishop of York, to the House of Lords, 30 January 1700)

In any society the law defines and limits what the individual may and may
not do. Different societies, of course, have different kinds of laws, and
differently constituted legislatures pass different kinds of legislation. In
some societies customary rules are of greater importance than statutory
laws – that is, enacted legislation. As the above quotation illustrates, the
law orders individuals specifically to do or not to do certain things, but it
also allows certain actions simply by omitting to forbid them. As a result
an individual living in a complex society often finds it impossible to find
his or her way along the law's labyrinthine lanes.

In both Britain and America from 1760 to 1900 the law was held in
high regard. No individual, be he president, monarch or prime minister,
preacher, publican or pauper, was above the law. The law was seen to
guarantee freedom against oppression. John Locke, the late seventeenth-
century philosopher and political theorist, made it abundantly clear that
without law there could be no true freedom.

But there were problems. One person's freedom guaranteed in and
by law could restrict another's; for example, if a factory owner could hire
and fire at will, the free speech of his workforce, particularly in the event
of a labour surplus, might be severely restricted. Pressure groups could
push through laws which impeded the freedom of large numbers of
individuals. One interest group might triumph over all others. If the state
was avowedly Christian, the atheist's or deist's right to free speech could
be limited. Thus George Jacob Holyoake was sentenced to six months in
Gloucester gaol in 1842 for blasphemy. If the political establishment of a
state felt threatened in time of war or by massive popular support for
some measure, it could legislate against public assembly and public criticism.

What then was the position of the 'democracy' – the people – in
relation to the law during this period? To what extent did the law protect
the interests of the 'individual' at this time? Did the law increasingly
favour particular interest groups within society as the period progressed
and, if so, which ones? Can we identify similar developments in both
countries? Well, obviously, we cannot hope to answer these questions of
enormous complexity in a brief essay. We can hope, however, to
introduce the problem and suggest some lines of inquiry.

Rights and liberties

How far were the people of Britain and America protected as individuals
by the law? There existed a variety of individual, and some would say

'fundamental', 'rights' which were not enforceable in either English or Scottish law. While eighteenth-century Englishmen certainly believed that they possessed these rights, the rights themselves depended rather more on convention and the observation of unwritten rules by government, Parliament and the courts than on statute law. Freedom from arbitrary arrest, freedom of speech, of publication, of assembly and even of property all fell into this category. The Habeas Corpus Act of 1679 (and the improved legislation of 1816) was a piece of legal machinery which enabled the legality of imprisonment to be tested in the courts; it was not a guarantee of freedom from arbitrary arrest. Furthermore, any act could be wholly or partially repealed by Parliament. Pitt's government suspended the Habeas Corpus Act for much of the 1790s. While only a small number of people were likely to be arrested without charge and without trial, there was the fear and, in some instances, the belief – which the government did nothing to gainsay – that the suspension was universal. Freedom of speech was not guaranteed by law, although it could be tested subsequently in the courts. Fox's Libel Act of 1792 authorized juries, as opposed to judges, to decide whether or not a libel had been committed. But it remained possible for the authorities to pack juries (hardly playing the game by the unwritten rules) or to use archaic machinery (such as *ex officio* information*) to ensure that 'offenders' were imprisoned and not brought to trial without punitive personal expense (Emsley, 1981, pp. 168–9). Freedom of assembly was a similar case and, perhaps more remarkably, so was and is freedom of property. The monarch and his servants cannot seize personal property, but Parliament can pass legislation restraining the exercise of any right having an economic value; generally Parliament will pay compensation but it is not required to do so. The revered exponent of eighteenth-century English law, William Blackstone, was well aware of the situation in this respect and noted it in his *Commentaries*.

* Such information was obtained on oath from the defendant by order of the court. This was therefore a compulsory, potentially self-incriminatory, device.

This was the situation in the abstract. But people believed that they had these rights. And this belief was shared by all. Governments only bent or broke the conventions in exceptional circumstances, such as with the fear of Jacobinism in the 1790s and the fear of radicalism and revolution in the period immediately following the Napoleonic Wars.

The American colonists shared this belief in British 'rights and liberties'. They felt that they had been the victims of just such action in exceptional circumstances. After they experienced what they perceived as threats to their rights as freeborn Englishmen by the British Crown, they demanded written guarantees of fundamental rights within the new state and federal constitutions. Specific rights were granted to individuals under the law by the original US Constitution, by the Bill of Rights (the first ten amendments of 1791) and by later amendments. These included freedom of speech and of the press; the right to assemble and to petition the government for redress of grievances; the right to bear arms; freedom from unreasonable search and seizure and from general, unspecific warrants; the right to trial by jury with expedition; the right to know of what one is accused and to confront prosecution witnesses, with advice of counsel; the right against self-incrimination; the right to reasonable bail; and protection from cruel and unreasonable punishment. These were seen to be fundamental laws which were not granted by man and which could not be removed by man. The rights were to be guaranteed against encroachment by the federal government, more particularly by Congress. As Thomas Jefferson put it: 'A Bill of Rights is what the people are entitled to against every government on earth, general or particular, and what no just government should refuse, or rest on inferences.' Nor was it only at the federal level that such rights were perceived as fundamental and inalienable; many individual states incorporated a bill of rights into their own constitutions. This belief in the existence of a fundamental law itself owed much to certain strands of English thought – to that of the Commonwealthmen, for instance – but it was separate from the common law strand of thought, which envisaged law as evolving in response to events despite the emphasis in common law upon precedent.

In addition to these fundamental laws guaranteed by the Constitution, the American federal and state governments also made new laws – laws of men. There was always the danger that fresh legislation might contradict or negate the fundamental rights of the individual before the law. What protection was there for the individual in America over and above the good will of governments – a protection which the Englishman also possessed? The Constitution did not assign the Supreme Court of the United States the role of watchdog, but it is clear from the writings of some American leaders that such a function was envisaged for it. In No. 78 of the *Federalist Papers* Alexander Hamilton argued that courts, the 'least dangerous' branch of government, should guard the Constitution by means of judicial review:

> ... the courts were designed to be an intermediate body between the people and the legislature, in order, among other things, to keep the latter within the limits assigned to their authority. The interpretation of the laws is the proper and peculiar province of the courts. A constitution is, in fact, and must be regarded by the judges as a fundamental law. It therefore belongs to them to ascertain its meaning, as well as the meaning of any particular act proceeding from the legislative body. If there should happen to be an irreconcilable variance between the two, that which has the superior obligation and validity ought, of course, to be preferred; or, in other words, the Constitution ought to be preferred to the statute, the intention of the people to the intention of their agents.

> (Quoted in Wright, 1961, p. 492)

In fact, the procedure of judicial review did not develop until Chief Justice John Marshall's court in the 1800s. Although the constitutional validity of the Alien and Sedition Acts (1798) was challenged by Jefferson and Madison among others, the case was never brought to law or before the Supreme Court for a decision. The case of *Marbury* v. *Madison* in 1803 represents the first occasion when the Supreme Court was asked to decide whether a law passed by Congress was unconstitutional.

The Supreme Court, indeed, has never initiated the process of review, and it was not until the early twentieth century that the Supreme Court acknowledged any ability to rule on the constitutional validity of legislation passed by *state* legislatures. Individuals who felt that specific federal legislation encroached upon constitutional rights could bring their case before the Supreme Court via the normal process of appeals; if the offending legislation was a state act, then they were advised to seek redress within that state. New legislation was not (and is not) *automatically* subjected to review. Even when a case was intended as a test to challenge the validity of the law, it had to follow the normal legal procedure through the various federal courts before being referred to this final court of appeal. The process, therefore, was both accidental and slow. The Supreme Court's decision was ruled by a majority vote of the justices.

By employing the Supreme Court in this way, Americans were harking back to the system whereby the English Privy Council had served as a review body for colonial legislation and also to the tradition of judicial interpretation of the law. English judges were accorded a large role in shaping the law, because so much case law was based upon precedent. Of course, when there was no written constitution, English judges could not brand a law as 'unconstitutional'. But they could and did employ common law to criticize statute law. In this way judges could take account of changes in society in advance of Parliament. For instance, in 1756 Lord Mansfield condemned the cornerstone of existing industrial policy, the Elizabethan Statute of Artificers, in the following terms:

> 1st ... This is a *penal law;* 2dly., it is in *Restraint of natural Right.,*
> 3dly., It is *contrary to the general Right* given by the Common Law
> of this Kingdom; I will add 4thly., The *Policy* upon which the
> Act was made, is *From Experience,* become doubtful.

It is possible to argue that the English system of judge-made law, combined with Parliament's ability to change the 'constitution' by legislation requiring a simple majority, was much more flexible than the American system. At the same time, however, it made it more difficult for English subjects to comprehend the true extent of their constitutional position and rights.

Equality before the law

Did all individuals have the same rights before the law? In England there was a hierarchy of statuses before the law: the natural-born subject (whose positive legal rights were not, as we have seen, specifically defined *en bloc*); the naturalized citizen; the denizen (foreigner admitted to residence and certain rights); the perpetual alien; the alien friend; the alien enemy – all stood in a different relationship to the law. For example, until the nineteenth century, natives of countries at war with Britain who were resident in England had restrictions placed upon their real property rights. Other aliens could not bring real actions in law and could neither exercise franchises nor hold offices to which property was attached. Recipients of parliamentary acts of naturalization were automatically possessed of the full legal rights of Englishmen. But those who were made denizens by royal patent received restricted rights – they could not inherit land or pass it on to children born before their denization. Until 1688 naturalized subjects enjoyed full political rights, whereas denizens did not. Hostility to the Dutch followers of William III led to naturalized subjects losing political rights at the Glorious Revolution. Intriguingly, however, the colonial charters acknowledged that the colonists were still English subjects who 'shall have and enjoy all liberties, franchises and immunities within any of our other dominions, to all intents and purposes, as if they had been abiding and born within this realm of England, or any other of our said dominions'. In 1740 a policy of liberal naturalization of colonial subjects, whether Protestant, Jewish or Quaker, came into operation. It was, in fact, much more liberal than that pertaining within England itself, where, for example, Jews were subject to various civil and legal restrictions.

In colonial America the hierarchy of differing statuses based upon types of subjection broke down. The colonies, anxious to maintain their European population levels, granted local naturalization with full rights before the law. Pennsylvania, for example, conducted a recruiting campaign in Europe, offering full legal rights in exchange for residence. In the eighteenth century the colonies were leaning backwards to make naturalization cheap and possible even for the conscientious objector.

Quite clearly, *the* right before the law which mattered most to these immigrants was the right to hold and pass on property. But the colonists also permitted naturalized and, occasionally, alien residents to vote and to hold political office. For instance, the Germans of Pennsylvania voted without naturalization. The English Parliament objected to such grants of naturalization and extension of rights and attempted to block local naturalization.

Attitudes to citizenship in England and America were developing along different lines. There was a growing belief in eighteenth-century America that all white inhabitants, whether native or immigrant, should receive equal rights in exchange for allegiance to the state. There was a contractual and volitional relationship between the individual and the community. This belief stood at odds with the English concept of subjection and the rights which pertained to subjects. It also raised the issue of whether or not English statute and common law ran in the colonies.

But if the Americans more liberally extended equal rights before the law to white immigrants from Europe than did their English counterparts, this by no means meant that all inhabitants of the new United States stood equal before the law. Several categories of people were discriminated against in both countries. Employees, for example, remained in an inferior position before the law throughout much of the nineteenth century. Under the Master and Servants Act of 1823, if an English worker broke his contract he had committed a crime which was punishable by three months in prison. If an employer broke the contract, he could be sued only in civil law. Generally speaking, American workers had even less protection than their British counterparts. Married women had no separate legal existence in either country. The Seneca Falls (New York) Convention for women's rights in 1848 issued a declaration, closely modelled on the Declaration of Independence, which asserted the status of married women as individuals guaranteed protection by the Constitution: 'We hold these truths to be self-evident that all men and women are created equal; that they are endowed by their Creator with certain inalienable rights; that among these are life, liberty, and the pursuit of happiness' (quoted in Brown, 1965, p. 153). The document specified as 'repeated injuries and usurpations' of these rights before the law the denial of the wife's right to hold property and to keep earned wages, unjust laws concerning marriage and divorce and the custody of children, and the denial of the right to vote. It might also have added the denial in practice of a woman's right to speak in public outside the religious forum. Between 1839 and 1850 most of the states passed legislation for married women to hold property in their own right, beginning with Mississippi in 1839. In general, these measures were achieved either by the efforts of large property owners who wished to safeguard bequests made to women or by those of a few liberal-minded and influential men, helped by small groups of committed and energetic women. Similar protection was granted women in England only by the passing of the Married Women's Property Act of 1870. America, unlike Britain, was faced with the problem of its attitude to thousands of black inhabitants, originally imported as slave labour, and to the indigenous Indian population. What were their rights? Were they equal before the law? The Civil War in the 1860s brought Americans face to face with the paradox of their attitude to human rights.

American liberal intellectuals (from the northern states of the Union) felt that the very existence of government was inconsistent with the quiet enjoyment of human rights; further institutional restrictions upon man's enjoyment of his life, liberty and property were to be abhorred. Yet many Americans were being denied that enjoyment by other Americans. Even the Supreme Court (in the case of *Dred Scott* v. *Sandford*, 1857) had denied the citizenship of black slaves and thereby their constitutional protection. In order to help destroy slavery, an institution which contradicted the American commitment to the extension of freedom, the reformers had to call upon the hated government for assistance. A Leviathan state was created to secure the Union. The creation of this state destroyed many individual liberties – those of slave-owners, for instance – and its very effectiveness suggested that there were disadvantages in viewing society as a conglomeration of self-acting individuals. A similar dilemma was encountered by English liberals during the late eighteenth and nineteenth centuries: there was an increasing commitment to government intervention as a means of winning legal rights for individuals (particularly for those from disadvantaged groups) and enforcing the same. This was as much a problem for the British as for the Americans, for both saw government as a necessary evil which had formerly been accorded a very restricted sphere of influence and direct intervention.

While it might seem that the American concept of citizenship based on voluntary membership of a community of allegiance admitted of none of the distinctions before the law which were acknowledged in Britain, in fact access to the rights which the constitutions of the Union and of the constituent states guaranteed citizens was considerably restricted. Ingenious arguments were put forward to justify this situation in terms of the theory of allegiance itself. The original reluctance to regard the vote as one of the fundamental rights of the citizen was used to good effect to exclude certain categories of person from participation in the political life of the nation. Attitudes to the status of freed blacks were confused. There was in theory no reason why freed black slaves should be denied the rights and privileges of citizenship, but in practice such a policy aroused tremendous opposition. When the Missouri Constitution of 1820 contained a clause denying entry to freed blacks and mulattoes, an opposition grew up which declared that, as they were neither aliens nor slaves, they were 'of consequence free citizens' with rights to property ownership and inheritance, religious freedom, personal protection and legal rights. Supporters of the clause were aghast. Emancipation, they argued, had

freed slaves but it had not naturalized them – Congress alone could do
that. By the Missouri Compromise, the Congress of the United States
agreed to admit Missouri to the Union on condition that this clause did
not deprive any free citizen of privileges and immunities granted by the
Constitution. But it shrank from defining *who* were citizens, thus leaving
the freed slave in as anomalous a position as previously.

In the northern states, attitudes to the position of the freed slave
developed in a novel way. In general freed slaves were accepted as citizens
with the same rights before the law as white Americans. They had rights
to property, liberty of person and conscience, and access to the courts
and their guarantees. They could appeal to the federal government if
their rights under the federal Constitution were infringed. But an earlier
tendency of the state courts to accept the suffrage as a natural right was
reversed: a determination to exclude adult male blacks from full political
rights was strengthened. Thus we note that opposition to granting full
civil rights to marginal groups led either to a denial of the citizenship of
members of the group or to a questioning of the nature of the rights
automatically extended to citizens.

The Indians were, in general, treated with as if they constituted
foreign nations when they lived on the periphery of white settlements.
Where they dwelt within white jurisdictions, they received protection but
were accorded a distinctly subordinate and separate legal status. There
were occasional experiments with the idea of creating separate Indian
states within the United States and of giving the tribes congressional
representation (for example, in the treaties with the Cherokees in 1875
and 1885). Sometimes Indians were naturalized as citizens if they specifically renounced their tribal membership. Clearly, although there were
occasional comments about the 'mental baseness' of the Indian, the true
stumbling block to admitting Indians to full rights as citizens lay in the
feeling that their primary allegiance was to the tribe. In 1823 Chancellor
James Kent of New York argued for the overturning of a lower court's
decision that an Oneida Indian could inherit property:

> Though born within our territorial limits, the Indians are con-
> sidered as born under the jurisdiction of their tribes. They are
> not our subjects, born within the purview of the law, because
> they are not born in obedience to us. They belong, by birth, to
> their own tribes, and these tribes are placed under our protec-
> tion and dependent upon us; but we still recognise them as
> national communities.

(Quoted in Kettner, 1978, p. 294)

Similarly, in the federal case of *Johnson* v. *McIntosh* of 1823, counsel
argued that Indians were 'of that class who are said by Jurists not to be
citizens, but perpetual inhabitants, with diminutive rights … an inferior
race of people, without the privileges of citizens, and under the perpetual
protection and pupilage of the government' (quoted in Kettner, 1978, p.
295). Americans moved more and more towards regarding the Indian
tribes as domestic, dependent nations in which federal law ran (and federal standards of justice), but in which birthright citizenship could be
denied because of the primary and potentially contradictory allegiance to
the tribe.

In theory, the Thirteenth Amendment to the Constitution (1865) and the Civil Rights Act of 1866 combined to affirm the freedom of all Americans and the natural-born citizenship of free men of any race or colour. The Fourteenth Amendment of 1868 finally asserted the primacy of national over state citizenship, recognized the principle of birthright citizenship, and guaranteed the immunities of all citizens against state encroachment and restriction. But, in reality, the position of American blacks in the legal, political and social sense worsened after the Civil War. On the one hand, the Constitution offered a shield but no sword to protect their rights before the law. For a variety of political reasons, the federal government slackened its efforts to enforce the political and civil rights of blacks. Between 1873 and 1898 the Supreme Court reached a number of decisions which curtailed the privileges and immunities recognized as being under federal protection. In the Civil Rights cases of 1883 it declared, moreover, that the Fourteenth Amendment gave Congress the power to restrain states, but not individuals, from acts of racial discrimination and segregation. American blacks were in no position to agitate for a sword to be wielded on their behalf.

When we examine the *theory* of citizenship and rights in the two countries, it often seems that the American system favoured equality before the law and the guarantee of certain fundamental individual rights much more positively than did the British. A closer examination of practice, however, suggests that the very heterogeneity of the American polity militated against effective equality before the law. At the time of the Revolution the true issue had been the rights of the white colonists before the law. The position of other groups had scarcely entered the picture. In the ensuing years, however, the rights of other groups – ex-slaves, poor European immigrants, and Chinese immigrants in the Far West as well as native peoples of the Americas – demanded attention. The white population responded by finding 'rational' arguments to support discrimination before the law. In Britain the theory of discrimination on citizenship grounds or, if we wish to be charitable, on grounds of hierarchy was always there. The relative homogeneity of British society, however, ensured that there was less need to discriminate against individuals on grounds of race or birth. We are faced with the paradox that there was more inequality before the law in this regard in the country most avowedly committed to equal rights.

Nevertheless, in Britain there was certainly gross inequality before the law. This inequality was class based, and men were 'more equal' than women. The employer and the landowner were 'more equal' than their employees. It would be possible to argue that in America also the origins of legal discrimination against certain groups within the population lay in their subordinate status. Black Americans were not only black, they were poor. Did the law act in the interests of all, or did it favour the interests of some against others? Well, we have offered a partial reply to this question. In both countries under discussion, some individuals and groups – blacks, Indians, women, children – were less protected by the law than were others. But this is only a partial reply. It is possible to argue that the law was an instrument of class oppression in the eighteenth and nineteenth centuries. It is also sometimes argued that new laws were passed during this period which directly favoured the property-owning classes and the new industrialists and entrepreneurs to the detriment of the 'small man'. Here we will look in a little more detail at such interpretations.

The law and property

Eighteenth-century Englishmen believed that they had certain rights and liberties. There was tremendous faith and pride in the law before which all were equal; there was no arbitrary arrest, and the accused were entitled to trial by jury. The reality may not have been identical to the belief, but it was the belief that mattered. Douglas Hay, who has probed both the belief in and the structure of the law in eighteenth-century England, has suggested forcefully that the law was primarily an instrument of class power which, 'more than any other social institution, made it possible to govern eighteenth-century England without a police force and without a large army' (Hay, 1975). How, according to Hay, was this effect achieved? Because, on occasion, noblemen and gentlemen suffered on the gallows or were transported for murder or other serious offences, it was possible for publicists to proclaim the existence of equality under the law. Thus, in May 1760 Lawrence Shirley, Lord Ferrers, was executed at Tyburn for the murder of his steward.

Yet in fact the law acted to protect not individuals but property. The number of capital statutes increased from about 50 in 1688 to about 250 in 1820, but nearly all of these concerned property offences. And who made this law which protected property? The ruling gentlemen of England who sat in Parliament – property owners to a man. Who administered this law? The ruling gentlemen of England who acted as magistrates in courts of petty or quarter sessions and sat as judges in the assize courts and central courts in London. Furthermore, within these courts these gentlemen had the power of discretion. The judges could make an example by publicly executing a criminal to discourage others from murder, rioting or theft; they could, and very often did, commute the sentence of death to demonstrate their own and the system's quality of mercy. Magistrates in the lesser courts, sometimes dealing with prosecutions brought by fellow landowners against poachers and petty thieves, were unable to impose the death penalty, but they could still temper their 'justice' with mercy. A magistrate could, for example, give charity to a wandering beggar or have him whipped and imprisoned.

> The private manipulation of the law by the wealthy and powerful was in truth a ruling-class conspiracy, in the most exact meaning of the word. The king, judges, magistrates and gentry used private, extra-legal dealings among themselves to bend the statute and common law to their own purposes. The legal definition of conspiracy does not require explicit agreement; those party to it need not even all know one another, provided they are working together for the same ends. In this case, the common assumptions of the conspirators lay so deep that they were never questioned and rarely made explicit ...
>
> However much they believed in justice (and they did); however sacred they held property (and they worshipped it); however merciful they were to the poor (and many were); the gentlemen of England knew that their duty was, above all, to rule. On that depended everything. They acted accordingly.

(Hay, 1975, pp. 52–3)

This hypothesis of the law as an instrument of class oppression has been criticized from several quarters. First, it is clear that the law was not used by the élite alone; people of all classes were victims, and people of all classes sought redress at law. Juries had a habit of committing what Blackstone called 'pious perjury'; on finding a guilty verdict they sometimes deliberately undervalued goods stolen to ensure that the charge was not capital (a hanging offence). Finally, there is no evidence that MPs drafted capital statutes in a conscious effort to plug all the gaps in the defences of property; moreover capital bills did not go through on the nod – they were seriously debated and could be defeated or talked out.

Traditionally the changes in the penal system at the end of the eighteenth and beginning of the nineteenth centuries – the abolition of many capital statutes, the rise of the prison as the principal form of punishment – were attributed to an enlightened humanitarianism rejecting a barbaric past. Some reforms sped through the system; for example, in 1808 a bill to abolish the death penalty for picking pockets went through all its stages in both Houses of Parliament and received the royal assent within six weeks of its introduction. The reforms of the Tory home secretary, Sir Robert Peel, in the 1820s can be understood in a similar way; Peel restructured and simplified much of the criminal law, sweeping away the 'Bloody Code' of the eighteenth century by repealing scores of statutes. Yet these reforms have also been subjected to historical revision. V.A.C. Gatrell has noted that from the 1780s the number of prosecutions and convictions began a steady rise; the increase became sharper with the end of the Napoleonic Wars. The government recognized that it could not continue to authorize the execution of a similar proportion of convicted offenders; the numbers would be such that the populace would not tolerate it. Yet a dramatic increase in the numbers pardoned or reprieved might only serve to make the law look even more of a lottery. The repeal of the capital statutes and Peel's reforms, in Gatrell's analysis, are less the result of an enlightened humanitarianism and more the result of a desire to restructure and thus preserve a system in danger of discredit, perhaps even collapse (Gatrell, 1994).

Michael Ignatieff suggests that during the 1820s the ruling élite was seeking 'to restore an older, nostalgically remembered social stability in a market economy' (Ignatieff, 1978, p. 184). This stability appeared to have broken down not only in the fast-growing urban, industrial areas but also in the rural districts where, farmers and gentlemen were protesting, labourers were refusing to show their former deference. Thus while, on the one hand, the legislators were reforming the 'Bloody Code', on the other hand they were authorizing certain officials to impose the discipline necessitated by the new economic order. So the Combination Acts, in force between 1799 and 1825, authorized employers to bring workmen on strike before magistrates for summary justice. Farmers who had once beaten offending workmen now brought such men before the magistrates for punishment. The creation of professional police forces, beginning with the London Metropolitan Police in 1829, can be seen as part and parcel of an attempt to restore social stability in a system under stress. Such an analysis makes Hay's vision of the effectiveness of the rule of law seem roseate. According to Ignatieff, contemporaries were aware of the weakness of the infrastructure of class rule, showing themselves eager to provide sufficient buttressing to support the changing superstructure of English society. Of course, it is possible to argue that Ignatieff has overstated his case. The combination laws were repealed in the mid-1820s. When Parliament debated the creation of a police force, it concentrated upon the need to suppress crime rather than upon the need for discipline in the workforce; and throughout the country the propertied complained of the burden which the new police put upon the rates.

Both Ignatieff and Hay assume the existence in Britain of a society divided along class lines. Hay suggests that the ruling class used the law in its own interests to the detriment of the non-property-owning class. He believes that the propertyless were intimidated and influenced by the law. The instrument, in his view, was honed to a fine point. It was employed to enable the ruling class to govern to their own advantage without undue opposition. Ignatieff modifies this interpretation by urging that the law as it stood in the eighteenth century proved inadequate to the challenge offered by the emergence of a new society and new social stresses. In the early nineteenth century the British ruling élite tried to produce a legal instrument suited to the new task, a hybrid of old and new policies.

Is it possible to apply these interpretations to the American case? Although American historians have not approached the issue quite in this fashion, it appears that few would agree with such a reading of the role of law in American society. In the early colonies society was bound together not by the rule of law, and especially not by the employment of the law by one class to control another, but by the communal ideal, often expressed in an ecclesiastical framework. There is every indication that when the church ceased to command the loyalty of all citizens, the communal ideal persisted and was regulated through the law courts – not by a law imposed from above but through party litigation which helped to define acceptable behaviour. In turn, these norms were themselves challenged, and the law was used by the triumphant interest groups to redefine social relations, acceptable behaviour and the goals of society.

One American historian, William E. Nelson, has argued that prior to the Revolution Massachusetts at least was a consensus society little in need of case law (Nelson, 1975). Although technically the law which applied in colonial Massachusetts (and the rest of the colonies) was the English common law, the law was in practice *jury law*. Juries decided not only factual issues in cases brought before them but also issues of law. The evidence of the power of juries in deciding points of law is fourfold: the witness of contemporaries such as John Adams; the fact that the panels of three judges who heard every case often gave conflicting instructions or no instructions at all to the juries; the fact that counsel was free to argue law to the jury in a way which often contradicted the opinion of the judges; the inability of the judges to set aside jury verdicts even when these went against the judges' own instructions. The decisions which juries reached were based upon their experience of either the common law as practised in their townships or some other customs which were observed as law. A consensus was built upon the fact that members of the juries shared the same ethical values and imposed these upon individuals who refused to abide by them voluntarily. Despite increasing religious diversity in Massachusetts, the legal system buttressed the idea that the church should set the moral standards for the community and ensure that those who transgressed were punished through the courts. Remarkable to the English eye are the large numbers of cases of breach of Sabbath observance brought before the local courts of the colonies. Similarly, the local courts made it very difficult for speculators in land: although it was possible to enter into certain sorts of speculative contracts if they were willing to go through the necessary formalities, these were made so cumbersome and expensive as to act as a positive deterrent. The inhabitants of Massachusetts regarded the establishment of a legal profession with suspicion. This hostility was rooted in their hatred of the oppressive English lawyers, but it was also founded in the belief that every man could be and was his own expert in a cohesive society such as their own. There was no need for a precedent law and no need for a legal profession to record and interpret it.

The study of the law in the colonies is not particularly well advanced, but it seems possible that the Massachusetts pattern prevailed elsewhere. Certainly, it was not until the end of the colonial period that Virginia, that most English of the colonies, was acquiring a small body of specifically American case law to which law students might be guided. It was in fact Thomas Jefferson who compiled careful reports of some 200 cases. Virginia had been a backward, immature and fledgling society, at first relatively unlitigious, and it had a backward, fledgling and immature legal profession to match. There was here the same hostility towards the recognition of a legal profession as in Massachusetts. Increasing commercial activity and the need to confirm land titles encouraged the establishment of a group of itinerant lawyers travelling the circuit from monthly court to monthly court. Nevertheless, at various points during the seventeenth century professional attorneys were actually barred from practising in the Virginia courts – for instance, between 1658 and 1680. By the eighteenth century the need for a professional bar was beginning to be recognized. Other colonies, notably Maryland and the Carolinas, had similar experiences.

Before the Revolution the courts in the colonies were agents of discipline enforcing a given moral code. As such they were agents of the community and can scarcely be viewed primarily as the defenders of individual or group rights. Of course, they were increasingly used for the registering of new land titles and for commercial work. And they were involved in the work of discipline. But it was a self-imposed discipline to a greater extent than in England. Litigation was not popular, moreover.

If the law was not big business in 1760, it certainly was by 1830. In 1760 not a single American law book had been printed; by 1830 nearly every state was publishing its own judicial reports. The first American legal periodical, *American Jurist*, was published in 1829. Several important legal treatises had been published in the United States. The law had become America's leading profession, dominating the 64 new colleges which had sprung up since the Revolution.

What had happened? Nelson claims that the old cohesive society was already under threat in the eighteenth century. The growing problem of pauperism, the plight of landless younger sons roaming the colonies in search of work, the increasing involvement in commerce and speculative activity were now joined to impatience with the old religious and political order. The law promoted stability for a while, but after the Revolution it acted as a force for change. The first big change occurred in the 1780s when agrarian debtors in western Massachusetts organized along political lines to object to judicial procedures which prejudiced their position when they were sued by creditors. Access to justice, they said, was one of the rights of men for which the war had been fought. Their access to the courts in debt collection suits was precluded by the very structure of the law and the legal profession. Their attacks, in the form of a petition to the Massachusetts legislature, was countered by a petition from the lawyers and creditors. For the first time, interest groups were ranged against one another over a fundamental legal issue. The next milestone was the political split which occurred in 1810 regarding the disestablishment of the church in the state. This marked the end of the period when the consensus was in favour of the imposition of a common set of values and standards upon all individuals in the community. This had a very marked effect, for example, upon attitudes to property ownership.

> In the colonial period, ethical standards, especially concepts of fair exchange associated with the law of contract, had insured that individuals would use their property consistently with the ethical sense of the community and with the preservation of the community's economic and social stability. In the nineteenth century, however, the demise of the old ethical standards left the owner of property free to use it as he wished. As a result, some owners began to argue in contract cases that they should be free to exchange their property even though the exchange was not fair or equal: when their arguments began to meet with success, they became able to improve their position in the community, at the expense of others, thereby upsetting the community's ancient order and hierarchy.

> (Nelson, 1975, p. 6)

The pre-revolutionary law protected individuals from unfair exchange; the post-revolutionary law did not recognize the existence of fair exchange. It was instead based upon the idea that a person could use his property as he pleased, even if he gambled it away, lost it or used it unscrupulously. It allowed individualism to run riot.

In the new situation, one in which interest groups pressured the legislature for new laws in line with their own needs, litigiousness was fostered. This was why the legal profession boomed. The power of the lawyers was increased even as that of the juries was diminished. For the first time, juries lost their right to decide points of law in civil cases: from the early nineteenth century onwards the law in Massachusetts was attorney- and judge-made.

As has already been suggested, the law itself changed after the Revolution. It now allowed, indeed encouraged, speculation. Before the war certain types of property such as water sources were regarded as the legal possession of the individual who first made use of them. After the war this law was seen to be impeding industrial and commercial activity – a farmer who owned a stream (by virtue of long use) might rightfully deny a mill owner the access to that water which he demanded. By the mid-nineteenth century the courts, in sympathy with this activity in the interests of the state's economy, overturned the inherited rules of property and introduced a new competitive ethic.

It might be argued that in making these changes American lawmakers were bringing American law more closely into line with English precedent. In the 1780 Massachusetts Constitution a clause provided for 'the continuing effectiveness of all law that had heretofore "been adopted, used and approved" in the Commonwealth'. The courts interpreted this as meaning that the entire common law and statute law of England at the time of the Revolution was now in operation, except for such parts as contradicted the new Constitution. The courts used English precedents to resolve cases, sometimes even referring to post-revolutionary English precedents. English law was adhered to rather closely in commercial cases, where interchangeability seemed most advantageous. But, in practice, common law precedents were often specifically rejected because of peculiar local circumstances.

There was certainly a tendency in all of the states to assume that rights before the law which were acknowledged in English statute or common law did pertain in the states of the Union. This was the case with the rights of Habeas Corpus, for example. The Habeas Corpus Act of 1679 specifically did not run in the colonies, but the assumption always was that the right itself rested in common and not statute law. In the early eighteenth century habeas corpus writs were customarily issued in the colonies, and it was assumed that individuals possessed this right under the Union as a result of common law precedent and local bail laws.

But what happened when the states legislated for themselves? Did they approach the issues in the same way as Britain? It seems that the law of contract and the law of negligence developed along parallel lines in Massachusetts and England. But the laws of civil and criminal procedure, the criminal law and the laws pertaining to debt developed in distinctive ways in the states. This was because the judges accepted English common law principles only when they were in accord with local needs.

It is, of course, dangerous to build a whole case upon the instance of one state. We need to know more about the actual operation of the law in the other states of the Union. Nevertheless, there do seem to be sufficient similarities after even a cursory glance to suggest that Nelson's thesis has more than a parochial relevance. If his thesis is broadly valid and is applicable to the United States as a whole, it would be possible to argue that legal changes after the Revolution produced a law which nominally protected the equal rights under the Constitution of propertied individuals but which principally facilitated the exploitation of one individual by another, fostered competition and encouraged the growth of corporations at the expense of the small, independent property owner. It describes the impact of capitalism upon society and the way in which the law was modified to answer the needs of the capitalists.

Conclusion

This discussion of the role of law in English and American society may well lead us to conclude that by the nineteenth century the law in both countries served the needs of particular interest groups rather than of individuals. This had been the case in England for many years – the law protected the propertied élite and, in so doing, discriminated against the propertyless poor. American historians paint an idyllic picture of early colonial society with its consensual politics and law. But they suggest that consensus had broken down by the late eighteenth century. After this point American law was changed to favour corporate enterprise at the expense of the 'small man'. It had become the instrument of 'class' oppression.

What we have sketched in here is in fact a crude Marxist view of the relationship between the law and society. The law is the instrument of the oppressors. Clearly, there is a very real sense in which the law was used in both societies in such a way. Unfortunately, matters are not so simple. It is equally clear that the law was also used to defend individual rights and that it did spring to the aid of the weak and defenceless on occasion. In fact, sufficiently often for the 'oppressed' to feel that in the law alone lay their guarantee of freedom from oppression. The myth of the freeborn Englishman's rights remained all pervasive. All classes of person in England subscribed to it without dissembling. In the 1790s the government sought to suppress popular radicalism by hauling its leaders before the courts on charges of treason. The charges were thrown out; juries refused to submit to the dictates of government. The English people at the time of the Civil War and the Revolution of 1688 appealed to the law as their defence against tyranny. Truly, the law was a two-edged sword: as capable of cutting as of defending its bearers. In America also the fundamental rights guaranteed by the Constitution and the birthrights conferred upon citizens were held up as a shining shield ever ready to protect all individuals. We present only one side of the story if we concentrate, as Hay and others have done, upon the use of the law as a sword to protect the interests of the ruling class and neglect its shielding properties.

References and further reading

Brown, Ira V. (1965) 'The Woman's Rights Movement in Pennsylvania', *Pennsylvania History.*

Emsley, Clive (1981) 'An Aspect of Pitt's "Terror": Prosecutions for Sedition during the 1790s', *Social History*, 6.

Gatrell, V.A.C. (1994) *The Hanging Tree: Execution and the English People 1770–1868*, Oxford University Press.

Hay, Douglas (1975) 'Property, Authority and the Criminal Law' in Douglas Hay, Peter Linebaugh, E.P. Thompson *et al.*, *Albion's Fatal Tree: Crime and Society in Eighteenth-Century England*, Allen Lane.

Ignatieff, Michael (1978) *A Just Measure of Pain: The Penitentiary in the Industrial Revolution, 1750–1850*, Macmillan.

Kettner, James H. (1978) *The Development of American Citizenship, 1608–1870*, Chapel Hill, University of North Carolina Press.

Macpherson, C.B. (1962) *The Political Theory of Possessive Individualism*, Oxford University Press.

Nelson, William E. (1975) *Americanization of the Common Law*, Cambridge, Mass., Harvard University Press.

Wright, Benjamin Fletcher (ed.) (1961) *The Federalist*, Cambridge, Mass., Harvard University Press.

1.6   Federal system and unitary state

During the last decade of the eighteenth century both Britain and the United States saw the enactment of repressive legislation aimed against aliens within their borders and against sedition. In Britain the threat posed by revolutionary France, combined with fear of unrest at home, led in 1793 to the passing of the Alien Act, which provided for the registration of aliens landing in Britain, restricted where aliens might reside, and required that people wishing to travel abroad – whether British or not – be issued licences and passports. This was followed a few months later by the Traitorous Correspondence Act, which made it a treasonable offence to aid the French war effort, to buy land in France or to travel to and from France without a licence or passport. During 1794 the Habeas Corpus Act was suspended, and the government began arresting considerable numbers of members of societies deemed to be subversive (see Essay 1.2). In the following year legislation extended the law of treason and limited the right of public assembly. These restrictions of the rights of the individual did arouse concern, however: in Parliament the opposition led by Charles James Fox fought these measures every inch of the way. Yet there the argument ended (at least among the political élite): Parliament was sovereign, and the only way in which such legislation could be overturned was for Parliament to overturn it. Fox and his supporters were so disillusioned that in 1798 they temporarily seceded from Parliament.

In the United States the 1790s witnessed the enactment of remarkably similar legislation during the administration of President John Adams. In 1798 a series of measures were passed which limited personal liberty: the Naturalization, the Alien, the Alien Enemies, and the Sedition Acts. These measures were designed to lengthen the period before aliens could be made US citizens (and thus participate in elections) and to prevent criticism of the government. Like the British government of the time, the Adams administration was both hostile to the revolutionary events in France and concerned to prevent the subversive and revolutionary contagion from spreading to its own shores. And, as in Britain, the legislation aroused considerable opposition. However, in the United States the form of the opposition was significantly different from that in Britain. In the US the Jeffersonian critics of the Adams administration attempted to use the federal structure of government and the written Constitution to frame resistance to what was regarded as a dangerous abridgement of essential freedoms. In 1798 and 1799 Thomas Jefferson and James Madison drafted a series of resolutions which their allies submitted to the legislative assemblies of Kentucky and Virginia. In these resolutions it was asserted that the central government, in passing the Sedition Act, had gone beyond the powers granted Congress by the Constitution and indeed violated the Fifth Amendment (which prohibited laws 'abridging the freedom of speech or of the press'). They denied that the central government had unlimited sovereignty, asserted that its sovereignty was limited both by the Constitution and by the federal system of government, and urged that the states assert their own sovereignty to prevent the central government overreaching itself. According to Jefferson, in the First Kentucky Resolutions, it should be resolved:

... that the several states composing the United States of America, are not united on the principle of unlimited submission to their General Government but that by their compact under the style and title of a Constitution for the United States and of amendments thereto, they constituted a General Government for special purposes, delegated to that Government certain definite powers, reserving each state to itself, the residuary mass of right to their own self Government; and that whensoever the General Government assumes undelegated powers, its acts are unauthoritative, void, and are of no force.

(Quoted in Cunningham, 1968, p. 140)

In Britain framing opposition to the repressive legislation of the 1790s in such terms would have been unthinkable, for the British state was structured very differently from the American. The Jeffersonian opposition to the Alien and Sedition Acts in the United States marked an important turning point, for it attacked the idea that the government had a right to suppress criticism of itself. Jefferson argued that in the American federal system the central government had no such rights. This points to a key difference between the American and British states: whereas Britain possesses a unitary state structure in which, in theory at least, sovereignty lies with Parliament and (until the government of the United Kingdom joined the European Economic Community and signed the Treaty of Rome) Parliament alone, the United States has a federal system of government in which sovereignty is vested at many levels, in which the law is very largely determined by the states, in which 'the state' is in effect an amalgam of many states, and in which power and authority are divided.

States' rights

Probably the most striking difference between the history of Britain and that of the United States in the last two centuries is presented by the American Civil War. There is no parallel to it in recent British history. Underlying this conflict were questions of states' rights, of sovereignty, of the nature of the federal system of government. The actual point of conflict, the reason why the Lincoln administration went to war in 1861, was the issue of whether any state had the right to secede from the Union. Lincoln's answer was clear: in his first inaugural address he forcefully asserted that 'no State upon its own mere notion, can lawfully get out of the Union' and that 'resolves and ordinances to that effect are legally void' (quoted in Stampp, 1980, p. 165). On the other side, the southern states tended to see the central government as the creation of sovereign states which chose freely to enter the Union and therefore could choose freely to leave it. In presenting their argument, exponents of the southern position referred to the Virginia and Kentucky Resolutions, in which Jefferson and Madison had stated that the Constitution was a compact to which 'each State acceded as a State'; the states had the right to judge when the central government overstepped its powers and then to 'interpose' their own authority (Stampp, 1980, p. 22). Clearly it was only a small theoretical leap from the arguments of Jefferson and Madison to the case for secession (although it should be noted that an aged Madison, shortly before his death in 1836, vehemently denied that he had condoned secession when he co-authored the Resolutions).

Perhaps the most formidable defender of states' rights against the encroachments of the central government before the Civil War was the senator from South Carolina (and vice-president under Andrew Jackson), John C. Calhoun. Although Calhoun began his Senate career as an exponent of nationalist policies during and after the War of 1812, during the 1820s his position changed together with that of popular sentiment in South Carolina to one of dogged defence of states' rights. In so doing, he buttressed his arguments with those of Jefferson and Madison in the Virginia and Kentucky Resolutions. Probably the clearest and most famous exposition of Calhoun's views is contained in his 'South Carolina Exposition' of 1828, a treatise on the Constitution written in response (and in opposition) to the 'Tariff of Abominations' passed by Congress in that year, which was published although not adopted by the South Carolina state legislature. In it Calhoun stated:

> Our system, then, consists of two distinct and independent Governments. The general powers, expressly delegated to the General Government, are subject to its sole and separate control; and the States cannot, without violating the constitutional compact, interpose their authority to check, or in any manner to counteract its movements, so long as they are confined to the proper sphere. So, also, the peculiar and local powers reserved to the States are subject to their exclusive control; nor can the General Government interfere, in any manner, with them, without violating the Constitution.

> (Crallé, 1968 edn, vol. vi, p. 36)

Calhoun was adamant that 'every one who is at least conversant with our institutions [must concede] that the sovereign powers delegated are divided between the General and State Governments'. According to Calhoun, however, while the central government exercised sovereign powers, these powers were only what had been delegated by the states for common benefit; sovereignty itself was not divided (in Calhoun's words: 'Sovereignty is an entire thing – to divide, is to destroy it') and it rested with the states. The federal system therefore was the agency through which divided 'powers of sovereignty' were exercised, but not through which sovereignty itself was divided. To antebellum advocates of states' rights, it was clear that the Constitution prohibited the central government from interfering with the activities of the sovereign states.

It is significant that such positions, which were bound up with the outbreak of the American Civil War, were made possible by the existence in the United States of a written constitution which outlined a federal system. The framework for the sorts of debates in which Jefferson, Madison and Calhoun were engaged simply did not exist in Britain. Of course, it would be misleading to suggest that the question of secession or the issue of where sovereignty lay was the *cause* of the American Civil War, and therefore to imply that because Britain was blessed with a unitary state structure she was spared a civil war in the nineteenth century. Debates about states' rights, about the right to secede from the Union, were a stage on which differing interests battled with one another. The American North and South had developed very different economic and social systems – the former based on family farming and manufacturing using free labour, the latter on large-scale agriculture dependent upon the institution of slavery – which were increasingly antagonistic. Economic issues, moral codes, cultural values and social conditions blended together to produce two fundamentally opposed systems battling within the federal system. Issues involving states' rights often were the arena in which the battles were fought, but they did not necessarily provide the reasons why the battles were fought.

In order to understand the constitutional and political issues which led to the Civil War, it is necessary to appreciate the federal structure of the American political system. The conflicts and increasingly precarious compromises which led to war largely concerned how the western territories of the United States would be admitted to the Union. As the law was primarily a matter for the states, the question of whether a state would permit slavery was decided by its own constitution. Thus with each new admission to the Union a new balance had to be found between slave and free states, a balance regarded as absolutely essential to both northerners and southerners in Congress. The federal structure – in which fundamental questions of law and rights were decided at state level – necessitated a series of difficult compromises at national level. When these compromises no longer sufficed, the federal system cracked, and it became necessary to fight a brutal and bloody civil war to restore it.

The American Civil War marked the end of an era in the relations between the federal government and the states, and put the federal system on a new footing. Questions of whether state sovereignty overrode the sovereignty of the central government and whether the United States was indeed indivisible were buried. However, this is not to say that the Union victory in 1865 was a triumph for centralized government. According to the Supreme Court in 1869 (*Texas* v. *White*), the United States was 'an indestructible Union of indestructible states'. The states remained the formulators and executors of most law, and continued to perform most of the functions associated with government. Thus, for example, the states continued to play a major role in the financing of American war efforts. Throughout the nineteenth century the states generally were responsible for raising, equipping and supplying troops, with the promise that they would be reimbursed by the central government after the hostilities were over (see Maxwell, 1946, pp. 43–4; Elazar, 1964, pp. 248–81). Even in the Civil War, in which the central government was engaged in a struggle against secessionist states, the Union armies were raised, organized and equipped largely by the individual states. According to the Act of Congress of 22 July 1861 which authorized the creation of a volunteer army of 500,000 men, 'The Governors of the States furnishing volunteers under this act shall commission the field staff, and company officers requisite for the said volunteers.' As one American historian noted in the 1920s:

> The principle of states' rights, as applied to the raising of an army, had prevailed. The federal government might call for the troops and assign the quotas, but the states would raise the men, organize the regiments and, to a great extent, control their destinies ... Numerous reasons might be presented to explain the superiority of the states in recruiting: the influence of local and state bounties; popular election of officers; the desire of volunteers to be organized in units with their acquaintances – all of which inducements would draw

recruits away from the regular army to the advantage of the volunteer army. But behind all these facts, lies the stronger reason, that states' rights had so strong a hold upon the minds of both of the major political parties, that they could conceive of no other way to create a large army, than by turning the work over to the agency of the states.

(Shannon, 1928, vol. 1, pp. 46–8)

It was only in 1863 that the conscription machinery came under the exclusive control of the central government. The system of centrally-funded state militias – called the National Guard by the beginning of the twentieth century – existing alongside a pitifully small federal armed force continued in effect until the eve of American entry into the First World War (when the 1916 National Defense Act finally extended effective central government control over the National Guard system).

Centralized and decentralized authority

Differences in the structure of the state may not have altered the underlying economic and social processes which have marked the histories of Britain and the United States, but they have determined to a considerable degree the differing *patterns* which many of these processes have taken. Particularly important in this regard are differences in the legal system: in the American federal system there are state legislatures and judiciaries as well as their counterparts at national level, whereas in Britain Parliament alone bears ultimate responsibility for the body of British law. This made for significant differences, for example, in how state regulations of work (hours and conditions) and trade unions came about. In Britain, thanks in part to extra-parliamentary pressure, there was significant factory legislation during the 1830s and 1840s. The 1833 Factory Act limited the number of hours that children were permitted to work and prohibited the employment of children under the age of nine (except in silk mills). An Act of 1847, by limiting the daily work of women and youths in factories to ten hours, effectively limited all factory work to ten hours since it was difficult for adult male workers to continue work unaided. It was parliamentary action which prescribed the limits of trade union activity, notably with the notorious Combination Acts of 1799 and 1800, and the repealing and amending legislation of 1824 and 1825. There was no question of a county authority legally being able to regulate trade unions or to establish minimum wage rates or maximum hours for that county alone. Such questions were decided at national level by the sovereign legislative body of the unitary British state.

In the United States the main thrust of such reform came on a state level, for it was the states which made and enforced most law in this field. Thus, for example, the regulation of working hours was a matter largely pushed in state legislatures and deliberated upon by state judicial systems. The pace of legislation differed in different states. In 1840 President Van Buren issued an executive order establishing a ten hour day for federal employees engaged on public works, but it was not until 1847 that a state (New Hampshire) passed a ten hour law, and other states followed suit only slowly. Child labour was similarly a state concern and was far less regulated in the southern states than the northern until the turn of the century; it was not until 1916 that a federal law governed child labour throughout the United States, and this related only to the production or distribution of goods passing from one state to another (and was declared unconstitutional in 1918). The federal government did not begin to play a major role in industrial relations until the 1930s.

While these differences may not have been of primary importance with regard to the underlying trends in labour history in Britain and the United States, they do help explain why particular economic and political struggles in the two countries took the forms they did. Issues which in Britain were dealt with essentially on a national level frequently were fought out at state or local level in the United States, not because the issues themselves were different but because the state and legal structures within which they were confronted were different. This was true not only for labour regulation and legislation regarding trade unions; it may also be seen with regard to the regulation of commerce, of education, of the criminal law, of who had the right to vote. Thus in the United States with its federal system – as opposed to Britain with its unitary state – it was largely the various states which determined and defined the relationship between the individual and the state, and not just the central government.

Political representation

At the root of the relationship of the individual to the state is the question of political representation, the right to vote. In both Britain and the United States there has been a considerable and significant extension of suffrage during the past 200 years, an extension which has meant bringing the right to vote to groups to whom it had been denied in the late eighteenth and early nineteenth centuries. However, the arenas in which this took place have been rather different. In Britain the right to vote was essentially a matter defined nationally by Parliament (at least since 1832), and extensions of the franchise were achieved in large measure as a consequence of successful agitation bearing fruit in the form of reforms enacted by Parliament. In the United States the question of the franchise was quite different, for the American Constitution drafted in 1787 expressly left the issue of suffrage to the states. (It was not until after the Civil War that the Constitution was amended to define voting rights nationally.) Regulating elections to national office – to the Presidency, to the Senate, to the House of Representatives – was left to the states. For the Presidency, each state was to appoint 'in such a manner as the legislature thereof may direct, a number of electors, equal to the whole number of senators and representatives to which the state may be entitled in the congress' (US Constitution, Article II, Section 1). The Senate was designed as the direct expression not of the American electorate but of the states; until 1912 senators were chosen not by the citizens of any particular state but by the state legislatures. Only the House of Representatives was intended by the framers of the Constitution to represent directly the will of the people, but even here they stopped short of prescribing a national definition of who had the right to vote:

> The house of representatives shall be composed of members
> chosen every second year by the people of the several states,
> and the electors in each state shall have the qualifications

requisite for electors of the most numerous branch of the state legislature.

(US Constitution, Article I, Section 2)

This is not to say that there were no regional variations in who in fact could vote in Britain; the injustices and idiosyncracies of the nineteenth-century voting system in Britain are well known. It is to say, however, that the ways in which the franchise was defined were different in the two countries. Unlike in Britain, in the United States it was a middle tier of government – the states with their own legislatures – which defined the right to vote. Therefore, whereas in Britain the campaigns to extend the franchise were essentially national, in the United States such campaigns also pressed forward at state level.

The general outlines of the extensions of suffrage are roughly similar for both Britain and the United States. During the eighteenth century, in the American colonies as in Britain, the possession of real property had been a prerequisite for being able to vote. By the mid-twentieth century the franchise had been extended to the entire adult populations of both the United Kingdom and the United States. Property qualifications had disappeared, religious restrictions no longer applied, the vote had been extended to non-whites, and the struggle for women's suffrage had been won. However, the steps along these paths were often rather different.

In Britain in the late eighteenth and early nineteenth centuries the voting system was a complicated combination of property qualifications, restrictions, corruption, and considerable differences in the ways different regions were represented politically. In the counties the rules governing the franchise were uniform and comparatively simple: men possessing a freehold worth at least 40 shillings could vote in the county where that freehold lay (thus men possessing 40 shilling freeholds in more than one county had more than one vote). In the boroughs, on the other hand, the system was immensely complex: in some the vote was tightly restricted to owners of certain types of property or to members of the corporation, while in others almost all adult males could vote. In some constituencies only Anglicans could vote; in others Nonconformists also could vote. This changed radically in 1832. As a result of the Reform Act of that year the franchise was settled on a uniform and regular basis throughout the country: the borough franchise was extended to men possessing a household valued at £10 per annum or more; the county franchise was extended to those with a 40 shilling freehold and to tenants-at-will who paid a rent of at least £50 per annum. (For details of the 1832 Reform Act, see Brock, 1973; for an overview of the extension of the franchise in Britain, see Hanham, 1971.) The next major extension of the franchise in Britain came in 1867 with the Representation of the People Act, which gave the vote in England to all householders of one year's residence in the boroughs and to farmers paying £12 or more annual rent in the counties; comparable reforms for Scotland and Wales followed in 1868. In 1884 the franchise was extended further, virtually doubling the electorate and bringing the right to vote to a much larger percentage of the rural population – and this reform pertained to Ireland as well as England, Scotland and Wales. In 1918 suffrage in Britain was extended to women. Of course, the extension of the franchise in Britain was in fact a much more complex process than so crude an outline as that above can indicate (and parliamentary reforms did not necessarily relate to municipal elections); however, the point here is that to a very great extent the broadening of the franchise in Britain was something which took place at national level.

In the United States, on the other hand, the extension of the franchise occurred largely at the state level. Despite the political transformations brought about through the American War of Independence, few changes were made initially in the ways in which suffrage was defined in the newly independent states; property or taxpaying qualifications remained in effect, and in four states – Connecticut, Rhode Island, Virginia and Delaware – suffrage qualifications inherited from the colonial period did not change at all. There had been some breakthroughs: for example, in 1787 all adult males in Connecticut and New York were permitted to vote for representatives to their conventions ratifying the federal Constitution. Nevertheless, by 1787 no state had divorced property completely from voting requirements, and real progress came only in the nineteenth century. Whereas in 1800 only three of the fifteen states.then in the Union allowed all white men to vote regardless of whether or not they owned property, 45 years later 23 out of the 30 states had thus extended the franchise. Although this development was not uniform or unblemished – for example, during the first half of the nineteenth century some southern states withdrew the ballot from free blacks, and in 1821 New York State retained property qualifications for black voters while abolishing them for whites – nevertheless during the early nineteenth century American office-holders were becoming more accountable to an increasingly broad electorate. (During this period state governors came to be popularly elected instead of being chosen by state legislatures, and in a number of states judgeships became elective positions.) Although the process of extending the franchise remained incomplete until the Fifteenth Amendment to the Constitution – ratified* in 1867 but not fully put into practice for nearly a century – extended the vote to blacks, and the Nineteenth Amendment – ratified in 1919 – granted women suffrage, during the early nineteenth century the general principle was established that voting should not be tied to property and wealth.

Amendments to the US Constitution have to be ratified by three-quarters of the states before they are accepted.

In broad terms this is similar to what happened in Britain, if in the latter progress was rather slower. However, in the United States until after the Civil War the definition of the franchise was left to the states. There was no American congressional counterpart to the Reform Act of 1832, for example. Removing property qualifications for voting came about as a result not of acts of Congress for the whole of the United States but rather of a large number of reforms in various states, reforms which together amounted to a democratic transformation of impressive proportions.

Taxation

For most people perhaps the most important, and probably the most annoying, point of contact with the state is the tax official. Here too the differing structures of state and government in Britain and the United States have played an important role. Whereas in Britain an essentially two-tier taxation system has evolved, in the United States there is another system of taxation: that of the states. Since the American states, unlike the English counties, have had their own wide-ranging powers to legislate and to levy taxes, they have enjoyed a considerable measure of financial independence. The American Constitution set few limitations upon the powers of the states to tax: states were explicitly prohibited from levying duties on imports and exports or levying tonnage duties, but that was all (US Constitution, Article I, Section 10). Of course, there also have been practical limitations: states imposing extremely high or burdensome taxes are liable to suffer the loss of industry and business to cheaper states; and the growth of the central government in the twentieth century has tended to circumscribe what the states can do, since so many potential sources of revenue are already tapped by Washington. Nevertheless, the American states have levied taxes in a variety and to an extent far beyond that attempted by local government in Britain. Thus states often impose their own income taxes, sales taxes, road taxes, petrol duties, duties on alcohol, etc.

The differences in taxation have to do with differences in the functions of the various tiers of government, which have been neatly summarized by M.J.C. Vile:

> In practice [the American states] exercise a wide range of functions, many of which are, in countries such as Great Britain, the exclusive province of central governments. In those areas of government activity which might be designated as the 'nineteenth-century' functions of government (apart from defence and foreign affairs), functions such as the maintenance of law and order, and the ordering of the general legal relationships within society, the States remain the major source of government action, and in some cases almost the sole source. In the field of 'twentieth-century' functions, economic regulation and social welfare, which require a relatively high degree of central control and initiative, the States have not been excluded; they remain as important partners in these aspects of government activity, sometimes junior partners it is true, but still exercising a degree of independent power and influence which is certainly not characteristic of local authorities in a unitary State. They remain responsible for the sole control of the structure of government itself at State and local level, a structure consisting [in 1961] of more than 116,700 units of government.

(Vile, 1961, p. 15)

This last point is important to keep in mind: it is the states, not the central government, which control the structure of local government in the United States. The American Constitution left the structure of local government for the states to determine, although often the individual state constitutions themselves limit the powers of the states to determine the shape of local government. This fact, together with the political strength of particular cities and the framing of many city government charters to permit the exercise of any powers not prohibited by the constitution or laws of their state, has meant that the cities and towns (as well as the states) in the United States frequently enjoy a status and independence far greater than that enjoyed by British local government authorities.

Conclusion

The argument underlying this essay has been that constitutional and state structures do matter, that historical development is not the expression exclusively of social and economic processes, but also of the constitutional structures within which these processes take place. When looking at the broad sweep of the histories of Britain and the United States, one is struck by similarities in economic development, in political development, and in social development. Whereas whether the state has been unitary or federal in structure ultimately may not have made much difference with regard to the general development of, for example, the capitalist industrial economies of Britain and the United States, structures of government and of the state have often determined the ground on which various conflicts have been fought. Without an appreciation of the structures of the state, not only does it become difficult to explain the location of particular conflicts, but the underlying historical processes can also become unintelligible.

References and further reading

Brock, Michael (1973) *The Great Reform Act*, Hutchinson.

Crallé, Richard K. (ed.) (1968 edn) *The Works of John C. Calhoun*, New York, Russell and Russell (first published 1888).

Cunningham, Noble (ed.) (1968) *The Early Republic, 1789–1828*, University of Southern California Press.

Degler, Carl N. (1984) *Out of Our Past: The Forces that Shaped Modern America*, 3rd edn, New York, Harper & Row.

Elazar, Daniel J. (1964) 'Federal–State Collaboration in the Nineteenth-Century United States', *Political Science Quarterly*, xxix, June.

Hanham, Harold John (1971) *The Reformed Electoral System in Great Britain 1832–1914*, Historical Association.

Maxwell, James A. (1946) *The Fiscal Impact of Federalism in the United States*, Cambridge, Mass., Harvard University Press.

Shannon, Fred Albert (1928) *The Organization and Administration of the Union Army 1861–1865*, Cleveland, A.H. Clark Co.

Stampp, Kenneth M. (1980) *The Imperilled Union: Essays on the Background of the Civil War*, Oxford University Press.

Vile, M.J.C. (1961) *The Structure of American Federalism*, Oxford University Press.

Williamson, Chilton (1960) *American Suffrage from Property to Democracy, 1760–1860*, Princeton University Press.

Part 2   Industrialization and Economic Growth to 1870

1.7   The Atlantic economy and Anglo-American industrialization, 1783–1865

The Industrial Revolution in the United States followed very closely after that in Great Britain, but it has been customary to treat them as largely separate events. In each case the pattern of economic growth reflected domestic constraints and endowments. However, in both countries the national pattern was transformed by the extensive flow of goods, ideas, skilled migrants and capital that developed in the 'Atlantic economy' in the late eighteenth and early nineteenth centuries. This essay suggests therefore that transatlantic connections are given an important role in British and American industrialization.

Pre-industrial Britain

The most important tension in pre-industrial Britain was between the growth of population and the productivity of British agriculture, with the population periodically coming up against fixed supplies of land worked by unchanging agricultural techniques. One severe demographic calamity associated with disease occurred in the fourteenth century, and there was another, milder crisis in the seventeenth century. By 1750, however, numbers were again rising rapidly, but this time Britain was able to meet the challenge because of the great improvements in agriculture dating from the mid-seventeenth century. The agricultural revolution seems to have occurred not only in the large part of England that was already enclosed but also on the common fields. (See Maps and Statistical Tables booklet, p. 5, for a map showing the progress of enclosure in Britain.) This revolution involved the introduction of mixed farming techniques – the use of root crops, clovers, grain and animals consecutively on the same land to improve arable output and increase herds. As a result agricultural output increased dramatically in the early eighteenth century, allowing the great mass of middle-income earners to buy amenities such as pots and pans, glass, cheap plates and cutlery, and linens. Not only was early industrialization encouraged by this demand, but the needs of agriculture also led to the improvement of rivers and canals, the growth of market towns and the creation of local capital markets.

Consequently many small, long-established industries began to grow more rapidly. The most important was woollen textiles, which was beginning to be concentrated in Yorkshire, although there was still a substantial amount of high quality production in the old textile areas of East Anglia and the West Country. The metal trades were well established in the West Midlands, and the output of coal and iron was starting to rise rapidly in areas such as Coalbrookdale in Shropshire, where Abraham Darby had discovered how to replace charcoal with coke. The old-established tin and copper mines in Cornwall and coal mines around

Newcastle were also expanding, and were beginning to use primitive steam engines to drain mines to greater depths. The cotton industry in Lancashire was, however, still small and overshadowed by imports from India. Despite considerable efforts, there was still no success in the search for ways of mechanical spinning.

Although the growth of these industries depended largely on the home market, foreign trade became increasingly important for Britain in the early eighteenth century. Traditionally Britain's leading export markets had been in Europe, but during the eighteenth century Britain, France and Holland all protected their domestic industries and developed commercial empires in the Americas and Far East. Britain found it increasingly difficult to sell in European markets, but was able to compensate by exporting to the American colonies. Whereas, in 1700, 80 per cent of exports of domestic manufacturers went to Europe, by 1798 60 per cent were going to North America and the Caribbean. The colonies could afford to buy only as much as they could sell, so the quantity of exports was limited by Britain's capacity to import colonial products such as sugar and tobacco. As these goods were semi-luxuries, this in turn was determined by how quickly rising efficiency in British agriculture lowered the price of the basic necessities of life. The colonial trade provided an increasingly valuable adjunct to British domestic commerce in the mid-eighteenth century, but was not yet an independent source of growth in its own right.

By the 1770s the British economy was on the verge of rapid industrialization. However, although agricultural output continued to increase rapidly after 1770, this by itself was not sufficient to maintain industrial progress. By 1800 the population was growing so rapidly that it was exerting a strong downward pressure on living standards. Furthermore the wars of the late eighteenth and early nineteenth centuries were financed by massive increases in taxation, borne not only by the gentry through land taxes but also by the poor through taxes on necessities. The domestic demand for industrial products on which industrialization had principally relied so far was potentially under threat. In addition, the population began to suffer great physical problems of congestion and sanitation in the new cities. Therefore, for about 50 years after 1770 Britain entered perhaps the most critical phase of its history, from which only successful industrialization saved it.

Pre-industrial America

The central problem of the pre-industrial British economy – the pressure of population on land and natural resources – was largely absent from the early American experience. The continent seemed so vast and the population relatively so slight that the real problem for American society appeared to be how to process resources effectively, rather than how to conserve them. Consequently the natural checks were relatively weak, and there was widespread approval of extremely rapid population growth. 'Malthus would not be understood here,' wrote one migrant in the early nineteenth century.* The critical problem for early Americans, therefore, was how to form their widely scattered population into a unified economic and political society, and how to link it adequately to effective markets. Initially this was achieved by the British colonial system. After

Malthusian population theory is discussed in detail in Essay 1.9, 'Population and labour in the USA and Britain'.

independence the internal linking between the states was provided by the federal system, but for overseas markets the United States still relied on the Atlantic economy.

When the colonists first arrived in the early seventeenth century, they were unable to deal with the harsh environment and relied on continual reinforcement from England. However, after they had adopted new crops and adjusted to the climate, their numbers increased rapidly. The population of the colonies was about 100,000 in 1670, 500,000 in 1720, two million in 1770, and five million by 1800 – implying a growth rate of about 3 per cent a year. This was faster than even Malthus thought possible. By comparison, the English population grew at about 0.3 per cent a year in the early eighteenth century, 0.5 per cent in the mid-eighteenth century and 1 per cent in 1800. The main reason for the difference lay in the higher birth rate, which was probably the result of a lower age and higher incidence of marriage. Mortality rates were also lower, and a large number of children survived to produce families in their turn. These factors were principally caused by the large surplus of land in the colonies. In England population growth was inhibited by frequent food shortages, and social practices adjusted accordingly – but this was not necessary in America. The other sources of American population growth were immigration of whites from Europe and of black slaves from the Caribbean and Africa – but after about 1670 these people formed a minor proportion of the total.

After the initial difficult 'starving time', the liberal amounts of land and timber available ensured the colonists a good standard of living. They were, however, lacking in most of the basic manufactures and services available in Europe. Many of these, such as clothes, could be made in individual households but only crudely and inefficiently. There had been occupational and regional specialization in cloth manufacture in England since the sixteenth century, but the small population and long distances between settlements made this impossible in America. Thus, despite the richness of the land, the colonists found themselves dependent on foreign trade for many necessities such as tools, glass, cutlery and weapons.

Accordingly, the southern colonies – Virginia, North and South Carolina, and Georgia – specialized in plantation crops such as tobacco, rice and indigo that were mostly sold in England. The middle colonies – New York, Pennsylvania, New Jersey, Delaware and Maryland – sold grain and foodstuffs to the British and French Caribbean islands, which themselves specialized in sugar for the British market. The African trade, of course, provided slaves for the West Indies and southern plantations, but was only a small part of colonial trade. The New England colonies – Maine, New Hampshire, Massachusetts, Connecticut and Rhode Island – specialized in providing shipping and services for the staple exports of the more fertile middle and southern colonies. Although several important cities developed – Boston, New York, Philadelphia and Charlestown – which serviced these trades and contained efficient merchant élites, 90 per cent of the population was still 'rural' in 1830 by comparison with only about 40 per cent in England.

The rate of growth of the colonies depended not only on the rate of growth of the population, but also on the rate of growth of trade. The volume of American exports was constrained in the eighteenth century by the limited ability of the British, European and West Indian markets to absorb American goods. In the late seventeenth and early eighteenth centuries exports of the leading southern staples expanded rapidly. However, by the 1770s, although rice exports were continuing to increase, tobacco exports to Europe had become stagnant and grain exports to the West Indies had overshot the growth of the local population. The final possibility of direct export of foodstuffs in bulk to Europe was not yet available because of the transport costs involved and the self-sufficiency of the British market in normal years.

The growth of population and trade obviously affected living standards, and there has been considerable debate about the standard of living of the colonists. The statistics for the American population and Gross National Product based on the decennial censuses show incomes per capita* to have grown at about $1\frac{5}{8}$ per cent since 1840. Colonial per capita incomes could not have grown at such a rate because if $1\frac{5}{8}$ per cent is deducted annually from the figure for 1840, the resulting figure for, say, 1770 is below subsistence. General descriptions of colonial life and detailed records such as probate inventories reveal a reasonably comfortable life-style. Therefore, after the initial settlement when living standards rose rapidly as organized farms and plantations were established, colonial incomes must have risen very gradually. The growth in trade and farming must have only just offset the huge growth in population that occurred. Even so, living standards were higher in the colonies than in England and growing as fast as in any pre-industrial society. They also varied markedly: the increasing sophistication of city life, on the one hand, contrasted with the poverty of the extending frontier, on the other. Similarly the plain, frugal life of small northern farmers was very different from the experience of the large plantation owners of the South. Historians therefore suspect that per capita growth rates were about 0.3 per cent per year in the eighteenth century and rose by degrees to $1\frac{5}{8}$ per cent in the mid-nineteenth century.

per capita = per person.

The reasons for this relatively slow growth in per capita incomes are obvious. Most importantly there was no agricultural revolution as in England. American farming methods remained relatively primitive until the 1850s, when labour-saving machines such as reapers began to be introduced to deal with extensive prairie farms. Nor was there much improvement in industrial technology. The largest American industries were iron making, shipbuilding and corn and timber milling. Iron making, despite the English example, retained its primitive charcoal technology until the 1840s. Shipbuilding remained an ancient craft until the 1850s, when the United States began to lose its strong position because of failure to modernize. In corn and timber milling, however, some very significant labour-saving devices were introduced at the end of the eighteenth century: these were early responses to the problem of labour shortage amidst abundant natural resources. Increasing productivity in the eighteenth century mostly resulted from small improvements in commercial organization and in agricultural techniques. There were also years when the demand for and prices of American staples were high (for example, 1745–1760).

It is difficult to know what the prospects would have been for the colonists had the political revolution in America and the Industrial Revolution in England not occurred. By 1770 the population was beginning to outrun the growth of trade as well as the easily available land east of the Appalachians. There were, of course, massive supplies of excellent new land in the area between the Appalachian Mountains and the Mississippi River that England had acquired in the peace treaty with France of 1763. (See the Maps and Statistical Tables booklet, p. 12, for a map showing the progress of eighteenth-century settlement.) Planters and farmers in these remote areas, however, found there were virtually no crops that would stand the cost of transport to market and that the land, however fertile, was useless for anything but immediate subsistence. The alternative to a hard pioneering life was to supplement an income from farming with domestic manufactures, and it was remarked as early as 1765 that 'many thousands rather than go further back into the country' were choosing instead to 'turn to manufacturing, and live upon a small farm, as in many parts of England'. Accordingly in the denser settled colonies, especially around the ports, simple manufacturing was developing by 1776.

In the long run, of course, this led to full-scale industrialization. In the short run, however, there was a danger of the 'Europeanization' of colonial life. In Boston, for instance, there was a gradual differentiation between the poorer labourers and seamen, and the wealthy mercantile élite. Simultaneously, the average size of New England farms gradually declined as land was divided. In other areas farms were deserted as the topsoils were destroyed by overcropping, and the owners crossed the Appalachians in search of new land. The possibility of manufacturing was distinctly limited by more efficient British competition and the costs of transport. A lively trade developed between the port cities based on relatively cheap seaborne commerce, but inland distances stifled enterprise. In addition, the generally easy living to be made on the land and the lure of the West reduced the potential supply of labour and made wages much higher than in Europe. Capital, too, was nearly all required for trade, and merchants did not show much interest in large-scale investments in manufacturing before 1812.

*See the chronology of economic legislation in the appendices to Teaching Unit 2.

The decade after the Revolutionary War revealed these problems. American exports, no longer restrained by the Navigation Acts* but no longer assisted by British preferences, expanded slightly in absolute volume but sank markedly per head. American manufactures, some of which had increased dramatically during the war, were hard hit when machine-made British products reappeared. The area under cultivation expanded with the growth of population, but there was no increase in productivity. Total output in the colonies was, therefore, a little higher in 1790 than in 1770, but as the population had grown by 50 per cent, per capita incomes were considerably less than in 1770.

On the other hand, all the ingredients for rapid expansion obviously existed. The trade of the colonial period had produced a well-educated and motivated mercantile élite with the capacity to organize future production. The population – about four million by the 1790s – was growing to the point where specialized production might take place. Finally, if only they could be brought together, there were massive supplies of raw materials such as timber, coal and iron, fertile soils to produce food and raw materials, and good water supplies for power. What was needed was commercial opportunity to expand trade and provide capital, and a prior example to provide the techniques.

The Atlantic economy and the British Industrial Revolution

The late eighteenth century was a critical period for both Britain and the United States. Modest development had been initiated in both economies, but it is clear that continued reliance on traditional industries and internal sources would not support much additional per capita growth. A range of possible outcomes was appearing, the worst of which was renewed Malthusian crisis in Britain and stunted development in North America. In the event, the increasing productivity of the Industrial Revolution more than offset the rise in population in Britain, and the British success provided the prior example and commercial opportunity needed by America. This more favourable outcome was the product of many factors, but perhaps the most important on the favourable side was the high levels of trade in the Atlantic economy.

The essence of the British Industrial Revolution was a series of linked technical innovations in textiles, iron, power and transport, together with great improvements in commercial and financial organization, and continued growth of population and accumulation of capital. The crucial factor was that although many of the inventions, and the parallel developments in capital accumulation and transport, had their origins earlier in the eighteenth century (and in this sense the Industrial Revolution was a long drawn out evolutionary process), they did not come together into a physically, geographically and organizationally close-knit and interlocking system of machinery, resources and power until the late eighteenth century. In this *combination* of factors it is suggested that the contribution of the Atlantic economy was vital.

The growth of Atlantic trade was particularly important after 1783 because of the relatively declining contribution of agriculture as a demand stimulus, the increasing pressure of population, and after 1793 the eruption of the French Revolutionary Wars. Only the Atlantic trade was clear and open to earn incomes for the new populations in the growing cities. It achieved this by drawing into action the modernizing industries of the late eighteenth century: cottons, woollens, pottery, iron, etc. It was only the growing productivity of these industries that offset the growth of population. Thus, from 1790 to 1860 the British population grew at about $\frac{1}{4}$ per cent per annum, but agricultural productivity over the same period rose at no more than one-half per cent per annum and the great mass of old-fashioned craft industries and services only marginally faster. In this mass, however, working to diffuse advanced industrial methods, were the new industries: cotton, whose productivity was growing at about $2\frac{1}{2}$ per cent per annum; worsteds 2 per cent; woollens 1 per cent; iron 1 per cent; canals and railways nearly $1\frac{1}{2}$ per cent, and shipping nearly $2\frac{1}{2}$ per cent.

By far the most important of these industries was cotton textiles. 'Whoever says Industrial Revolution says Cotton,' claims one historian. The evidence for this interpretation is the almost miraculous increase in raw cotton imports and manufactured cotton exports that began in the 1780s, and the growth of the factory system which until the 1830s was principally in Lancashire. The vast development of Manchester, which has been called the 'shock city' of the early nineteenth century, embodied all the dramatic symptoms of industrialization. By 1820 cotton was employing 5 per cent of the workforce and contributing 7 per cent to

Gross National Product (GNP) and, even more important, influencing many other activities. Its methods were copied by the other textile industries, and by the 1830s it was the main user of steam engines in the country and had generated a substantial engineering industry. Cotton also stimulated many other ancillary activities, such as chemicals for bleaching and dyeing, and used large quantities of iron for building and gas and coal for lighting and heating.

Moreover, cotton was more than a manufacturing industry, and some of the largest merchants in Britain as well as important foreign firms were drawn into the trade. Manchester and Liverpool became part of an international network of commerce and finance linking New York and New Orleans in the west with Bombay and Alexandria in the east. As the scale of transactions increased and markets developed, many aspects of commerce gained in sophistication and efficiency. Cotton was a bulk crop that generated substantial shipping and port development. Ships on the Atlantic route grew rapidly in tonnage and efficiency in the early nineteenth century, mostly because of the size and regularity of the cotton trade from the American South to Liverpool. Grain and migrants did not become important cargoes until the 1840s, and the timber trade used older vessels. Cotton was usually shipped by American vessels, but British interests were often involved. The profits from the cotton trade were probably as great as from cotton manufacturing and went into commercial credit, building in Lancashire, British railways and American securities.

The new industries were soon critically dependent on foreign trade for the scale of their output. Initially cotton developed in the mid-eighteenth century as an import substitute for foreign textiles. By the late 1790s the industry was exporting more than 50 per cent of its finished product overseas. The extra volume that this provided was not essential for internal economies of scale, as most firms were small relative to the industry as a whole. However, the rapid growth and eventual size of exports made entrepreneurs install the latest equipment, and created large external economies of scale in Lancashire which became an efficient complex of interlocking factories, skills, services, markets, etc. Similarly, exports built up the efficiency of woollens in Yorkshire. By 1805 cotton formed 42 per cent of British exports, and by the 1830s textiles as a whole formed about 80 per cent. Thus although exports were only about 15 per cent of GNP in the early nineteenth century, their importance was far greater than this because of the leading industries involved.

The income from these exporting industries moderated the pressure of the population on food resources, as well as the physical and psychological hardships of life in the new industrial cities. Foreign trade now provided some form of insurance for the nation in bad harvest years. In addition, many simple household goods like clothing and soap were becoming so cheap that even the poorest classes could benefit. Imported timber placed cheaper housing and furniture within their grasp. Industrial expansion, buoyed up by export demand, also helped alleviate the desperate pockets of unemployment that frequently developed in the early nineteenth century as technical change inevitably destroyed old crafts.

The most important foreign market during the critical phase of the Industrial Revolution was undoubtedly North America. The American

Revolution only temporarily interrupted a rapidly rising trend. The extremely rapid growth of the American market at first more than offset the gradually increasing proportion of American manufactures produced at home. The other side of the coin – the increasing difficulty of exporting to Europe – was made even worse after 1793 when the French wars began. Markets in Latin America and Asia were still underdeveloped and only available intermittently. It is not surprising that North America took 37 per cent of Britain's cotton exports in the 1780s, 61 per cent in the 1790s, and 53 per cent in the 1800s. The bulk of these exports went to the United States although the West Indies also took large quantities. Similarly, large proportions of woollen exports went to the United States – 43 per cent in the 1790s and 47 per cent in the 1800s. Many other British trades benefited from the American market, and it was claimed in 1812 that 'in Birmingham one third, or one half of the total trade, in Sheffield one third; in the potteries one fourth ... in Leeds one half or one third ... in Manchester one third or one fourth' was sent to the United States. After 1815 many British industries remained painfully susceptible to American demand, gaining in the booms of the 1830s and 1850s but suffering in periods of contraction. However, the general level of the trade sank after 1820 as American industrialization began – but by then the most difficult period of British industrialization had passed.

The Atlantic economy and American economic growth

The Industrial Revolution in Great Britain relied significantly on the development of the Atlantic economy, but British industrialization also had significant effects on American development. North America was the first of a series of primary producing areas drawn into the British industrial system to supply raw materials and buy manufactures from the late eighteenth century onwards. The United States, however, was distinguished from most of the other extra-European primary producers by the facility with which it acquired the benefits available from the British connection while avoiding the costs.

Americans sensed the potential threat implicit in British commercial dominance in the mid-eighteenth century. Dislike of Britain's mercantilist system was one of the causes of the Revolution. The Navigation Acts which regulated colonial trade did not impose large burdens on the colonists generally, but did hurt some specific groups. Similar interests were also alienated by the progressively increasing intrusiveness of British commerce. For instance, until the 1750s merchants in Boston, New York and Philadelphia handled most consignments of British manufactured goods, but in the mid-eighteenth century agents of large British merchant houses began to sell direct. Similarly in Virginia Scottish factors, representatives of leading Glasgow houses, increasingly controlled local markets for tobacco, manufactured goods and credit. In both cases colonial consumers and producers benefited from substantial reductions in marketing costs, but local merchants and planters lost trade and status and feared future trends. It was, of course, the British imperial system that permitted this free competition and prevented local businessmen winning trade privileges from the colonial Assemblies. Not unnaturally American businessmen soon began to attempt to change the system and give America its own protective mercantilism.

Consequently, as soon as the federal government was firmly established by the Constitution of 1787, Congress enacted its own navigation laws and tariff system, and created a Bank of the United States modelled on the Bank of England. The forging of these new weapons did not determine exactly how they would be used, and the eastern cities generally argued in favour of a strong, relatively centralized state with encouragement for commerce and manufacturing, while the farmers favoured a more decentralized rural federation. This debate continued into the early nineteenth century and became an important element in the constitutional crises of the early 1830s and late 1850s, the South arguing for free trade with Britain and the North for industrial protection. (Part 1, especially Essays 1.3, 1.4 and 1.6, discusses these developments in more detail.)

The winning of independence and the creation of an American mercantilist system would not have led to industrialization without a rapid growth of demand. The basic factor affecting demand was population growth, spurred on by the same influences as were present in the eighteenth century and, after 1840, by much increased migration. As Table 1 shows, crude population increase was supplemented by increasing per capita income growth after about 1820, suggesting that the economy was undergoing qualitative change. The first signs of this are difficult to detect. The revolutionary period brought only a temporary flowering of craft manufacture, and American trade in the 1780s did not grow as rapidly as the population. The passage of the Constitution increased confidence in the new republic, but while trade around the seaboard increased, interior commerce was hampered by high transport costs. In 1800 it was still possible to imagine the continent developing into several independent nations.

Table 1   Growth of population and income in the United States

	1800	1820	1840	1860	1880	1900
Population (millions)	5.3	9.6	17.1	31.5	50.3	76.1
Gross National Product (in billions of 1860 dollars)	0.3	0.6	1.6	4.1	8.4	17.3
Income per capita (in 1860 dollars)	61	64	95	130	167	227

Of far greater immediate importance to development was American participation in the great growth of European and colonial trade in the late eighteenth century. Until 1776 the colonies had participated in Britain's increasing share of this trade, but after 1783 France and Spain gained at the expense of Britain, and American trade stagnated. However, when the European wars broke out in 1793, Britain once again isolated France from her colonies and seized much of her overseas trade. Britain, however, was hampered by naval requirements and consequently American shipping grew dramatically from 1793 to 1806. Nevertheless, although this stimulated commerce and finance in the east coast cities, British manufactures continued to threaten existing crafts and western agriculture remained relatively untouched. Finally, after 1806 the United States was gradually drawn into the European conflict, and between 1812 and 1815 it was at war with England. This temporarily destroyed American trade, and her maritime commerce and shipping were never as important relative to other activities again.

The other and longer lasting stimulus to American economic growth in the early nineteenth century was the cotton trade. At first in the 1770s and 1780s the mills in Lancashire drew most of their cotton from the non-American colonies, but by 1802 imports from the United States had overtaken other sources. The cotton trade had immense effects on the South, pushing the frontier back from the Appalachians to Texas between 1790 and 1860. (See the Maps and Statistical Tables booklet, p. 5.) Plantations struggling to market tobacco or discover new crops found in cotton an ideal staple which grew rapidly in the hot climate, could be cultivated by slaves, and was cheap to transport. The influence of the cotton trade on the rest of the United States is more questionable, since exports as a whole – of which cotton formed 50 per cent – were only 5 per cent of GNP. They almost certainly indirectly brought the upper Mississippi valley into the market economy in the 1820s and 1830s as a source of provisions for the slaves, and also stimulated the early development of east coast commerce and banking. However, it is also clear that after about 1840 the South was easily able to feed itself, and that the most active internal trade was between the industrial Northeast and the agricultural Midwest, increasingly bypassing the South.

British demand also influenced other areas of North America. The most important was the vast St Lawrence Basin, whose timber came from both sides of the US and Canadian border, and formed 75 per cent of Canadian exports in the 1830s. Finally, after the repeal of the Corn Laws in 1846, Britain began to buy sufficient American wheat to influence the development of the Midwest.

Demand from Britain also strongly influenced the *rhythm* of American development in the early nineteenth century. The amount of additional cotton and other staples raised each year depended on the growth of the population and the amount of new land opened up. However, if supply overshot demand and prices for raw materials dropped significantly in Liverpool, the frontier process slowed dramatically. This happened three times in the early nineteenth century, after the great frontier booms of 1815–19, the middle 1830s and the middle 1850s. American merchants therefore closely watched prices in Liverpool, and this concern and its consequent effects were reciprocal. In 1837, for instance, the Bank of England became alarmed at the volume of trade credit flowing to the United States and put pressure on the leading Anglo-American merchant banks. These in turn withdrew credit from their correspondents in the eastern ports, and this precipitated a commercial crisis that ultimately led to the depression of the early 1840s.

The scale of staple production necessitated British capital not only for short-term credit but also to help finance an improved transport system. The coast of North America lies in a great half circle around the staple producing interior, and the ports from Montreal and Quebec in Canada, through Boston, New York, Philadelphia and Baltimore in the East, down to Charlestown and Savannah in the South and through Mobile and New Orleans on the Gulf vied to secure this trade (see the Maps and Statistical Tables booklet, p. 5). The most dramatic development in the deep South was the opening up of the Mississippi River by steamboats in the 1820s and 1830s. All the firms were American, but their success ultimately depended on the cotton trade and on liberal credit from British merchants. Similarly the first railroads in the South were built from Charlestown and Savannah to capture the cotton trade of upland Georgia and South Carolina, and since they found it difficult to raise money directly, they were often financed by state governments who sold their own stocks in London. In the Northeast, canals and railroads were often built for local purposes such as bringing coal down from the Appalachian mines to the coastal cities, but larger projects like the Erie Canal in New York or the Baltimore and Ohio Railroad were built principally to win western trade for their respective cities, and were partly financed by British capital.

The result of these transport improvements was that by about 1850 the Mississippi valley and the Midwest had been effectively connected with the Northeast, and a well-organized system of inter-regional trade had been stimulated. Western provisions travelled south and east, northern manufactures south and west, and southern staples, especially cotton, north and to Europe. Within particular regions or states, too, rich rural areas were now more closely related to their rapidly growing urban centres such as Philadelphia or Chicago. The wealth of American agriculture and natural resources combined with its burgeoning population could now begin to bear on industrial growth.

American industrialization

Increasingly attractive markets created great opportunities for American entrepreneurs. At first, they chose products and methods of manufacturing that took full advantage of American conditions to replace particular British goods. This toehold was then widened out until imports had been reduced to a small share of the market. Like all new countries wishing to industrialize, they borrowed from British experience, but they also rapidly adapted existing technological ideas and in some respects improved on them.

Initially American manufacturers were fortunate in the timing of their industrialization. In the early nineteenth century they were shielded by high tariffs and substantial transport costs. Many small artisan shops in the Appalachian backcountry in the 1810s, or around the Great Lakes in the 1840s, enjoyed local monopolies just because of their remoteness, and simple manufacturing skills became widespread. Even so, it was not always easy to copy British machinery. The general principles were easy to grasp, but it was much more difficult to know the detailed operational settings and tolerances required. In addition, the new technology was by no means foolproof. Many machines today are so well designed that unskilled operators can use them effectively, but the machinery of the early Industrial Revolution was often haphazardly made and required frequent manual intervention by skilled mechanics. Instruction by skilled British migrants or American visiting of British factories was often a vital ingredient for success.

The most important industry required by the United States in this period was cotton textiles. The problems were formidable. The technology in Britain was developing rapidly, and there were many different machine builders producing individual machines that were constantly modified to meet local standards. There were no adequate printed descriptions of the machinery before the 1830s, and the British government attempted to prohibit the export of both machines and skilled workers. Nevertheless, New England had acquired a power spinning industry by 1800, a power weaving industry by 1820, and by 1840 had become the second largest centre of cotton textiles in the world. As in Lancashire, textiles stimulated many other industries such as engine building and machine tools, and these in turn were crucial to the start of the general Industrial Revolution in the United States.

The American cotton industry was by no means an exact copy of the British. For instance, the large new American mills built in Massachusetts in the 1820s and the 1830s specialized in the volume production of strong plain cloth. This cloth could be woven effectively on power looms by relatively unskilled workers. Good quality raw cotton was required to stand up to the powerful machinery, but this was available relatively cheaply in the United States. The crude cloth was acceptable to farmers, slave owners and sailors, and if necessary could be colour printed cheaply but effectively. By contrast, British mills produced a finer yarn and employed skilled hand or power loom weavers to introduce colours and patterns into the fabric, which would then command a premium in British and foreign markets. In this way manufacturers accommodated their product to the relative availability of raw materials, labour and machinery and the nature of their markets.

The early American railroads, too, were a modification of the British example, and inevitably the Americans with their vast distances to cover adopted them rapidly. The problem of transfer was easier than with textiles because the British were keen to export capital equipment and to show American purchasers their products. A key role was played by the leading Anglo-American merchants, many of whom were civic leaders in the coastal cities and were determined to gain access to the interior. American railroads soon adapted to the local environment. In Britain railways could expect a heavy density of traffic between established communities, and the gradings, tracks, bridges, etc. were well built from the start. In America by contrast, especially in the South and West, railroads – if they were to be built at all – had to be built very cheaply because the expected density of traffic in such sparsely populated areas was inevitably low. Hence they were often very poorly built with many curves and flimsy wooden bridges. This was a general frontier characteristic; capital and labour were scarce so most construction work was crudely and impermanently done. American engines also reflected local conditions not only in their smoke stacks (the use of wood instead of coal) and cowcatchers (reflecting the high labour cost of building fences to keep animals off the track), but also in their ability to deal with tight curves and badly laid track. Naturally, as the country developed and traffic density increased, these early characteristics were modified.

In some areas of production American entrepreneurs rapidly overtook their English rivals. They were assisted by the continual pull of the market, which grew much more rapidly than in Britain and gave manufacturers repeated opportunities to enlarge their plant and introduce the newest machines. They were also stimulated by the need to bid for labour against the lure of the frontier. They probably did not lose many of their own workers to western farming because manufacturing workers found agriculture hard. However, skilled workers frequently drifted off to western cities, and New England farmers often chose to migrate to the frontier rather than become wage earners. After 1840, with the Irish and later migrations, labour shortages in the East eased. However, by then a distinctive type of American mechanization had appeared which was later called 'the American System'. This involved the early mass production of clocks, watches, guns, sewing machines, etc. made of interchangeable parts. Capital costs were high for manufacturers because of the speed of the country's expansion and weaknesses in the American banking system. This, however, also imposed a useful discipline on manufacturers, making them very conscious of the dangers of overbuilding machinery.

America did not take all the ingredients of the classic British Industrial Revolution. As in Britain, her leading industry in 1860 was cotton textiles, but there was much less coal, iron and steam employed than in Britain's tightly woven industrial areas. Many of the New England mills still relied on waterpower, and steam was mostly used to drive steam boats or railroad engines and simple processing plants on the flat prairies or southern delta lands. The iron industry was backward, relying mostly on charcoal, and wood was still the major construction material rather than brick or iron. Other important sectors of American manufacturing were even more basic – the local processing of the profusion of crops by cotton gins, grist and saw mills, tanneries and liquor distilleries. By 1860, while the total manufacturing output of the United States was rapidly catching up with that of Britain and the quality of its light engineering was in advance, it was in many other respects still far behind, particularly in iron and steel production, chemicals and heavy engineering.

Conclusion

In 1860 the old description of Britain as the 'workshop of the world' was still accurate, and the American economy remained in many respects complementary rather than competitive to Britain. Thus *The Times* declared in 1851, 'For all practical purposes the United States are far more closely united with this Kingdom than any one of our colonies, and with us they keep up a perpetual interchange of the most important good offices; taking our manufactures and giving us in return the materials of industry, of revenue and of life.' As late as the 1850s, when about 20 per cent of British GNP was exported, about 20 per cent of this went to the United States. Moreover, in certain areas the proportion was much higher: in wool textiles 33 per cent, linen 36 per cent, pottery 53 per cent, iron and steel 43 per cent, hardware and cutlery 29 per cent. In iron rails in particular, American railroad demand in the 1850s absorbed the huge surplus output of the British mills built during the British railway mania of the 1840s. As a nation with continental resources, the United States was potentially far less dependent on foreign trade than Britain, but as indicated earlier British demand was still critical for certain important American trades and regions.

Possibly even more important for good transatlantic relations than the sheer volume of trade was the way in which it was organized. This was achieved in the early nineteenth century by merchants in the leading ports. Some of the leading names of the time such as Barings, Rothschilds, Brown-Shipley or Phelps-Dodge are still well known in the City of London or on New York's Wall Street. Manufacturers within Britain and planters within the United States relied on merchants and merchant-controlled institutions like the early banks and exchanges for essential credit and marketing services. The mercantile community, however, was also very tightly linked across the Atlantic. Because of the slow communications of the time and the large sums involved in transactions, the leading British merchants had to have carefully controlled agencies in the American ports. Very often only trusted relatives were given these duties because the firms' credit at difficult times might hang on their agents' ability to act quickly and judiciously. Therefore the closely knit skein of trading and credit relations that already existed in the Atlantic economy was supplemented by a web of personal relationships that tied the whole system together.

These trading links helped to produce close social and political relationships in the 1840s and 1850s. In the early nineteenth century there had been considerable hostility between Britain and the United States, and the depression of the late 1830s inevitably embittered many trading relationships. The last surge of American territorial expansion in the 1840s had also led to friction when American claims to the continent inevitably ran up against British and Canadian interests in the Far West. However, relations improved substantially from the mid-1840s. The Ashburton Treaty of 1844 and the Oregon Treaty of 1846 settled the Canadian frontier. The moderate American Walker Tariff of 1844 and the repeal of the British Corn Laws in 1846 opened up fresh trade possibilities. The vast migration from Ireland and the growing migration from Britain demonstrated how America could help solve Britain's population problems. The large capital export of the early 1850s showed how the British surplus could supplement American capital formation. Finally, the long American expansion of the late 1840s and early 1850s symbolized by the Gold Rush in California and the building of the railroads changed British views of America and helped cement political relationships. It was no wonder that in the decade before the Civil War there was great mutuality of consumer, literary and artistic tastes as well as philosophical and political ideas across the Atlantic: an Atlantic society as well as an Atlantic economy.

Further reading

Albion, Robert G. (with J.B. Pope) (1939) *The Rise of New York Port, 1815–1860*, New York, Scribners.

Bourne, Kenneth (1967) *Britain and the Balance of Power in North America, 1815–1908*, Berkeley, University of California Press.

Bruchey, Stuart (1990) *Enterprise: The Dynamic Economy of a Free People*, Cambridge, Mass., Harvard University Press.

Chapman, Stanley (1992) *Merchant Enterprise in Britain: From the Industrial Revolution to World War I*, Cambridge University Press.

Coleman, Terry (1972) *Passage to America: A History of Emigrants from Great Britain and Ireland to America in the Mid-Nineteenth Century*, Hutchinson.

Crafts, N.F.R. (1985) *British Economic Growth during the Industrial Revolution*, Oxford University Press.

Davis, Ralph (1973) *The Rise of the Atlantic Economies*, Weidenfeld and Nicolson.

Davis, Ralph (1979) *The Industrial Revolution and British Overseas Trade*, Leicester University Press.

Farnie, Douglass A. (1979) *The British Cotton Industry and the World Market*, Oxford, Clarendon Press.

Habakkuk, H.J. (1962) *American and British Technology in the Nineteenth Century*, Cambridge University Press.

Hindle, Brooke and Lubar, Steven (1986) *Engines of Change: The American Industrial Revolution, 1790–1860*, Washington, DC, Smithsonian Institution Press.

Jeremy, David (1981) *Transatlantic Industrial Revolution: The Diffusion of Textile Technologies between Britain and America, 1790s–1830s*, Oxford, Blackwell.

Lower, Arthur (1973) *Great Britain's Woodyard: British America and the Timber Trade, 1763–1867*, McGill-Queen's University Press.

McCusker, John J. and Menard, Russel R. (1985) *The Economy of British North America, 1607–1789*, Chapel Hill, University of North Carolina Press.

Morison, Samuel Eliot (1921) *The Maritime History of Massachusetts, 1783–1860*, Boston and New York, Houghton Mifflin.

North, D.C. (1961) *The Economic Growth of the United States, 1790–1860*, Englewood Cliffs, Prentice-Hall.

Potter, Jim (1960) 'The Atlantic Economy, 1815–60, the USA and the Industrial Revolution in Britain' in Leslie S. Presnell (ed.) *Studies in the Industrial Revolution*, Athlone Press.

Ratner, Sidney, Soltow, James, and Sylla, Richard (1993) *The Evolution of the American Economy: Growth, Welfare and Decision Making*, Macmillan.

Temin, Peter (1989) *The Jacksonian Economy*, New York, Norton.

Thistlethwaite, Frank (1959) *The Anglo-American Connection in the Early Nineteenth Century*, University of Pennsylvania Press.

Wilkins, Mira (1989) *The History of Foreign Investment in the United States to 1914*, Cambridge, Mass., Harvard University Press.

1.8   British and American agriculture to the 1860s

Agriculture and the economy

This essay looks at agriculture in the British and American economies before the 1860s – a useful dividing line because of the growing import-ance of international markets after that date. Clearly agriculture occu-pied a much more important position in the two economies in 1850 than it did a century later, as Table 1 makes clear.

Table 1   Proportion of labour force engaged in agriculture, 1850–1950 (with forestry and fishing)

	1850 %	1900 %	1950 %
Britain	22	9	5
USA	64	38	12

By the middle of the nineteenth century, American farming employed 64 per cent of the labour force and represented a slightly smaller proportion of the national income. In Britain the comparable figures were about 20 per cent – only a third of the American proportion. Earlier in the century agriculture had represented a larger slice of the national income, but it is worth stressing that the British agricultural labour force reached its peak in absolute numbers about 1850 and thereafter declined, while in the United States the peak was not actually reached until 1910.

Moving from labour and national income to social structure, we find that in Britain there were three pretty clearly defined agricultural classes: landowners, farmers (only 12 per cent of farm occupiers were tenants by 1870), and labourers. In the United States the picture was more complicated and open-ended, but with a similar hierarchy of big farmers, plantation owners, land speculators, owner-occupiers, tenant farmers (or share-croppers), homesteaders and – at the bottom of the heap – slaves on the southern plantations. With the exception of plan-tation slaves, there was probably more movement between the groups than was likely to occur in Britain, where class boundaries remained more rigid.

The relative decline of the labour force, a decreasing contribution to national income, and slowly changing social structures all reflect a much longer-term decline in the agricultural sector than during the period which concerns us here. Before the 1860s agriculture contributed substantially to industrialization in both Britain and the United States, for the expansion and modernization of agriculture went hand-in-hand with industrial development in both countries. A checklist of the main ways this was achieved would need to include the following points:

1   Agriculture increased *food supply* for a larger proportion of non-agricultural producers through improved efficiency.

2   It helped provide *labour* (consequent on 1 above) with movements from agricultural-rural sectors into industrial-urban ones.

3   It provided *capital* through increased returns for the development of industry and transport.

4   It was a *source of demand* for industrial manufactures, hence stimulating that sector (both 3 and 4 are mentioned in a later essay in this part, 'Capital').

5   It was a *source of foreign earnings*, though you should note the contrast between Britain and the United States here. Britain became increasingly dependent on grain imports after industrialization got underway, while America was already a major exporter by the time of the Civil War.

6   It contributed to *scientific and technical change* through biological, chemical and mechanical innovation (note the link with 2 above, for more efficient methods of production and greater mechanization reduced labour inputs).

Moreover, many industries depended on agriculture for their raw materials, notably processing activities like milling, tanning, soap making, brewing and distilling – often using factory-style production and quickly working to mass production to meet the demands of an expanding market. In both Britain and America there were other interesting links from agriculture to industry and transport. Often landowners with an enthusiasm for improving or modernizing their estates were also interested in mining, quarrying, roads, canals and railways. Many of the newly planned rural communities in Britain had their parallels across the United States. They combined a variety of agricultural and manufacturing functions, and in both countries the intimacy of the relationship serves to emphasize that the modernization of agriculture was part of more general economic growth. Once serious industrialization got underway in both Britain and America, many processing industries became urbanized, but they still maintained close links with the land which supplied the necessary raw materials.

Comparative themes and debates

Since agriculture was an important sector in the economy and played a significant role in the process of industrialization, the 'agricultural revolution' has long been a subject of scholarly research in both countries. You may recall some of its features in Britain: the great landowning pioneers of 'modernization' or 'improvement' struggling against traditional methods, the open fields giving way to consolidated holdings during the era of enclosures, the experimentation with new breeds of livestock, crops and farm machinery, and the creation of a landless labour force working in conditions of relentless toil or driven to the towns in search of alternative employment. Less familiar perhaps are developments on the other side of the Atlantic, where agriculture was unburdened by the same traditions. It was dominated by the rapid spread of tobacco in Virginia and of cotton in the South (using indentured and slave labour in both contexts), the exploitation of western lands by land-hungry settlers (accompanied by the near-extermination of Native American peoples), and the expanding market for farm products both in the United States itself and for export to Europe. As in Britain technological innovation played a part, for Yankee ingenuity produced machinery on a scale appropriate to the extensive nature of much American farming.

While empirical studies of agricultural history in both countries are vital to expanding our understanding of development on the ground, the wider political, economic and social questions are of greater interest to us. Take, for example, a study of English agriculture in the period 1815 to 1873, in which Eric Jones (1968) focused attention on what he saw as issues worth further exploration:

- Agricultural output continued to rise during a period of deflation from 1815 to 1836, a period formerly depicted as one of crushing depression. How could this paradox be explained?

- After the repeal of the Corn Laws (1846) had apparently stripped cereal producers of tariff protection, arable farming seems to have remained remarkably prosperous for at least 25 years. Why should this be so?

- Was the so-called 'golden age' of British agriculture (1846–73) all that prosperous? Was agriculture perhaps becoming over-capitalized, depressing the rewards of land ownership as early as 1850? Did landowners stick with it for non-economic reasons?

- What was the true condition of farm labourers during the period? What were wage rates and their standard of living, and how did they compare with industrial workers?

Other British scholars have addressed themes like agricultural enclosures, the position of the rural poor, rural–urban migration, agrarian protest, the role and influence of landowners, the profitability of agriculture, the problems of Ireland and the Scottish Highlands in the eighteenth and nineteenth centuries. Some have looked at much wider problems of agriculture and economic growth in general. As with industrialization, a lot of attention has been given to the timing and impact of the changes, and all the indications are that the agricultural revolution was a much longer-term business than previously thought, for many developments once ascribed to the magical eighteenth century had much earlier origins – dating back in some instances to the seventeenth century. These examples indicate the wide-ranging nature of agricultural history and the way it impinges on wider economic, social and political history in Britain in this period.

In the United States historians have posed similar questions:

- Agriculture and the frontier: how did domestic demand and the western movement affect farming?

- Did public land policy advance or retard agriculture? Did it favour rich speculators or railroad barons at the expense of poor homesteaders? What was the role of the railroads and the speculators in the development of American agriculture?

- Were railroads critical to agricultural growth in the United States after about 1840? (The wider economic questions are considered by Michael Drake in Essay 1.11.)

- Was the southern plantation system – and slavery in particular – profitable? What changes did the slave economy undergo in the period 1800 to 1860?

All these issues, we should note, were of continuing significance *after* the Civil War.

You can see how closely many of these problems and controversies about American agriculture relate to the wider development of the United States before the Civil War. We also need to bear in mind that our discussion has an even wider context, as agricultural commodities were increasingly traded in the emergent *international* economy during the nineteenth century. Obviously the development of agriculture in the lands of recent settlement in North America, Australia, New Zealand and Argentina had a big impact on European farming. By the middle of the century it was already being affected by cheap imports, notably grain and wool (and later meat was added to the list). However, while our concern is with some of the broader historical issues, we need first to know something about the lands and their respective products.

British agriculture to the 1860s

Soil and climate are obviously the major determinants of agricultural land use; thus British farming in the period before 1870 can be divided into three broad regional categories:

- Pastural, stock rearing and fattening with dairying, essentially in the wetter west and north, including much of northern England, Wales, Ireland and Scotland.

- Arable, cereal production, mainly in the English Midlands, East Anglia, south-east England, and including parts of southern Ireland and the Scottish lowlands.

- Mixed farming in much of the rest of the country, especially south-west and northern England, and around growing urban, industrial centres where there was an increasing demand for meat, vegetables and dairy products.

These categories were probably more marked in the eighteenth and early nineteenth centuries than today.

Within this broad division there were clear regional specializations – often the result of the spirit of commerce and land rationalization that accompanied the capitalist revolution in agriculture during the eighteenth century. East Anglia (where so many of the early 'improving' landowners, including the famous Coke of Holkham, were active) was barley country, while Kent and Worcester produced hops, both important raw materials in the rapidly expanding urban brewing trade of the metropolis and elsewhere. In Wales, the North and especially the Scottish Highlands, landlords with an eye on the growing demand for both meat and wool had introduced sheep, so that by the early 1800s vast new areas were being given over to pasture. Not only did this mean enclosure and land improvement, it often spelt disaster for those peasant farmers and crofters moved to make room for sheep. While there is evidence that at least some of the early 'clearances' involved brutal eviction (some crofters left for North America of their own volition, particularly before 1815), this sort of treatment was more prevalent after the 1820s. Still later in Scotland sheep were replaced in some instances by deer as the increasingly anglicized (and often absentee) lairds developed their estates for the sporting rich. The Irish peasantry also suffered similar deprivations, and by the early nineteenth century they joined the Scots and many English and Welsh in the great transatlantic and colonial migrations to

Australia, New Zealand and elsewhere. In general, the arable-pastural mix became a feature of areas near centres of expanding population, such as the West Midlands and south Lancashire, where canals and later railways with their cheap transport brought improved returns for products like grain, pork, vegetables and dairy products. In addition, towns and cities supplied the land with human and industrial waste (like spent grains from breweries and distilleries), which both fertilized the land and provided livestock feeding. Brewing is an excellent example of a large-scale urban consumer industry (in cities like London, Edinburgh and Dublin) which maintained long-established links with agriculture and the countryside. Though manufacturing a traditional product, it was at the forefront of mass marketing and new technology.

Three main elements were relatively new to agriculture after 1750:

- large-scale capital investment

- land rationalization, enclosures and extension of cultivable areas

- scientific methods and new technology.

Investment of capital on a larger scale than previously came from landowners and bigger farmers anxious for greater returns. Soon bankers, lawyers, and increasingly the successful merchant-capitalists and entrepreneurs of the Industrial Revolution also began to plough their profits into land. The Bristol, Liverpool and Glasgow merchants are good examples from the mid-eighteenth century, while Richard Arkwright, the shrewd inventor and textile magnate who bought himself an estate and country seat near his cotton spinning village at Cromford in Derbyshire, is another from the Industrial Revolution era. Capital was sunk in the consolidation of holdings, enclosures, farm buildings, roads, plantations, and the new technology which gave better crop yields and improved livestock. These measures not only raised productivity but made further investment attractive in the longer term – especially given rising demand as industrialization gained speed after 1780.

Enclosure of open fields, common lands and wastelands (often not previously cultivated) is sometimes seen as the key to experiment with crops, livestock and machinery. Certainly it was pursued with enthusiasm during the eighteenth and early nineteenth centuries (see the Maps and Statistical Tables booklet, p. 5, which shows the geographical spread of parliamentary enclosure), so that by 1850 most agriculture was undertaken on consolidated holdings (except in parts of the Scottish Highlands and Ireland where subsistence crofter-peasant farming prevailed). Farm mechanization was slow and British farming – unlike American agriculture – remained essentially labour intensive, so the major innovations really came in livestock, crops and husbandry.

The period of the Revolutionary and Napoleonic Wars from 1793 to 1815 brought with it a dramatic expansion in British agriculture, partly to counter the loss of European grain imports and partly in response to rising domestic demand. High agricultural prices and a spate of bad harvests made marginal cultivation attractive; hence large areas were either put under the plough or enclosed for pasture. Some agricultural historians say that more land was utilized for productive farming in that period than at any time since, including, you might be surprised to learn, both world wars.

After the Napoleonic Wars there was some painful adjustment to new conditions. The high wartime costs were no longer matched by high prices, although the agrarian distress that resulted (with its accompanying social protest) was far from general. Work on the agricultural depressions of 1813–36 suggests that the cereal districts were worst hit, whereas those areas lucky enough to embrace large urban markets barely suffered at all (Jones, 1968).

It comes as no surprise that a parliament of landlords should enact the Corn Laws of 1815 in consequence of a government committee's recommendation that foreign grain should be imported free of duty only when the price of home-produced wheat had climbed to 80 shillings (£4.00) a quarter (the average price from 1820 to 1845 was about 58 shillings a quarter). But paradoxically agricultural output continued to expand during this period – a product of continuing investment by progressive landowners combined with new methods of farming light soils. At the same time, recent work on the Corn Laws suggests that a price-cost squeeze encouraged many farmers at this time to adopt mixed farming or move out of cereals altogether into pastoral farming, where the prospect of profits was relatively more attractive because there was less competition from imports (Vamplew, 1980).

Rising farm prices from the late 1830s heralded the 'golden age' of British agriculture, which can be placed between the repeal of the Corn Laws in 1846 and the 'Great Depression' that set in with the rise of cheap American cereals after 1870. You will notice my use of inverted commas here because historians of agriculture during the second half of the nineteenth century have been revising many previously held notions about the economic condition of farming after repeal. Historians have often taken the view that this was a tranquil and prosperous time for farmers, especially cereal producers, though it seems paradoxical that this belief should have been so long held, given that an end to protection was meant to reduce grain prices dramatically – as the Anti-Corn Law League hoped. Yet the evidence seems to indicate that the sharp rises and falls in grain prices over the 30 years or so after 1846 virtually cancelled each other out. Given the increasingly mixed nature of farming (with the possible exception of eastern England), it was rather the rising trend of *livestock* prices which underpinned the 'golden age' before 1870.

Repeal had only minimal impact on British cereal producers because until the 1870s foreign competitors were in no position to undercut them. In the 1840s European cereals were generally in short supply; in the 1850s the Crimean War interfered with Russian exports; and, more significant in the longer term from our point of view, Britain remained isolated from American exports due to high transport costs across the Atlantic. At the same time industrial prosperity and enhanced employment in Britain created an increased demand for farm products. So, as Jones (1968) indicates, while the growth of supply was interrupted or retarded in bad years, demand grew more vigorously and steadily.

The condition of labour in the late eighteenth and nineteenth centuries remains a field of active investigation by both social and agricultural historians, though we still need to know a lot more about household incomes (often desperately low), rural poor relief, migration and emigration during and after the Industrial Revolution. There have been attempts by an 'optimistic' school of economic historians to paint a

more favourable picture of rural conditions than that presented by earlier historians, with much of the debate focused on the merits or
demerits of the old Poor Law. Detailed studies of localities before 1834
are beginning to help us appreciate the wealth of regional differences,
but the controversy continues. The new Poor Law apparently did not
change matters all that much, for structural unemployment due to the
lack of other opportunities in the countryside was omnipresent, even in
mid-Victorian times. After the 1850s things certainly improved, bringing
higher wages and fringe benefits (see Table 2).

*Table 2   Regional wage movements, 1850–72 (national average
1850–1 = 100)*

	1850–1	1869–70	1872
Northern counties	130	165	188
Midland counties	104	138	161
Eastern counties	84	114	138
South and southwestern counties	83	111	131

If the 'golden age' was based on the expansion of mixed farming rather
than cereals, coupled with the drift to the towns and to industrial
employment, then higher wages were clearly offered to hold labour on
the land. In some localities labour shortages occurred at harvest time,
though it is easy to exaggerate this because seasonal unemployment was
for long a feature of rural life. Certainly the emergence of unionism
among farm labour – apparently so long delayed – was triggered in the
early 1870s when the wage ceiling had been reached and some landowners and farmers actually began to cut wages.

　　While there were many earlier developments dating back (in some
cases) to the seventeenth century, the agricultural revolution of the late
eighteenth and early nineteenth centuries transformed British farming by
reorganizing land use and applying new technology to increase production and feed rising populations. Modern research has certainly
changed our perspective of the timing and impact of these changes, dis-
pelling old myths about the primacy of a few 'improvers', new farm gad-
getry or animal breeding techniques. Now we can see the processes in a
wider perspective, and start to understand how important *economic* forces
were in shaping changed attitudes throughout the farming community –
not just amongst an élite.

American agriculture to the 1860s

If, on balance, regionalism was hardly significant in British agriculture,
the same could certainly not be said of the United States, where section-
alism shaped so much of the historical process before the Civil War. The
United States of 1783 was a distinctly commercial and agricultural nation,
and until the Civil War agriculture – despite industrialization in the
North – remained dominant in the economy. At the same time it is
impossible to study the history of American agriculture in the first half of
the nineteenth century without constant reference to the westward movement. For in an era of general optimism and expansion two significant
themes emerge:

- a vast and rapid extension of agricultural land (bearing no comparison with the British experience)

- investment in new technology and scientific farming (deriving much from Britain and Europe but again on a more dramatic scale).

So, while it may be said that British agriculture in this period was intensive (in terms of both land use and deployment of labour), American agriculture was extensive in land area but scarce in labour and ultimately large-scale in capital investment.

Above all, environment shaped land use and farm products in the same way we saw in microcosm in Britain. Three major divisions or sections had emerged in the colonial era: the South, the middle colonies, and New England. Antebellum expansion broadly reflected the established pattern, though clearly prairie cereal farming or far-western ranching were significant sectional specialisms which reflected their own particular environments.

The old South produced goods – cotton, rice, indigo and tobacco – which fitted ideally with British requirements: commodities that could not be produced at home and which Britain and other countries wanted. Plantation agriculture was ideal, but these commodities required not only abundant land but also an abundance of labour, and the latter was scarce and expensive. Migrants were needed all over the colonies, but most pressingly in the southern plantations. Resort was soon made to slavery as a means of supplying cheap labour. By the end of the eighteenth century, plantation agriculture had expanded well beyond the boundaries of the old South (see Maps and Statistical Tables booklet, p. 5), although the main surges into the new Southwest came between 1815 and 1860. The economics of slavery have been hotly debted by historians, and are referred to further in the essay on '"King Cotton" in Britain and America'. Certainly, the plantation system, with its production of export commodities, especially cotton, had a critical role in the industrialization of both Britain and the United States. So it deserves attention not just as a system of agriculture or social organization.

Turning to the middle colonies we find a very different environment. By the 1800s the fertile areas of New York, Pennsylvania and New Jersey supported a prosperous mixed agriculture of grain and livestock. Much of the land had access to navigable rivers and to growing urban centres like New York and Philadelphia. With increased settlement and the building of roads, canals and railroads, farmers in this section were well placed to help fulfil demand for food products until commercial agriculture became established. The mixed agriculture of the middle colonies also came to typify Ohio and other new states as far west as the Mississippi valley, often initially dependent on the labour of the whole household (Craig, 1991).

New England was totally different again for, apart from the river valleys like the Connecticut, the land was relatively poor. Much of the region was typified by subsistence agriculture, and this was often marginal enough to force settlers to look to the sea for their livelihood – hence the development of fishing and whaling, which were already significant by independence. Later, when the cereal lands were opened up, New England and eastern farmers in general were unable to compete, though it is worth noting that increasing urban industrial demand forced a switch from grain to dairy and fruit products – much as it did in farming areas near urban centres in Britain.

The West – at first the 'old Northwest' comprising Ohio, Indiana, Illinois, Michigan and Wisconsin – soon established its own pattern of agriculture, though the immense potential of this vast area was not fully exploited until the transport revolution brought canals and railroads. By 1860, however, the five states, with their ideal cereal growing soils, produced half the nation's wheat crop. Wheat and cattle were subsequently to become the great staples of agriculture beyond the Mississippi, when the frontier was pushed into the western prairies. In Iowa, another great granary of the Midwest, early settlers on the farming frontier who stuck it out enjoyed rates of growth in their income considerably above the national average (Galenson and Pope, 1989).

Against this background we can begin to appreciate how sectional interests reflected not only environment and land use but also general socio-economic attitudes. It comes as no surprise that the biggest single issue, the westward movement, was viewed very differently by each of the three sections – broadly the South, the East and the West – and it is to this that I would like to turn briefly now.

American agriculture and the western frontier

So all-pervading is the westward movement in the history of the United States during the nineteenth century that one might assume it was absolutely critical to economic growth. But from what you have read in other essays and what has been said here about agriculture before 1860, you might conclude otherwise given the relative success of different farming systems in the older, longer-established areas of the United States. On the other hand, would American agriculture have remained as prosperous without apparently limitless land resources, and would expansion have been slowed or even checked completely?

The 'counter-factual' approach (i.e. 'what if...?' – used by Robert Fogel to examine railroads in the nineteenth-century American economy and discussed in Essay 1.11, 'What price railways?') could only be extended to such a broad sector as agriculture with some difficulty, but it might serve our purposes for the moment to look at why agriculture expanded so fast with the frontier before the Civil War – and speculate on what might have transpired *without* the westward movement.

Sectional attitudes are readily assessed. Generally the East (New England and most of the middle colonies) opposed rapid westward expansion because it caused labour scarcity, depressed land values, and brought stiff competition from cheap western produce. Yet the East benefited substantially from the West (as it did from the South) in its industrialization, in the growth of commerce, services and transport, and in the financing of internal improvements. The products of eastern industry – from stoves to railroad engines – were much in demand in the West.

The West, always a 'debtor' area, demanded low interest rates, liberal policies and more internal improvements – especially transport – so that the products of the new lands could be moved cheaply to urban markets in the East or down the Mississippi to southern plantations or rapidly expanding centres like New Orleans. The West (like the South again) always seemed to be claiming that land was rapidly being 'used

up', when in fact the so-called 'frontiersman' was primarily a land specu-
lator and only *afterwards* a farmer. After long agitation a Homestead Law
was passed in 1862 to make free entry into the public lands possible. But
despite the high hopes held for it, the law was not able to curb the
activities of land speculators, nor did it encourage large numbers to
become homesteaders.

Sectional interests in the South were irretrievably bound up with
slavery and the plantation system – and ultimately with 'King Cotton', the
most important product. Like the West, the South was a 'debtor' society,
often dependent on northeastern capital, with the plantation owners and
farmers living on credit from banks or merchant houses. Slave-owning
planters also had an insatiable 'land hunger', but were ever conscious of
the need to defend the 'peculiar institution' of slavery from attack.
Hence the southern obsession with the creation of Slave States within the
Union on a one-for-one basis with the Free States established in the
Northwest. The importance of the cotton plantations to the American
economy needs little emphasis, for by 1860 cotton represented two-thirds
of total exports.

The westward movement greatly influenced patterns of agricultural
expansion before 1860. The major surges of movement into new lands
occurred in 1816–18, the 1830s and the 1850s, each induced by expanding demand for farm products and by rising prices. As Douglass North
says: 'It is well to keep this in mind, because such market influences do
not appear as decisive in many descriptions of western settlement'
(North, 1974, p. 122). Essentially, agriculture expanded to meet demand.
The West at first mainly satisfied the expanding urban East, and once
canals and railroads penetrated the interior, it increasingly looked to foreign exports. The South also expanded its plantation system westward
into the 'new Southwest', especially Louisiana and Mississippi where conditions were well suited to cotton culture. Here, too, expansion reflected
the apparently insatiable demand during the first half of the nineteenth
century for cheap cotton textiles at home and abroad.

Without the westward movement it seems likely that agriculture in
the United States might well have been arrested by the early 1800s, and
the old colonial-style system might have been maintained for much
longer. A logical extension of this idea is the argument that the sectional
struggle might have reached crisis point long before the 1860s. For as
long as the new lands of the West were open to exploitation, the socio-
economic 'safety-valve' operated to the benefit of the economy *and*
nation.

Conclusion

Some of the main points you should have grasped from this discussion
are that:

- Agriculture played a significant role in the economies of both Britain
  and United States before 1860, and expansion was part and parcel of
  the general process of economic growth.

- Expansion was everywhere a reflection of increased demand from a
  rapidly rising urban and industrial population.

- Both agricultures had a series of regional specializations, which were generally more vulnerable to market forces than mixed producers. Specialization remained more important in the United States, while Britain began to swing towards mixed farming after the mid-century.

- Britain and the United States had their 'frontiers', though the American westward movement hardly bears direct comparison with the more modest general enclosure movement in Britain (much of it from former waste land, heath, fens and moors). Both certainly represented attempts to expand agricultural output to meet rising demand. The colonies of Canada, Australia, New Zealand and South Africa were Britain's real frontiers during the nineteenth century.

- Regional or sectional interests were far more significant in the United States than in Britain – and always seemed more likely to generate conflict – ultimately on a big enough scale to plunge the country into civil war. Conflict was certainly present in Britain in a variety of forms – economic, social and political protest – typified by the 'swing' riots of the 1830s in southern England, when agricultural labourers revolted against mechanization on the farm by smashing up threshing mills, or crofters' riots against evictions in Ireland and the Scottish Highlands during much of the period. Such protest was often more than local in its impact, but even then hardly on the scale of civil war.

In the longer term, regional or sectional interests in both countries were swallowed up in the rapidly emerging international economy, to the extent that American cereal farmers in the Midwest or cotton plantation owners in the South were just as exposed to international market vagaries as wheat producers in the East Midlands or stock farmers in Devon. Certainly, the expansion of agriculture in the American West and the export of prairie wheat after the 1870s were to have a profound and long-term effect on British agriculture at least until 1914, when the outbreak of World War I brought a return to the artificial conditions experienced during the Revolutionary and Napoleonic Wars a century before.

Finally, agriculture remains a useful barometer of socio-economic conditions in general. For despite the rise of industry, the introduction of new technology, and the transport revolution brought by canals, railways and steamships, the natural cycle still maintained its timeless influence on life and work for large sections of the British and American people before the 1860s. Some of the other essays discuss aspects of agricultural capital, agriculture's contribution to industrialization, farming on the frontier, and the southern plantation system, so these and other topics could be followed up in greater depth either in your course material or the further reading cited here.

References and further reading

Chambers, J.D. and Mingay, G.E. (1969) *The Agricultural Revolution 1750–1880*, Batsford.

Church, R.A. (1975) *The Great Victorian Boom 1850–1873*, Macmillan.

Craig, L.A. (1991) 'The Value of Household Labor in Antebellum Northern Agriculture', *Journal of Economic History*, vol. 51, no. 1, pp. 67–81.

Galenson, D.W. and Pope, C.L. (1989) 'Economic and Geographic Mobility on the Farming Frontier: Evidence from Appanoose County, Iowa, 1850–1870', *Journal of Economic History*, vol. 49, no. 3, pp. 635–55.

Hudson, P. (1992) *The Industrial Revolution*, Edward Arnold (especially ch. 3).

Jones, E.L. (1968) *The Development of English Agriculture 1815–1873*, Macmillan.

North, D.C. (1974) *Growth and Welfare in the American Past: A New Economic History*, 2nd edn, Englewood Cliffs, Prentice-Hall.

O'Brien, P.K. and Quinault, R. (eds) (1993) *The Industrial Revolution and British Society*, Cambridge University Press.

Temin, P. (1975) *Causal Factors in American Economic Growth in the Nineteenth Century*, Macmillan.

Thernstrom, S. (1989) *A History of the American People, Volume One: To 1877*, New York, Harcourt Brace Jovanovich (especially chs 11 and 12).

Vamplew, W. (1980) 'The Protection of English Cereal Producers: The Corn Laws Reassessed', *Economic History Review*, XXXIII, no. 3, August, pp. 382–95.

Walsh, M. (1981) *The American Frontier Revisited*, Macmillan.

1.9   Population and labour in the USA and Britain: a comparative approach

Introduction

In 1984 we celebrated the 150th anniversary of the death of the greatest social scientist England has ever produced. His main interest was demography (the study of populations), and the theory which he propounded in a spirited little occasion piece in 1798, and which he elaborated through a further five editions over the next 30 years, still commands respect. In some ways his reputation is higher today than it has ever been. The year 1979, for instance, saw the publication of not one but two biographies (James, 1979; Petersen, 1979 – these were the first ever to appear); whilst in 1980 the French government hosted an international conference of great size and complexity in his honour at the UNESCO headquarters in Paris. He was discussed throughout the 1980s in a steady stream of articles by historians, economists, theologians, political scientists and geographers. Then – the ultimate accolade! – a sumptious collected edition (the first) of his entire output appeared in 1987 (Wrigley and Souden, 1987).

   In this essay we shall be using the work of the Reverend T.R. Malthus (1766–1834) to provide the framework for a comparative investigation into the population and labour histories of the USA and Britain. We feel this approach has several advantages. First, examining the various facets of the subject (e.g. growth rates, age at marriage, levels of fertility) within the context of one theory (or explanation) serves to highlight the similarities and differences between the two countries. Second, central to Malthusian theory is the relationship between production and population, and with labour being one of the three factors of production (the other two being land and capital), we are necessarily brought straight away to the core of our discussion. Third, it so happens that in articulating his theory Malthus drew very much on the historical experience of the two countries with which we are concerned.

   Our comparative analysis does, however, pose a couple of problems. The first concerns the data available to us. On the whole both the primary sources and the secondary sources are much richer in Britain (more especially England) than in the USA. Thus we cannot compare like with like as precisely as we would have wished. The second problem concerns the timing of our comparison. Strictly speaking, the demographic experience of the two countries is only comparable from about 1880 when both were undoubtedly populous countries, heavily urbanized, with large industrial workforces. From this point we can compare the demographic responses of the two countries under broadly similar conditions: we are no longer talking about 'chalk and cheese'. In order to do this before 1880, however, we must go further back in time in the case of England than in the case of the USA. In that way we can compare the demographic response of the two countries in the pre-industrial and industrializing phases of their development.

The population theory of Malthus

Malthus, as he put it, 'sketched the general outline of [his] argument' in the first chapter of his *Essay on the Principle of Population, as it affects the Future Improvement of Society with Remarks on the Speculations of Mr Godwin, M. Condorcet and other writers.* Quoting from that chapter we find the essence of his case to be as follows:

> I think I may fairly make two *postulata*. First, that food is necessary to the existence of man. Secondly, that the passion between the sexes is necessary and will remain nearly in its present state ...
>
> Assuming then my postulata as granted, I say, that the power of population is infinitely greater than the power in the earth to produce subsistence for man.
>
> Population, when unchecked, increases in a geometrical ratio. Subsistence increases only in an arithmetical ratio. A slight acquaintance with numbers will show the immensity of the first power in comparison of the second. By that law of our nature which makes food necessary to the life of man, the effects of these two unequal powers must be kept equal.
>
> This implies a strong and constantly operating check on population from the difficulty of subsistence ...

> (Malthus, 1970 edn, pp. 70–1)

It might be interjected here that Malthus took a good degree in mathematics at Cambridge, so he perhaps overestimated the numeracy of his audience. He did, however, spell out the difference between the two ratios elsewhere in his essay: the geometrical ratio leading to an increase of the order 1, 2, 4, 8, 16, 32, etc. and the arithmetical one of 1, 2, 3, 4, 5, 6, etc.

In chapter 4 Malthus describes this 'constantly operating check', or rather he divides it into two:

> ... a foresight of the difficulties attending the rearing of a family acts as a preventive check, and the actual distresses of some of the lower classes, by which they are disabled from giving the proper food and attention to their children, act as a positive check to the natural increase of population ...

> (p. 89)

A visual summary of Malthus's position appears in Figure 1 (overleaf). This is a copy of Figure 11.1, 'The positive and preventive checks', which appears in Wrigley and Schofield's *The Population of England 1541–1871: A Reconstruction* – a book of immense erudition, about which more anon.

The diagram consists of two loops: the outer one represents the operation of the positive checks, the inner one that of the preventive checks. The circles containing a plus or a minus sign indicate whether a particular relationship involves a negative or a positive correlation. Thus, if population rises (as we shall see shortly), food prices rise; if population falls, food prices fall. In other words, there is always a positive correlation between the two, i.e. both move in the same direction. On the other hand, there is always a negative correlation between food prices and real income, since if the former *rises,* the latter *falls.* And if food prices *fall,* real income *rises.*

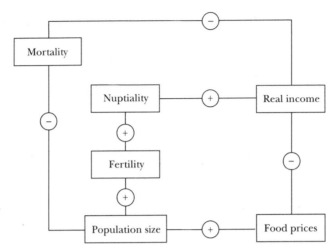

Figure 1
The population theory of
Malthus (Wrigley and Schofield,
1981, p. 458)

We shall now go round this 'wiring diagram' quickly before examining each link, in the context of the British and American experience, in more detail. We start with the box marked 'population size'. Let us suppose this is increasing. If so, it will not be long before food prices rise owing to human inability to raise food output as rapidly as people can reproduce (the arithmetic versus the geometric rate of growth). If food prices rise, then real income will fall (other things being equal). If this happens, food consumption will be curtailed, which will lead to a rise in mortality either through diseases associated with malnutrition or, in extreme cases, through famine. A rise in mortality will then lead to a fall in the rate of population growth or, if it is high enough, to an actual fall in population. This in turn will lead to a fall in food prices, a rise in real income, a fall in mortality, and an increase in the rate of population growth – and so on and so on. Here we have a classical negative feedback, with each change in the system setting off further changes, each of which *tends* to restore the original state of equilibrium. Malthus, of course, never went so far as to say that no progress was ever made. That would have been patently silly since it was obvious that the population of his world was greater than it had been 2,000 years earlier. Nevertheless, he argued, the actual growth of population had been extremely slow when compared to its potential for growth.

Turning now to the inner loop, we share the initial linkages with the other one, i.e. population size to food prices to real income. If real income falls, then, argued Malthus, people (of all classes) will be hesitant about embarking upon marriage. Thus nuptiality (the proportion of the population living in the married state) will fall; the age at marriage will rise (so the amount of time a woman is exposed to childbearing whilst still fertile will also fall), and the fertility of the population will be reduced. A fall in fertility means a diminution in the number of new members being added to the population and so, other things being equal (no immigration, for instance), a fall in its rate of growth. Conversely, a rise in real income will encourage more people to get married and at an earlier age, which will lead in turn to higher fertility. And so we will get a higher population.

Malthusian theory and the English experience

Our ability to see the extent to which Malthusian theory explains the English experience has been very much helped by the study of Wrigley and Schofield (1981). For the first time we have an appropriate set of statistics in which we can be reasonably confident. Let us look at our wiring diagram again in the light of the Wrigley and Schofield findings.

Population size

Malthus argued that the 'principal states of modern Europe ... though they have increased very considerably in population since they were nations of shepherds ... require three or four hundred years or more' to double their populations (p. 89). He contrasted this with the doubling every 25 years of the population of those North American colonies which had become the USA in his lifetime (p. 74).

Current research findings suggest that Malthus was not far from the truth in his thinking on this point, though somewhat paradoxically the rate of population growth in England (a country he believed exemplified the rest of Europe) had begun to increase very sharply in his lifetime. Before the Black Death struck in 1348, the population of England was of the order of 4.5 to 6 million (Hatcher, 1977, p. 68). By 1377 it had fallen to between 2.5 and 3 million (Hatcher, 1977, p. 68) and had got no higher than 2.8 million by 1541 (Wrigley and Schofield, 1981, p. 531). Although it all but doubled in the next 100 years (5.1 million in 1641 and 5.3 million in 1656, its highest point in the seventeenth century), it did not actually do so until 1745 (Wrigley and Schofield, 1981, pp. 532–3). It then began to grow rapidly, reaching 8.4 million in 1798, the year Malthus published his essay. Only another 50 years was to elapse before the population doubled again, a rate of growth that was to be all but maintained to the end of the nineteenth century (see Table 1).

Table 1   Population of England and USA, 1700–1980

Year	England	USA
1700	5,027,000	275,000
1750	5,739,000	1,207,000
1800	8,606,000	5,308,000
1850	16,516,000	23,192,000
1900	30,509,000	76,094,000
1950	41,159,000	150,697,000
1980	46,221,000	226,505,000

Sources: England 1700–1850, Wrigley and Schofield, 1981, pp. 533–5; England and Wales 1901–81, Office of Population Censuses and Surveys, 1982, p. 13; USA 1700–1850, Potter, 1965, pp. 638; USA 1900–80, *The Statesman's Year Book*, 1981–2, p. 1373.

Food prices

As with the rate of population growth, Malthus also 'got it right' as to the relationship between population growth and food prices. Wrigley and Schofield use an index of consumables prepared by Phelps-Brown and Hopkins (1956) to indicate this relationship in England. They conclude that during the 250 years before the appearance of Malthus's essay, whenever population growth rates increased, food prices rose too and at a faster rate – just as Malthus predicted they would. 'Between 1541 and 1656, the population of England almost doubled while the price series more than tripled' (Wrigley and Schofield, 1981, p. 402).

After 1656 population and prices fell. Between 1731 and 1811 the population again doubled, but prices increased by two and a half times. But then – as with the rate of population growth – there came a remarkable change. Wrigley and Schofield (1981, pp. 403–4) again:

> Between 1811, when the price index turned down, and 1871, population doubled yet again, maintaining an even higher rate of growth than in the preceding 60-year period, but the price of the consumables basket first fell and then levelled out. The historic link between population growth and price rise was broken; an economic revolution had taken place. And by an ironic coincidence Malthus had given pungent expression to an issue that haunted most pre-industrial societies at about the last moment when it could still plausibly be represented as relevant to the country in which he was born.

Real income

On the food price–real income relationship, Wrigley and Schofield conclude (p. 409) that not until the end of the eighteenth century was the English economy able to sustain a rate of population growth in excess of 0.5 per cent per annum (a rate of this order would lead to a doubling of the population in 140 years) without bringing about a fall in real income. A rate of population growth below that figure was accompanied by a rise in real income. As with the population–food price relationship, a dramatic change occurred at the beginning of the nineteenth century when population rose by 1 per cent per annum and real income rose too.

Real income and mortality

We now come to the core of Malthusian theory: the 'positive check'. Malthus argued that population growth was checked periodically by a rise in mortality, the result of insufficient food. Frankly we do not have adequate data to test this in England. For instance, we lack accurate information as to cause of death. Historical demographers have had, therefore, to settle for second best and have tried to tease out the cause of death from the magnitude and timing of the fluctuations in burials recorded in the Church of England's parish registers. The discussion has become enormously complex, and to summarize it in a few paragraphs is to do scant justice to the many historians who have laboured long over it. Briefly, then, it would appear that:

1   Burials did often rise sharply, sometimes to three or four times their average level (see Figure 2 – p.120).

2   Such 'mortality crises', as they have been called, were usually fairly local in their extent. Wrigley and Schofield, for instance, found that even the worst crises affected less than 40 per cent of the parishes in their national sample, whilst the norm was between 7 and 15 per cent (1981, p. 670).

3   The crucial question remains: were the upswings in burials associated with high food prices? The evidence is mixed. For the northwestern parts of the country in the sixteenth and early seventeenth centuries, a strong case has been argued by Appleby (1978) for linking food shortages, brought on by harvest failures and depressions in the woollen cloth industry, and high mortality. Key years here are 1586–8, 1596–8 and 1623. Elsewhere, however, years of exceptionally high food prices appear not to have had any impact on the number of burials. Thus, for instance, Chambers (1957, p. 25) noted as long ago as 1957 that the years 1708–10 witnessed the highest grain prices until the 1790s, yet burials rose only slightly in the many Nottinghamshire villages he studied. On the other hand, there is a good deal of   evidence to suggest that mortality crises occurred as a result of epidemics of such diseases as plague and smallpox, which were only slightly, if at all, connected with food shortages. Chambers noted the years 1727–30 were in this category, a finding underlined by Wrigley and Schofield (1981, pp. 681–4). Devastating crises associated with plague were also found in the years 1603–4 and 1665–6. So far as England was concerned, then, the pattern of mortality does not seem to be as monocausal as Malthus assumed.

4   Yet another blow to the Malthusian theory was struck by Wrigley and Schofield (1981, p. 414) through their findings on the long-term links between mortality and real income (up to now we have only been looking at the short-term relationships). They believe that the expectation of life at birth (a far more sophisticated measure of mortality than the crude death rate, which sadly through lack of data we normally have to use) was high at the end of the sixteenth century at a point when the real wage index was at its lowest, having fallen sharply since the 1550s. Indeed so high was expectation of life at birth (at about 40 years) that it was not to reach the same level again before 1870! During the seventeenth century the expectation of life at birth fell, to reach its nadir in the late seventeenth and early eighteenth centuries despite rising real wages. This topsy-turvy situation (at least in Malthusian terms) continued in the eighteenth century, with rising expectation of life at birth going hand-in-hand with falling real income. When real income turned sharply upwards in the nineteenth century, expectation of life at birth levelled off!

Two conclusions may be drawn from this evidence. First, the data are faulty. Alternatively, real income in England, from at least the early seventeenth century onwards, was so high that mortality was barely affected by changes in it. The many food riots in England were not, then, the expression of a starving population but of one that was marginally distressed.

Mortality and population change
We will leave a comment on this until we come to look at the relationship between fertility change and population change.

Real income and nuptiality
We now move to the preventive check: the inner of our two loops. As the inner and outer loops cover the same elements to begin with, we need

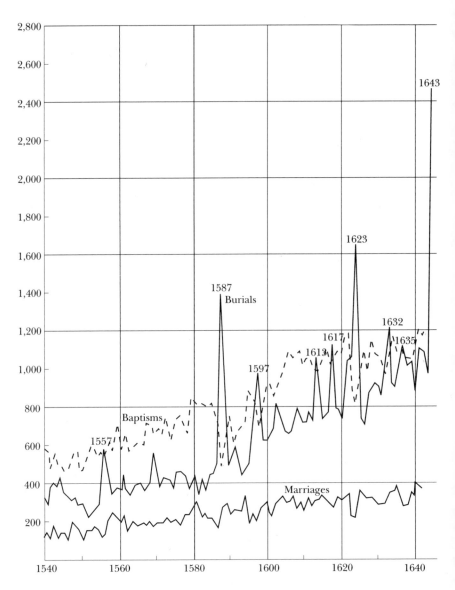

Figure 2
Baptisms, marriages and burials
in the Wapentake of Morley,
1540–1643

not go over them again. Our investigation of the working of the preventive check in England is severely hampered by lack of evidence. Not until the mid-nineteenth century, for example, do we have censuses which allow us to calculate the proportions married, single and widowed in the various age groups. As for age at marriage we are usually dependent, until about the same time, on the occasional marriage register recording ages consistently and – even more rarely – the occupation of the bridegrooms. Recently, however, our evidence on age at marriage has been enlarged by the results of a dozen or so *family reconstitution studies.* Such studies involve the linking of entries from baptism, marriage and burial registers (rather in the manner of a genealogist) to produce life histories of individuals. From these it is possible to work out mortality rates, fertility rates and age at marriage. Wrigley and Schofield (1981, p. 255) have aggregated the findings of twelve reconstitution studies which give age at marriage from 1600 to 1849. From 1600 to 1749 the mean age at first marriage of men remained remarkably stable at around 28 years and of women at 26 years. Then it fell, reaching 26.4 for men and 24.9 for women in the half-century 1750–99 and 25.3 and 23.4 respectively in the half-century 1800–49.

How can these changes be explained? Malthus no doubt would have laid the fall partly at the changing employment opportunities associated with what we now call the Industrial Revolution. New jobs in industry, commerce, even in agriculture which did not involve waiting on dead-men's shoes and which paid maximum wages at young ages gave people the opportunity to marry earlier, an opportunity they appear to have taken. Malthus, too, no doubt would have blamed the iniquitous Poor Law system (iniquitous, that is, in his eyes) which, until it was 'reformed' along Malthusian lines in 1834, encouraged people to marry by relating the amount of relief to the price of bread and the number of children in a family.

Specific evidence linking industrial employment with age at marriage is rare, but where it does exist supports the argument just presented. Despite this there does appear to be a fundamental contradiction in the evidence: namely, that age at marriage fell at a time when real incomes were falling, whilst in the seventeenth century when real incomes were rising, the age at marriage remained stable at a high level.

Nuptiality and fertility

We come now to our penultimate linkage. Logic would suggest that fertility must rise and fall in line with changes in nuptiality. Yet the matter has been argued over for a quarter of a century (because of the intractability of the data). It has been suggested that changes in the age at marriage have been too small to affect fertility significantly; that any increases in fertility have been wiped out by rising infant mortality; even that the earlier a woman married, the earlier she stopped bearing children. Wrigley and Schofield are, however, firmly of the opinion that fertility was affected quite dramatically by changes in the proportion of women who were married and in their age at marriage. The preventive check in their eyes was as powerful as Malthus supposed.

Fertility and population size

For over 40 years historical demographers have argued over the relative importance of fertility and mortality in bringing about the rise in England's population which began so dramatically in the late eighteenth century and continued at an unprecedentedly high level for a century. Which of Malthus's two checks was eased the most? The answer would seem to be – a bit of both, with the preventive check probably accounting for the lion's share. Over the whole period from the mid-sixteenth century to the mid-nineteenth centuries, Wrigley and Schofield actually give pride of place to the preventive check. Others have favoured the positive check (see Razzell, 1994).

We have now completed our survey of England's demographic history from the mid-sixteenth century to the last quarter of the nineteenth century. Malthus would appear to have been remarkably perceptive on developments up to his own time. Ironically, from about that time his theory appears to have broken down – at least to the extent that it no longer appeared to explain the facts of the English demographic scene. But what of America?

Malthusian theory and the American experience

When Malthus wrote the first edition of his essay in 1798, he took the experience of America as his limiting case. Of course, the positive and preventive checks operated there too, but they were far weaker than anywhere else. Thus he believed that a doubling of population every 25 years was about the maximum likely in any society. Malthus writes:

> In the United States of America, where the means of subsistence have been more ample, the manners of the people more pure, and consequently the checks to early marriages fewer, than in any of the modern states of Europe, the population has been found to double itself in twenty-five years. This ratio of increase, though short of the utmost power of population, yet as the result of actual experience, we will take as our rule, and say, that population, when unchecked, goes on doubling itself every twenty-five years or increases in a geometrical ratio.
>
> (p. 74)

Thirty years after writing the above, Malthus published *A Summary View of the Principle of Population*. He did so because, as his publishers noted in introducing the pamphlet, 'it has frequently been remarked, that no work has been so much talked of by persons who do not seem to have read it as Mr Malthus' *Essay on Population*'. In this, Malthus returns to the situation of the United States, noting that:

> We should expect to find the greatest actual increase of population in those situations where, from the abundance of good land, and the manner in which its produce is distributed, the largest quantity of the necessaries of life is actually awarded to the mass of society.
>
> Of the countries with which we are acquainted, the United States of America, formerly the North American colonies of Great Britain, answer most nearly to this description. In the United States, not only is there an abundance of good land, but from the manner in which it has been distributed, and the market which has been opened for its produce, there has been a greater and more constant demand for labour, and a larger portion of necessaries has been awarded to the labourer, than in any of those countries which possess an equal or greater abundance of land and fertility of soil.
>
> (p. 226)

Malthus was able to use the results of the US Census (the first took place in 1790) to substantiate his view. Thus between 1790 and 1800 the population grew at a rate which would lead to a doubling in just over 22 years; between 1800 and 1810 the rate was equivalent to a doubling in 22 years, and between 1810 and 1820 to one of 23 years and seven months (p. 227). But what of the earlier period? Some earlier censuses of the individual colonies enable us to make estimates of growth rates as far back as the seventeenth century. Thus New York appears to have grown by 3.1 per cent per annum between 1698 and 1771, Virginia by 4.9 per cent per annum between 1624 and 1703, Rhode Island by 3.2 per cent per annum between 1708 and 1774 (Wells, 1975, p. 260). In each of these cases, the population was doubling in less than 25 years. (To calculate the number of years precisely, one divides the annual growth rate into 70.) Unfortunately we do not know to what extent this growth was the product of high birth rates, low death rates, immigration or some combination of all three. Nearer to the time that Malthus wrote, however, what evidence we do have suggests that immigration played a very minor role, whilst the crude birth rate was an astronomical 50 or more per 1,000 (Coale and Zelnik, 1963, p. 34). This figure – taken together with the growth rates recorded in the censuses of 1790 to 1820 – would indicate a crude death rate of around 20 per 1,000. This compared with crude birth rates of around 40 per 1,000 and crude death rates of around 25 per 1,000 in England at the same time (Wrigley and Schofield, 1981, p. 529).

Our desire to point up the differences between the English and American demographic experience has caused us to miss a few of the stages we examined when looking at the former. Unfortunately, too, the state of American demographic records, being less satisfactory than those of England, makes it impossible for us to supply the equivalent amount of detail. The division of the country into colonies, later to become states; the lack of a national church which in England, however imperfectly, provided the basis for the measurement of birth, death and marriage rates; the late flowering of interest in these matters amongst historians – all conspire against us.

On this latter point – and in parenthesis as it were – it is interesting to note that Malthus also complained that 'one principal reason' for his not being able to document to his satisfaction the population history of ordinary men and women was that 'the histories of mankind that we possess are histories only of the higher classes' (p. 28). Thus we cannot supply the detail of mortality and fertility experience. On one issue – namely, the age at marriage – we do appear to have evidence comparable to that of England. Thus in the colony of Plymouth the mean age at first marriage of men in the years 1600–25 was 27.0 and of women 20.6. By 1675–1700, however, the figures were respectively 24.6 and 22.3 (Demos, 1979, p. 58). The convergence of the male and female ages at marriage would seem to be due to changing sex ratios. In the early days of the colony women were in short supply so their chances of finding a marriage partner early were high. Later the balance became more equal and even moved against the women, as single men moved west in search of new land. Evidence of other studies shows a similar pattern of convergence, though with somewhat higher ages overall. For example, in the Massachusetts community of Hingham, age at first marriage before 1691 was 27.4 years for men and 22.0 years for women. By 1781–1800 the corresponding figures were 26.4 years and 23.7 years. One must admit, however, that in the intervening period the trend was by no means linear (Smith, 1979, p. 39).

An even more startling example of the rise in the mean age at marriage of women, but this time accompanied by a rise (though of a somewhat smaller size) in that of men, occurred in the Massachusetts community of Sturbridge. This community, founded in 1730, was economically based on agriculture. In the years 1730–59 the mean age at first marriage of women was 19.54 years, of men 24.84. By 1780–99 the figures were 23.84 (women) and 25.61 (men). By 1849 they were 25.50 (women) and 28.93 (men) (Osterud and Fulton, 1979, p. 403) .

It will be apparent from these rather disparate comments that the American demographic experience was very different from the English. How far, then, can Malthusian theory throw light on it? To go back to our wiring diagram, it would appear the American colonies that were later to become the United States maintained a high rate of population growth from their founding in the seventeenth and eighteenth centuries until well into the nineteenth. Indeed, they lived up to Malthus's maximum rate of growth of a geometric progression leading to a doubling every 25 years. They appear to have done so because an abundance of good land and ready access to it meant that food was plentiful and real wages high. The positive checks did not operate to anything like the same extent as in the long-settled European states. As for the preventive check, the age at marriage of women was very low to begin with (by which is meant when each new community was settled) but tended to rise as the sex ratio became more balanced. The age at marriage of men tended to fall or remain relatively stable, but was in any case lower than in England (once the sex ratios became balanced), though it tended to increase towards the end of the eighteenth century and into the nineteenth. Thus fertility as measured by the crude birth rate was higher than in England around 1800, even though at that date English fertility was just about at its all time maximum.

We noted earlier that, with one or two exceptions, Malthusian theory explained much of the English experience up to about the time he wrote. This would also appear to be true of the United States. And there, it would seem, his theory retained its power. For from 1800 fertility began to decline and was to continue to do so virtually without a break until the 1940s. From around 50 births per 1,000 in 1800 (a guesstimate this) it had fallen to 42 per 1,000 by 1860; 34 per 1,000 by 1880; 29 per 1,000 by 1900 and 17 per 1,000 by 1933 – its lowest point (Coale and Zelnik, 1963, pp. 21–3).

Two sets of explanations have been put forward for this long and uninterrupted decline in the American birth rate. The first seeks to link it with urbanization and industrialization. According to this argument (which has also been used to account for the decline in the English birth rate from the 1870s onwards), children, if looked at as a production good, were less valuable in an industrial-urban setting than in an agricultural-rural one. In other words, they could not earn their keep until they were in their teens (especially as industry moved from the domestic hearth to the factory floor) and so parents stopped having so many. So far as the United States is concerned, however, there are a number of flaws in this argument. First, the country remained very much one where people lived in rural communities, dependent upon agriculture, until well into the second half of the nineteenth century. Thus, in 1860, 80 per cent of the population lived in communities with fewer than 2,500 inhabitants and 60 per cent of the working population were engaged in agriculture (Vinovskis, 1979, p. 615). Second, it would appear that fertility declined in both urban and rural areas.

A more plausible explanation would appear to be the one put forward by Yasuba (1961). It is very Malthusian. Yasuba argued that as the nineteenth century progressed access to land became more and more difficult (despite the constant westward movement of the 'frontier'); hence marriage was delayed and farmers already married restricted the size of their families, in order more easily to provide what children they did have with a livelihood. Very high rates of immigration also pushed up the price of land, even though comparatively few immigrants moved directly to the frontier.

Conclusion

Our exploration of the demographic histories of the United States and England from the seventeenth to the late nineteenth centuries has inevitably been brief (through lack of space) and patchy (through lack of evidence). No attempt, for instance, has been made to incorporate the experiences of the black population of the USA, first as slaves and later as second-class citizens. These experiences do not, in fact, appear to have been as different from those of lower-class whites as one might at first sight suppose. We would argue that the use of Malthusian demographic theory as a framework for our analysis has served its purpose in that it has provided a common set of explanations for what appear to be two very different societies. To do this it has been necessary to go back in time, for in demographic matters (as, indeed, with many other socio-economic phenomena) a straight comparison between two or more countries at the same point in time can lead to no more than a descriptive listing of characteristics, e.g. the birth rate in A is so-and-so, in B so-and-so.

Postscript

From 1880 onwards the demographic experiences of England and the USA have converged. By that date fertility was at about the same level in both countries, though, as we have seen, it arrived there by very different routes. Mortality rates too were similar. Both fertility and mortality fell, the former reaching its lowest point in the early 1930s, whilst the latter (in crude terms) has continued to fall to the present day. Fertility rose after World War II, as it had been expected to, but then quite unexpectedly it continued at a comparatively high level until the 1960s. Explanations of this 'baby boom' (which was more pronounced in the USA than in Britain) have varied – demographers being rather put out that what they thought had caused the long secular decline in fertility (higher living standards and falling mortality) were now more evident than ever, yet the birth rate rose! To some extent the rise was the result of earlier marriage and the growing propensity to have one's children over a shorter span of time. The effect of this was to cause birth rates to rise in the short term without involving any increase in the size of completed families. Another explanation involved a switch from viewing children as a production good to viewing them as a consumption good. According to this, earlier falls in fertility were brought about by children no longer being sources of income for the parents (we have already noted an urban-industrial environment provided less opportunity for child labour than a rural-agricultural one), especially as ever longer years at school, together with earlier ages at marriage, reduced the time when they could provide an income for their parents. Furthermore, children were less and less likely to provide financial help for their parents' retirement years, the state and occupational pensions taking on this role. Children could, however, be seen as consumption goods in the same way as cars, houses, stereos, etc. Thus, the more income one had, the more children one could afford and – so the argument goes – would have. There is evidence in the USA that better-off families did increase the number of children they had in the 1950s and early 1960s. But the introduction of the contraceptive pill (one of the most rapidly accepted innovations ever) coincided with a downturn in the birth rate. Today both the USA and Britain are set on a course towards nil or negative population growth.

References

Appleby, A.B. (1978) *Famine in Tudor and Stuart England*, Manchester University Press.

Chambers, J.D. (1957) *The Vale of Trent 1670–1800: A Regional Study of Economic Change* (*Economic History Review Supplements* no. 3), Cambridge University Press.

Coale, Ansley J. and Zelnik, Melvin (1963) *New Estimates of Fertility and Population in the United States*, Princeton University Press.

Demos, J. (1979) 'Notes on Life in Plymouth County' in M.A. Vinovskis (ed.) *Studies in American Historical Demography*, Academic Press.

Hatcher, John (1977) *Plague, Population and the English Economy 1348–1530*, Macmillan.

James, Patricia (1979) *Population Malthus: His Life and Times*, Routledge and Kegan Paul.

Malthus, T.R. (1970 edn) *An Essay on the Principle of Population* ..., ed. Antony Flew, Penguin.

Office of Population Censuses and Surveys (1982) *Census 1981, Preliminary Report*, HMSO.

Osterud, Nancy and Fulton, John (1979) 'Family Limitation and Age at Marriage: Fertility Decline in Sturbridge, Massachusetts 1730–1850' in M.A. Vinovskis (ed.) *Studies in American Historical Demography*, Academic Press.

Petersen, William (1979) *Malthus*, Heinemann.

Phelps-Brown, E.H. and Hopkins, Sheila V. (1956) 'Seven Centuries of the Prices of Consumables Compared with Builders' Wage-rates', *Economica*, new series, vol. 23.

Potter, J. (1965) 'Growth of Population in America, 1700–1860' in D.V. Glass and D.E.C. Eversley (eds) *Population in History*, Edward Arnold.

Razzell, P. (1994) *Essays in English Population History*, Caliban Books.

Smith, Daniel Scott (1979) 'The Demographic History of Colonial New England' in M.A. Vinovskis (ed.) *Studies in American Historical Demography*, Academic Press.

Vinovskis, M.A. (ed.) (1979) *Studies in American Historical Demography*, Academic Press.

Wells, Robert V. (1975) *The Population of the British Colonies in America before 1776: A Survey of Census Data*, Princeton University Press.

Wrigley, E.A. and Schofield, R.S. (1981) *The Population of England 1541–1871: A Reconstruction*, Edward Arnold. (First paperback edition with new introduction, Cambridge University Press, 1989.)

Wrigley, E.A. and Souden, D. (1987) *The Works of Robert Malthus*, Pickering and Chatto.

Yasuba, Y. (1961) *Birth Rates of the White Population in the United States, 1800–1860*, Baltimore, Johns Hopkins University Press.

1.10   'King Cotton' in Britain and America, 1780–1860

Cotton and industrialization

This essay examines the cotton industry in the late eighteenth and nineteenth centuries, linking the development of manufacturers in Britain and the northeastern United States with those in the southern states, where the raw material was produced. The central theme is the role of cotton in economic growth, in British and American industrialization, and in the expansion of the southern plantation economy before the Civil War.

The economic fortunes of Britain and the United States were inexorably linked by cotton production and manufacture during much of the period before the Civil War. Cotton textile manufacture played a significant role in British economic growth during the late eighteenth and early nineteenth centuries (coincident with the critical early phases of industrialization), while in the American South cotton was the basic export of a rapidly expanding plantation economy. In American industrialization, by contrast, while the introduction of the cotton industry marked the beginnings of industrial growth before 1830, the later development of transport services and the iron industry were more important to its overall industrial development.

The role of cotton in the British economy during the late eighteenth century has been the subject of lively debate amongst historians, notably since the publication of Rostow's 'take-off' theory of economic growth. In his words, 'the take-off consists, in essence, of the achievement of rapid growth in a limited group of sectors, where modern industrial techniques are applied'. He identified cotton textiles as the leading sector in British 'take-off', and defined the 'take-off' period as 1783–1802, citing spectacular increases in the import of raw cotton in the decades 1781–91 (319 per cent) and 1791–1801 (67 per cent) as evidence (Rostow, 1960, p. 53). Other historians – notably Phyllis Deane in *The First Industrial Revolution* (1965) – took a more cautious view, and perhaps like them you may take a lot of convincing that *one* industry could be as important as Rostow apparently makes out. The debate about cotton's role certainly needs to be seen in a more general context (addressed in a related essay on 'Industrialization and expansion' in Book 2, Part 1).

During this phase of growth the characteristic feature of the industry was the rapid expansion of factory-based spinning, with an extensive accumulation of plant and capital equipment (discussed further in Essay 1.12 on 'Capital'). The weaving section of the industry – lacking the same degree of innovation – still retained the organization and technology of the proto-industrial era, particularly in its use of household labour and the handloom. For technical and financial reasons the power loom was relatively slow to develop.

Although exports of cotton products were far from negligible, the British domestic market seems to have generated the main stimulus to growth before the 1790s. But thereafter the evidence provided by customs data indicates a surprising surge in exports – even during the difficult times of the Revolutionary and Napoleonic Wars in the 1790s and early 1800s – so that by 1805 and for some years after they accounted for two-thirds of production.

In the second phase of expansion from 1825 onwards, one of the key features of the British cotton industry was the integration of weaving into factory production and the consequent decline of the handloom weaver. The industry became even more capital intensive as a result. Though developed initially in Britain, the power loom was taken up more readily by American industrialists after 1820, with the result that the American cotton industry tended to have more large integrated spinning and weaving factories than was the case in Britain.

During the post-war period in the 1820s and 1830s, the share of exports declined to somewhat over 50 per cent: the home market seems to have increased its share, but in a massively expanded world market for cheap cloth. Europe, Britain's overseas empire, and other areas such as Latin America were as avid consumers of cotton goods as the people of Britain. After the mid-1840s the growth of both production and export volumes slowed down, but the former much more than the latter, while export values increased sharply. Thus export's share of the value of the industry's production rose again, reaching over 60 per cent by 1850. American industry, on the other hand, grew very largely on the basis of an even more rapidly expanding domestic market, which was protected by tariffs from British competition from 1820 onwards.

The demand for raw cotton broadly followed the needs of the British textile industry, which given its early lead dominated the international scene even after the industry developed in New England and on the Continent, notably in France and Belgium. In the early stages of extraordinarily rapid growth in the British industry, serious difficulties of supply forced up the price of cotton. So British merchants sought to encourage the development of new sources, especially of cotton of improved quality, as it became apparent as early as the 1780s and 1790s that the West Indies and Levant were approaching the limits of their capacity.

The expansion of cotton output in the southern states was often underpinned by British capital directly or indirectly through American merchant houses. Thus the United States quickly became a big supplier, and after the Anglo-American War of 1812 the British cotton industry settled down to rapidly increasing dependence on American supplies. From 1815 the price of cotton fell rapidly, due mainly to extended production in the American South, economies in the use of the cotton gin which facilitated preparation of raw cotton for export, and the decreasing cost of transport.

By the time of independence the southern agricultural economy was based firmly on the growth of specialist commercial crops – tobacco, rice and cotton – cultivated mainly by black slave labour. From at least 1820 onwards, cotton was the main cash crop of the South; it was grown on over half the farms and plantations from Tennessee and North Carolina southward by 1860, and slaves accounted for around 80 per cent of the labour used in growing it. Cotton production – more so than the growth of any other plantation crop – is central to one of the great historical debates about the economy of the American South: the system of slavery and its profitability.

The cotton industry

The growth of the cotton textile industry in Britain and America during the Industrial Revolution was essentially a function of new technology and increased demand, though which was most significant continues to be a subject of debate. Certainly there was a remarkable coincidence in the growth of demand for cheaper cottons *and* the technological breakthroughs that made mechanized production possible. As Deane showed, the invention of cotton spinning machinery combined with a more systematic application of prime movers – water power and steam engines – made mass production of yarn in large mills possible. But it would be a mistake to think that the new technology of cotton spinning necessarily implied large-scale factory production, for much of the evidence now indicates that domestic organization remained more significant than previously realized. Even as late as the 1790s, a large proportion of cotton yarn was produced on hand jennies in craft workshops, loomshops or small factories rather than on water frames or jennies powered by steam engines. Nor was steam as significant as might be imagined, for many of the larger units were actually country spinning mills located on prime water-power sites, such as those in Lancashire or the west of Scotland. These districts were notable for old-established textile skills and had easy access to the ports of Liverpool and Glasgow, which had secure trading links across the Atlantic to the West Indies and America. Modern research adds weight to previous notions about the relatively limited impact of steam power on the cotton industry, at least before the 1800s – pointing in general to industrialization *without* steam in textiles. The same was true of early New England where British technology was used to establish mills on the Pawtucket, Merrimac and Saco Rivers (Jeremy, 1981). It was not until railroads brought cheap coal after the Civil War that steam became the predominant source of power.

But the new technology could never have been harnessed on the scale that occurred without substantial inputs of capital. And it is easy to see why cotton textiles, formerly a luxury cloth now capable of mass production, should prove such an attractive investment. The textile entrepreneurs like Richard Arkwright (whose skillful licensing of his patent water frame made him a fortune) soon attracted backers and partners in many parts of Britain, notably from the merchant communities of Liverpool, Manchester, Glasgow and Bristol, and from landowners on whose estates the new cotton spinning communities were built. Often partnerships united textile masters, merchants (many in the West Indian or American trade), landowners (who often held the water rights), bankers and lawyers in mutual self-interest – for the profits of successful enterprise, as Robert Owen for one showed, were quite considerable. (For further discussion see the essay on 'Capital'.)

Given the new technology, substantial inputs of capital, and dynamic business management of the kind which apparently characterized many cotton enterprises, there remained the problem of labour. Did people flock to work in the country spinning mills (often water powered and consequently in remote locations) or what were ultimately to become the 'dark satanic mills' of urban centres like Manchester, Glasgow or Lowell, Massachusetts? Much of the evidence indicates not, so mill owners had to resort to inducements such as relatively high wages, housing or other social provisions. Arkwright's village at Cromford in Derbyshire and Dale and Owen's New Lanark on the River Clyde in Scotland were classic examples of the genre – planned industrial villages designed as much for business efficiency and labour management as the ostensible philanthropy so admired by contemporaries.

Yet with this said, many myths surround labour conditions in the early cotton mills, particularly those of women and children. The factory system in cotton textiles created job opportunities for all the family, even young children. David Dale collected pauper children from the Glasgow and Edinburgh workhouses, though this was later stopped by Robert Owen when he took charge of the mill. William Kelly, Dale's manager at New Lanark, actually developed lightweight machinery that could be readily worked by children; even those who stayed at home could be usefully employed spinning on hand jennies or helping out at the loom (Donnachie and Hewitt, 1993). Early American factories like Almy and Brown's in 1801 brought together over 100 children aged between four and ten under the supervision of a single overseer. Many mill owners found useful work for small hands, for often the only way to attract labour was to offer work to the whole family to supplement adult wages. Exploitation was perhaps inevitable given the new time discipline, but was this better or worse than back-breaking farm labour in all weathers or being closeted in a loomshop for long hours to earn a pittance?

The second stage of growth, which we previously identified as beginning in the 1820s, saw a shift to integrated mills, mainly steam powered though many of the older water-powered spinning mills continued as before. This shift was even more pronounced in New England, with the diversion of substantial capital from foreign trade into the cotton industry in these years. Moreover, the survival of the 'domestic' or proto-industrial sector of the trade was quite remarkable, and even after more general adoption of the power loom by the 1830s, large numbers of hand-loom weavers were still at work. In 1833, for example, there were 100,000 power looms in Britain, compared with 250,000 handloom weavers – a reflection both of poor wages and of comparative costs favouring a commitment on the part of mill owners to the old hand methods. Yet in the longer term the handloom weaver was doomed – one of the first major victims of technological change in the process of industrialization. In America, where there had been fewer weavers, the growth of power weaving was very rapid indeed.

While water wheels provided most of the power before 1820, the switch to steam was significant by 1835 in Britain (see Table 1), though not in the United States. By that time, steam accounted for three-quarters of the power used in the industry.

Table 1 Cotton mills and power, 1835

	No. of mills	Steam horsepower	Water horsepower
Northern England	934	26,513	6,094
Scotland	125	3,200	2,480
English Midlands	54	438	1,200
Total	1,113	30,151	9,774

Source: Chapman, 1987, p. 19.

The dominance of the North (Lancashire and adjoining districts of Cheshire, Derbyshire and the West Riding) was clear; even at the close of the eighteenth century the area had accounted for around 70 per cent of cotton output, and by 1835 it had reached 90 per cent. Concentration on the Lancashire coalfield reflected the importance of steam power as the prime mover, as much as the industry's traditional association with Manchester and Liverpool.

If we use raw cotton imports as an indicator of the volume of output (see Table 3, p. 136), we can deduce that apart from the period of remarkable innovation at the end of the eighteenth century, the cotton industry's peak period of growth was during the 25 years or so following the end of the Napoleonic Wars. In the first quarter of the nineteenth century it increased threefold, while between *c.*1816 and *c.*1840 the multiplier was 7. By comparison in America, mill-produced cotton goods were growing at an average annual rate of 16 per cent between 1815 and 1833, giving a multiplier of 14. Although the rate slackened in the late 1840s, the industry (protected by tariffs) was still growing apace until the cotton famine brought about by the Civil War. An unprotected American industry, Harley (1992) concludes, could not have competed.

The plantation economy

Turning to the American South, the significance of the rise of cotton was that it opened up a much broader area to commercial agriculture and the profitable use of slaves – and hence contributed substantially to economic growth (see also Essay 1.8 on agriculture). Thus the South offers a case study of almost colonial-style economic growth based essentially on agriculture under an alternative institutional system (see the essay on 'Industrialization and expansion' in Book 2, Part 1 for a discussion of the colonial status of the United States *vis-à-vis* Britain). This contrasts markedly with the British experience of paid labour in the new cotton mills, though you might think that the spinner was just as much a slave to his or her machine as the African-American to the cotton bed. Certainly the outstanding feature of the southern plantation system was its overwhelmingly labour-intensive character – unlike the British or American cotton industries with their mix of large-scale investment in machinery and labour.

The emergence of cotton as the leading southern plantation crop is typically dated from Eli Whitney's invention of the cotton gin in 1793, but it now seems clear that the development of the gin was only a dramatic episode in a process which had its origins in market demand. The older machines could not cope with short-staple greenseed cotton which grew inland in the South, and it was Whitney's innovation – using the same principles as the threshing machine developed about the same time in Britain – which provided the critical breakthrough. From this time on, the fortunes of the southern economy were closely tied to the progress of the British textile industry.

On the supply side the rise of cotton and slavery was influenced by two highly significant factors. First, cotton could be successfully cultivated anywhere south of the 37th parallel; second, the particular combination of soils, temperature, rainfall and growing season found in the cotton belt was uniquely suited for the production of those varieties of cotton most in demand. Cotton allowed slavery to escape its narrow geographical confines on the coast. It could also be grown on a small scale, for nonperishability and high value to weight made it economically feasible quite far inland. As Gavin Wright shows in his study, *The Political Economy of the Cotton South*, cotton gave the South 'a prosperity, growth and unity that it could not otherwise have had' (Wright, 1978, p.15).

The plantation economy employed large areas of land – in the new South sometimes running to hundreds and even thousands of acres. It was also very labour intensive, and the slaves that made up much of the labour force therefore represented a major 'capital' investment. Between 1802 and 1860 the price of a prime field hand rose from about $600 to $1,800, an increase which reflected the slave's value in plantation cropping generally and the cultivation and picking of cotton in particular. One can also readily appreciate the potential of slave breeding, though economic historians still argue about the degree to which breeding existed and its contribution to overall viability. The westward expansion of cotton proceeded with remarkable speed, as the map on p. 5 of the Maps and Statistical Tables booklet indicates. After 1815 planters and slaves moved in a series of surges that coincided with rising prices, resulting in rapid population growth in the new South (shown in Table 2).

Table 2 Population of free (black and white) and slaves of Alabama, Arkansas, Florida, Louisiana and Mississippi, 1820–60

	1820	1830	1840	1850	1860
Alabama					
Free	85,622	191,978	337,224	428,779	529,121
Slave	41,879	117,549	253,532	342,892	435,080
Arkansas					
Free	12,638	25,812	77,639	162,797	324,335
Slave	1,617	4,576	19,935	47,100	111,115
Florida					
Free	–	19,229	28,760	48,135	78,680
Slave	–	15,501	25,717	39,309	61,745
Louisiana					
Free	83,857	106,251	183,959	272,953	376,276
Slave	69,064	109,588	168,452	244,809	331,726
Mississippi					
Free	42,634	70,962	180,440	296,698	354,674
Slave	32,814	65,659	195,211	309,878	436,631
Total					
(Free and slave)	371,125	727,105	1,470,869	2,193,300	3,039,383

Source: North, 1974, p. 88.

The main surge into the new South occurred between 1833 and 1837, although land sales in the late 1850s did expand modestly. One might conclude that the whole process of expansion was induced by demand, notably from Britain and the northeastern United States. Significantly, the new plantations had lower production costs and tended to be more specialized than those of the old South, with cotton and sugar the main crops.

In comparative terms, cotton production was the most obvious option for southern planters, who correctly believed that their income from cotton would be higher than if they devoted their land, slaves and capital to other activities. Even when cotton prices were low, the plantation could continue to be viable (though less profitable) by a simple switch to corn or other crops. Cotton production stamped its mark on the southern economy in other ways, for it severely limited both industrial and commercial development. Planters had only to get their cotton bales to one of the many waterways, where they could pick up any imported goods needed. Further, the system under which northern or British merchants purchased cotton provided most of the South's goods in return, as well as the necessary shipping. Nor must we overlook the fact that many plantation owners were interested in commerce or banking only so far as these affected their incomes – preferring to settle for the life-style and status they held amongst the southern élite (Collins, 1985).

Clearly a major issue for historians has been the profitability and viability of slavery, and there is still debate about the exact statistics needed to resolve the profitability issue, as well as about the extent of slave breeding. But slavery, on balance, seems to have been both viable and profitable, forming the basis for an economy that achieved substantial *growth* (if perhaps not *development*) in the first half of the nineteenth century – thanks essentially to the demands of the British and northeastern cotton trades.

An Atlantic trade

The interdependence of the British and American economies during much of the period between 1780 and 1860 is almost self-evident. For despite political differences, many factors combined to encourage economic intimacy between them. More than any other single factor, the unifying agent of the Atlantic economy until 1860 was cotton. The nineteenth-century cotton trade was fundamentally different from the earlier tobacco trade of the eighteenth century. Then the tobacco import and re-export trades were highly profitable enterprises, but they had little direct effect on the economy. By contrast, as we have seen, the growth of the cotton industry depended wholly on imports of raw cotton, and at the same time the American market was opened up for a wide variety of British manufactures. From the 1820s to the outbreak of the Civil War, cotton was king not only of the southern states but also of the Atlantic economy. During this period the British cotton industry relied on the United States for more than 75 per cent of raw cotton supplies. For most of the period after 1820 raw cotton accounted for more than half the value of total American exports, and as Figure 1 shows, by 1860 this had risen to nearly two-thirds of the total, an enormous dependence on a single export commodity. But the growth of domestic manufacturing in the United States was also providing that country with means for escaping from any dependent role relative to Britain. By the end of the nineteenth century this had been substantially achieved. Some statistics can help us to fill in the details both on British imports from the United States and on the export performance of the cotton industry as a whole. Turning first to imports, we can see from Table 3 (overleaf) the importance of the United States as a source of supply, even when production was expanded in the Near East and Asia. Notice, too, the steady growth in the re-export trade, mainly to Europe. (Notice in Figure 1 the rapid, if erratic, growth of wheat exports, mainly to the British market after the repeal of the Corn Laws, United States railroad construction and the opening of the West post-1850.)

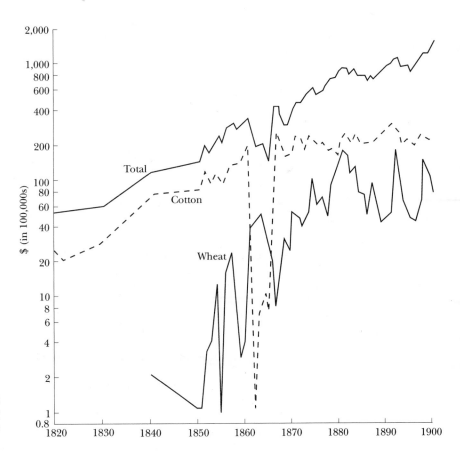

Figure 1 Total exports and wheat and cotton exports, 1820–1900

Table 3   British imports, exports and re-exports of raw cotton, million lbs

Country of origin	1784–6	1794–6	1804–6	1814–16	1824–6	1834–6	1844–6	1854–6
Latin America		4.3	4.3	24.1	23.2	26.2	19.6	22.6
West Indies	8.4	12.1	19.2	16.4	6.3	2.1	1.6	19.6
USA		1.5	24.7	33.0	118.8	280.8	516.1	728.1
Canada		1.2	.1					
Asia		.4	1.4	5.7	19.4	50.1	60.6	148.4
Africa						1.8		.5
Near East[1]	1.7	2.4	.2	.1	12.2	2.3	10.6	30.1
Europe[2]	6.3	9.7	8.6	4.2	2.6	2.3	3.3	2.8
Total imports[3]	16.4	27.4	58.7	84.1	182.7	365.6	611.8	934.6
Retained	16.3	26.6	58.0	77.4	164.4	335.9	559.8	803.3
Re-exported[4]	.3	.8	.7	6.7	18.3	29.5	52.0	131.3
Average price[5] per lb (*d*)			16.25	22.75	9	9.5	4.5	5.75

1 The early supply was from Syria, but Egypt is included under Near East rather than under Africa, and was one of the main sources of the increased supply of the mid-nineteenth century.
2 None of this was produced in Europe.
3 Excluding Ireland – from which the import was trivial.
4 Including Ireland.
5 American prices from B.R. Mitchell and P. Deane (1962) *Abstract of British Historical Statistics*, Cambridge University Press, pp. 490–1.

Source: Davis, 1979, p. 41.

Table 4 shows the relative importance of American supply to total British imports in greater detail: as early as 1815 over half the cotton used in Britain came from the United States, and at one point in the late 1840s the proportion exceeded 80 per cent.

Table 4   Imports of raw cotton into the UK, 1815–61 (average annual quantity in each five-year period)

	1815	1816–20	1821–5	1826–30	1831–5	1836–40	1841–5	1846–50	1851–5	1856–60	1861
Total imports (million lbs)	100	141	169	229	314	461	612	615	872	1,129	1,25?
From USA (million lbs)	54	66	114	174	246	368	485	499	683	869	82?
US supply as % of total	54	48	68	76	78	78	79	81	77	76	6?

Source: Potter, 1969, p. 22.

As we noted at the outset, British cotton exports were quite modest before the mid-1790s, when they represented about 16 per cent of the total. Notice in Table 5 how quickly cotton supplanted wool in the early 1800s. (It represented over 40 per cent of total exports until at least 1850.) It is interesting to compare cotton's export performance with those of other commodities, and Table 5 is particularly illuminating on that score, since it shows that cotton was an export leader throughout the period despite its slow start.

Table 5 Exports and production in three industries (ratios of the value of exports to the value of the industry's final product)

	Wool %	Cotton %	Iron %
c.1695	c.40		
c.1760		c.33	
c.1772	c.45	c.22	
1781–3		16	
1787–9		23	
1795–7		37	
1799	c.55		
c.1805	31 or 37		18
1805–7		66	
1815–17		58	
c.1818			26
1819–21		54	
1820–4	23		18
1829–31		56	
1830–4	19		21
1839–41		52	
1840–4	19		30
1849–51		62	
1850–4	25		40
1859–61		64	
1860–4	30		40
1869–71		67	
1871–4	43		38

Source: Crouzet, 1980, p. 86.

As regards British exports to the United States, Table 6 provides a useful picture, though we need to qualify the data with a few words of explanation. First, the American cotton industry was well established by the 1820s, particularly in New England, where the first spinning mills on British lines had been built in the 1790s. Second, US tariff legislation in the Acts of 1816, 1824 and 1828 all provided protection for domestic manufactures, including textiles. The 1816 tariff imposed a duty of 25 per cent on imports of manufactured cottons, and this clearly hit British exports of cheaper, coarser cloths. With this protection the American industry made such progress that by the early 1830s it had little to fear from foreign competition in cheaper cottons at least. British exports to the United States were therefore increasingly of more expensive printed and patterned cloths, while colonial markets in Asia, Africa and elsewhere absorbed the enormous volume of cheaper cottons.

Table 6   Exports from the UK distinguishing cotton and other manufactures: annual average declared value in each five-year period

	1816–20	1821–5	1826–30	1831–5	1836–40	1841–5	1846–50	1851–5	1856–60
Total exports (£m.)	40.3	37.3	35.9	40.4	50.0	54.0	60.8	88.8	124.1
Total exports of cotton manufactures (£m.)	16.4	16.7	17.2	19.2	23.7	24.1	25.3	31.8	38.3
Cotton manufactures as % of total exports	41	45	48	47	47	45	42	36	31
Cotton manufactures exported to USA (£m.)	1.8	2.0	1.9	2.1	1.7	1.0	2.0	3.1	4.6
Cotton manufactures exported to USA as % of total exports of cotton	11	12	11	11	7	4	8	10	10
Cotton manufactures as % of total exports to USA	26	32	33	26	22	16	18	17	20
Total exports less cotton manufactures	23.9	20.6	18.7	21.2	26.3	29.9	35.5	57.0	85.8
Exports to USA less cotton manufactures (£m.)	5.2	4.3	3.8	5.8	6.7	5.1	8.9	15.6	15.9
US share of total exports less cotton manufactures %	22	21	20	27	26	17	27	28	19

Source: Potter, 1969, p. 31.

Cotton and the economy

We turn now to an assessment of cotton's contribution to economic growth, where in Britain much debate centres on whether the industry was a key sector in the whole process (this is also discussed in the essay on 'Industrialization and expansion' in Book 2, Part 1). Rostow regarded cotton as the 'leading sector' in the first push to industrialization, while earlier the economist Joseph Schumpeter went as far as to claim that 'English industrial history can almost be resolved into the history of a single industry.' Deane, as we noted, was one of a group of historians who subjected Rostow's claim to critical analysis, hence her caution. Deane and her associate Cole calculated it was unlikely that cotton contributed more than 5 per cent of national income by the end of Rostow's 'take-off' phase (*c.*1802). Yet as Chapman indicates in *The Cotton Industry in the Industrial Revolution* (1987), if this figure is correct, it shows what a substantial contribution cotton was already making to the economy. However, other studies indicate that the iron industry was making the same contribution to the economy during the period, and if these calculations are accepted, it is difficult to see how cotton could claim to be *the* leading sector. Chapman points out the 'highly tentative' nature of such calculations and shows fairly convincingly that the results might substantially underestimate the value of the cotton industry, particularly if the contribution of related finishing trades like bleaching, dyeing and printing is taken into account. He estimates that cotton was already contributing over 7 per cent of the national income by 1797 – a figure reached only in 1810 according to Deane and Cole's estimates.

Statistics aside, Rostow also suggested, quite sensibly in my view, that the dramatic growth of cotton stimulated other activities by 'forward linkages' – shipping, inland transport, commerce and banking, the chemical, coal, iron and engineering industries. But if it is difficult enough to assess cotton's contribution to the economy, it is virtually impossible to measure in any meaningful way the impact of cotton on other sectors of the economy. It is certainly possible to demonstrate direct connections between the cotton industry and other activities, especially iron founding, engineering and chemicals. Many firms in these trades in Lancashire, the west of Scotland, and the West Riding grew in response to the stimulus of cotton in Rostow's 'take-off' period. Deane and Cole, on the other hand, took a much wider view, identifying the other periods of expansion I have described rather than confining themselves to the period 1780–1800. It is clear that cotton continued to play an important part in the British economy, and especially so in the 'peak period of growth' between 1815 and 1840 (Rostow, 1960). Set against this is the fact that agriculture was still the largest single industry at mid-century and that the heavy industries had expanded rapidly during the second stage of industrialization.

In the United States the cotton industry pioneered industrialization in New England and contributed to the demand for machinery, steam power and iron. However, its quantitative impact was perhaps less than in Britain, and less than that of railroads and the iron industry in the development of the American economy. Before the Civil War the South was wealthy, prosperous, expanding westward, and growing at rates that compared favourably with those of the rest of the United States. After the war and emancipation the same region was poor, backward, and growing only slowly and irregularly. Accounting for this change in fortunes is far more difficult than simply describing the contrast, the major obstacle being the historical coincidence of three developments of the 1860s: the Civil War, the end of slavery and, of greatest significance for this discussion, the end of a long period of rapid growth in demand for cotton. The fundamental question remains. Is it necessarily true that slavery was responsible for antebellum growth, or are other factors of equal or greater importance?

On the economic side, demand for cotton was the main impetus to growth, a factor largely beyond the control of the planter since it was almost wholly sustained by British textile production. Significantly, the rapid growth of the textile industry in Britain was over by 1860, and indeed the industry stood on the threshold of a major crisis of overproduction which would have brought stagnation had it not been overshadowed by the cotton famine of the 1860s. Whether the growth which occurred between 1815 and 1860 would have been possible in the plantation system *without* slaves is more problematic. For labour was always in short supply everywhere – a reflection of new opportunities in a rapidly expanding country. Certainly constraints on growth within the slave system were beginning to operate long before the Civil War; the slave labour force could not be expanded greatly, and further the environmental limits of cotton growing – given available technology – had probably been reached.

On the political side, there was continuing friction throughout the whole period between North and South, Free and Slave States. Whether or not the origins of the Civil War lay in economic or moral differences, there seems little doubt that confrontation was inevitable. Not only this, there were continuing tensions in the slave South, particularly between the slave owners and the free white workers. The latter were not hostile to slavery as an institution, though their attitude might have been very different if slaves had been shifted into crafts and industries on a larger scale than occurred.

So if economic, social, environmental and political factors are taken into account, it is difficult to imagine how slavery could have survived for much longer; even if it had done so, it would inevitably have had to pay an increasing price for its survival. It is hard to escape the conclusion that slavery contributed to southern *growth* at least until the 1860s. But the South's experience of growth was very different from the *development* which occurred in the North. The North (and ultimately the Northwest) was a region of diverse activity with expanding industry, commerce and transport – a picture in marked contrast to the agrarian South where cotton alone was king.

Finally, it does not seem unreasonable to describe the southern plantation economy as an appendage of the British cotton industry, so the unresolved problems of slave profitability and the growth of the southern economy in general can hardly be seen in isolation. By the same token, any assessment of cotton's contribution to British economic growth, either during the classic industrialization era or the longer period from 1780 to 1860, really needs to be made in the context of a wider Atlantic economy.

References and further reading

Chapman, S.D. (1987) *The Cotton Industry in the Industrial Revolution*, 2nd edn, Macmillan.

Collins, B. (1985) *White Society in the Antebellum South*, Longman.

Crouzet, François (1980) 'Toward an Export Economy: British Exports during the Industrial Revolution', *Explorations in Economic History*, vol. 17, no. 1, pp. 48–93.

Davis, R. (1979) *The Industrial Revolution and British Overseas Trade*, Leicester University Press.

Deane, P. (1965) *The First Industrial Revolution*, Cambridge University Press.

Donnachie, I. and Hewitt, G. (1993), *Historic New Lanark: The Dale and Owen Industrial Community since 1785*, Edinburgh University Press.

Harley, C.K. (1992) 'International Competitiveness of the Antebellum

American Cotton Textile Industry', *Journal of Economic History*, vol. 52, no. 3, pp. 559–84.

Jeremy, D.J. (1981), *Transatlantic Industrial Revolution: The Diffusion of Textile Technologies between Britain and America, 1790s to 1830s*, Oxford, Blackwell.

North, D.C. (1974) *Growth and Welfare in the American Past: A New Economic History*, 2nd edn, Englewood Cliffs, Prentice-Hall.

Parish, P.J. (1979) *Slavery: The Many Faces of a Southern Institution*, British Association for American Studies.

Potter, J. (1969) 'Atlantic Economy, 1815–1860: The USA and the Industrial Revolution in Britain' in A.M. Coats and R.M. Robertson (eds) *Essays in American Economic History*, Edward Arnold.

Rostow, W. (1960) *The Stages of Economic Growth*, Cambridge University Press.

Wright, G. (1978) *The Political Economy of the Cotton South*, New York, Norton.

1.11   What price railways? The nineteenth-century experience of England and the USA

Introduction

Today a number of alternative transport systems compete directly with railways – notably cars, buses and planes for passenger traffic and lorries for goods traffic. And the merest glance at the reduction in the size of Britain's rail network since 1900, the levelling off in passenger miles, and the fall in ton-miles carried indicate the impact of this competition on the railways (Figure 1). But what of the situation prior to 1900?

Surely if any age were to be labelled 'the age of the train', it would be the nineteenth century or – to be more precise – the last half of it. Here surely we are dealing with a claim shared by *all* economic historians. Was it not the case that alternative means of transport were patently inferior? For passengers the horse-drawn coach was both slower and far less comfortable, whilst for freight the canals could compete on neither speed nor range. Railways were also in profit, and almost every index one chooses produces a graph whose shape is beyond that of a sales manager's wildest dream.

If you think there is no case to answer, if you subscribe to the view that, as far as England and the USA were concerned, the late nineteenth century was 'the age of the train' to the extent that without railways the history of the two countries would have been so different as to be all but unrecognizable, then read on. For our purpose is to sow some seeds of doubt. In particular we shall be focusing on the contribution of the railways to *economic growth*. This is partly on the grounds that, in the period with which we are concerned, economic growth was greater than it had ever been before and is thus a legitimate object of study in itself, but also because without such growth much else that happened was unlikely to have done so.

Along the way we shall examine one or two economic concepts with which you may not be altogether familiar, i.e. 'social saving', 'national income' (see the appendix at the end of this essay for a discussion of total output, Gross National Product and national income). We also hope to make our contribution to the arguments in favour of comparative studies, of which this course is an example. Above all, we shall pursue this topic through the work of one of the major economic historians of the late twentieth century (Robert Fogel, who was awarded a Nobel Prize in 1993) and one of his disciples (G.R. Hawke). We hope that after studying nineteenth-century railways you will not only have increased your knowledge of this subject but also have gained some familiarity with a way of looking at the past which may influence your future studies.

We begin by examining some railway statistics. We then present some opinions of contemporaries and of historians on the impact of railways. Following this we present Fogel's thesis and then go on to look at his argument in detail. Hawke's case, which amounts to an application of the Fogel thesis to the English situation in the years 1840–70, is then given.

Some railway statistics

Wagons and coaches drawn by steam-driven engines along iron rails appeared first in England. Although there is some dispute as to the precise place and date of the first occurrence of this event, it is sufficient for our purposes to note the opening of the Stockton and Darlington line in 1825 and of the Liverpool and Manchester line in 1830. The 1830s witnessed spectacular growth in the number of lines built, as did the 1840s. From 97 miles of track in 1830, the figure rose to 1,498 miles in 1840, 6,084 miles in 1850 and 9,069 miles in 1860. By 1927, when the network had reached its greatest extent, 20,412 miles were in operation (see Figure 1). The American experience was similarly spectacular. Starting with 23 miles of line in 1830, the track totalled 35,000 miles by the end of the Civil War and 181,000 miles by 1895 (Fogel, 1964, pp. 3–4).

Figure 2 shows the amount of freight and passengers moved on American railroads in the period 1840–1970. As with the position in Great Britain, the breathtaking growth of the nineteenth century was sharply checked in the twentieth.

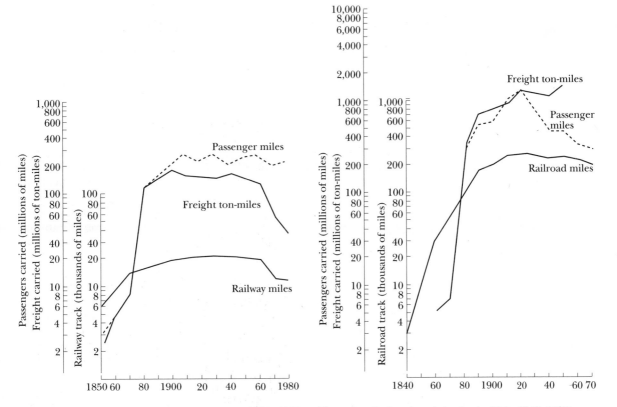

Figure 1   *Railway statistics for Great Britain, 1850–1980*   **Figure 2**   *Railroad statistics for the USA, 1840–1970*

Opinions on the impact of the railways

To a greater or lesser degree the judgements passed by the two commentators quoted below echo those of contemporaries and historians. These quotations refer to the American experience. But they could be repeated many times for England too.

> In 1867 the *North American Review* surveyed the effects wrought by railroads and found that they were stupendous. 'With perhaps two exceptions,' it said, the railroad was 'the most tremendous and far-reaching engine of social revolution which has ever either blessed or cursed the earth'. It was this innovation that 'made our century different from all others – a century of greater growth, of more rapid development'. The railroad, the distinguished journal held, had peopled the 'wilds of America' and turned 'the very Arabs of civilization' into 'substantial communities'. It made the nation cosmopolitan; removed the old distinctions between classes, changing both dress and manners; 'abolished' the Mississippi River; crushed the southern rebellion; made the grass grow in the once busy streets of small commercial centers, like Nantucket, Salem and Charleston; robbed 'New Orleans of that monopoly of wealth which the Mississippi had promised to pour into her lap'; and simultaneously turned New York into 'an overgrown monster'. The 'iron arms' of the railroad, the *Review* concluded, 'have been stretched out in every direction; nothing has escaped their reach, and the most firmly established institutions of man have proved under their touch as plastic as clay'.
>
> (Fogel, 1964, pp. 3–4)

> The growth of the United States west of the Alleghenies during the past fifty years is due not so much to free institutions, or climate, or the fertility of the soil, as to railways. If ... railways had not been invented, the freedom and natural advantages of our western states would have beckoned to human immigration and investment in vain. Civilization would have crept slowly on, in a toilsome march over the immense spaces that lie between the Appalachian ranges and the Pacific Ocean; and what we now style the Great West would be, except in the Valley of the Mississippi, an unknown and unproductive wilderness.
>
> (Dillon, 1891, p. 443; cited in Fogel, 1964, pp. 5–6)

To move from contemporaries to present-day historians, we have the testimony of W.W. Rostow. In an influential and at the time widely acclaimed work, *The Stages of Economic Growth*, Rostow argued that all countries undergoing an industrial revolution passed through certain stages. The most important of these was what he called 'the take-off into self-sustained growth'. This was a period of around two decades during which 'both the basic structure of the economy and the social and political structure of the society are transformed in such a way that a steady rate of growth can be thereafter regularly sustained'. Rostow believed that three conditions were necessary for 'take-off'. One was 'a rise in productive investment from, say, five per cent or less to over ten per cent of *national income*' (emphasis added – see appendix for an explanation of this term); a second was 'the development of one or more substantial manufacturing sectors, with a high rate of growth'; a third condition was 'the existence or quick emergence of a political, social and institutional framework which exploits the impulses of expansion in the modern sector and the potential external economy effects of the take-off and gives to growth an on-going character' (Rostow, 1960).

It is only the second of these conditions that concerns us here. For Rostow argued that in the USA the take-off stage occurred in the years 1843–60 and that in this process the railways were 'decisive'. For, he argued, the take-off in the USA was 'the upshot of two different periods of expansion; the first, that of the 1840s, marked by railway and manufacturing development' in the east of the country; 'the second, the great railway push into the middle west during the 1850s' (cited in Fogel, 1964, pp. 113–14).

Fogel's thesis

Faced with a welter of opinion stridently proclaiming the crucial role of the railways in the destiny of England and the USA during the later nineteenth century, Fogel's stand would seem breathtakingly perverse. For Fogel argues that so far as the US economy was concerned, they played by no means so great a role as has been alleged. Indeed he goes so far as to state that even without railroads the American economy was likely to have reached almost the same level of output as it did with them! His argument hinges on calculating what he calls the 'social saving' brought about by railroads. Fogel defines 'social saving' as the difference between the actual cost of shipping a certain bundle of goods in any given year and the alternative cost of shipping exactly the same bundle of goods between exactly the same set of points without railroads (p. 208). Fogel is critical of historians for basing their arguments in favour of the importance (indeed of the indispensability) of the railroads merely on 'descriptions of what the railroads did' (p. 10) and wholly ignoring what alternative means of transport could have done. Fogel then challenges historians to examine what lies implicit in their case: namely, what it says about other means of transport. He insists on the examination of what he calls the 'counter-factual' position: 'counter-factual' because, of course, these alternative means of transport *did not, in fact*, take on the role of the railroads.

Fogel's argument in detail

Fogel's argument is long and complex, involving many assumptions, some of breathtaking magnitude. Indeed one of the major criticisms of his thesis involves the nature of these assumptions. Much of his argument also involves an understanding of economic theory not usually to be found amongst historians. What will be attempted here, therefore, is no more than a rudimentary account of some of the key elements in Fogel's argument, the aim being to enable you to understand the main thrust of his case to the point at which it becomes intelligible enough for a stand to be taken on it.

By the late nineteenth century American railroads were obviously an important carrier of goods and people, and had created a significant demand for the products of the iron industry. But what do we mean by 'important' and 'significant'? Both words imply numbers. They are examples of what is called 'implicit quantification'. Such terms are widely used by all of us. Fogel says that when historians use them they ought to endeavour to make them explicit. Fogel himself gives a very good example of what he means. First, he cites a *qualitative* description of the effects of the railroad on the development of the American economy and then draws out the *quantification* implicit within it.

First, the qualitative description:

Regional concentration of industries and specialized crops, though dependent on many factors, could not have developed so fully without railroad transportation. New England could find national markets for its textiles and shoes. Pennsylvania, with its coal and easy access to iron, could concentrate on basic iron and steel, shipping products wherever they might be wanted. Iowa could, with its specially adapted soils and climate, become a corn and hog country.

(Soule, 1952, p. 103)

Then Fogel's critique:

This apparently qualitative description is permeated with implicit measurements. The 'regional concentration' of industry referred to in the first sentence can only be defined in quantitative terms; the phrase implies the existence of a measure of the spatial distribution of productive activity. The sentence as a whole implies that the difference between the cost of transportation by railroad and the next most favourable medium was of such a magnitude that the absence of the railroad would have reduced regional concentration by a detectable, and, therefore, measurable amount. [In a footnote Fogel adds, 'To be precise, the sentence implies that such a measurement has in fact been performed.'] The term 'national market' (second sentence), if it is to have anything but a trivial meaning, implies that the amount of shoes and cotton goods sold by various firms beyond some region specified as local was large relative to their total output. The only significant economic interpretation of the phrase 'easy access' (third sentence) is that the cost of obtaining iron in Pennsylvania was lower than in other designated areas. The statement that Pennsylvania 'concentrated' on the production of basic iron and steel implies a system by which the amounts of the qualitatively different products of the state can be aggregated and against which the state's production of iron and steel products can be measured. Finally, the statement that Iowa's soil and climate were 'specially adapted' to corn production (fourth sentence) presumes the existence of a measurable relationship between corn yields on the one hand and rainfall, temperature, and various soil properties on the other.

(Fogel, 1964)

This passage by Fogel indicates one aspect of his thought pattern and provides a useful entry into the substantive elements of his thesis. The example chosen here forms chapter two of his book, *Railroads and American Economic Growth: Essays in Econometric History*, and is entitled 'The inter-regional distribution of agricultural products'. Here Fogel focuses on the shipment of agricultural products between states – more particularly between what he calls the primary and secondary markets. He notes that by the 1890s the distribution of the agricultural surpluses of the Midwest involved three stages. The first involved the carriage to the great primary markets. In the case of grain 80 per cent went from the farms to the cities of Chicago, Minneapolis, Duluth, Milwaukee, Peoria, Kansas City, St Louis, Cincinnati, Toledo and Detroit. The second stage involved the shipment of the grain from these primary markets to 90 secondary markets in the East and South; the most important were New York City, Baltimore, Boston, Philadelphia, New Orleans, Albany (NY), Portland (Maine), Pittsburgh, Birmingham and Savannah. The third stage involved the distribution of the grain within the territory immediately around the secondary markets or to countries overseas. Meat products followed a similar path, though in their case the first stage of the process was dominated by only four cities: Chicago, St Louis, Kansas City and Omaha.

Given this situation Fogel now sets out his hypothesis. Before giving this it is perhaps illuminating to cite a couple of sentences from a passage which appears at the head of his chapter. 'To say that the thing happened the way it did, is not at all illuminating. We can understand the significance of what did happen only if we contrast it with what might have happened' (Cohen, 1959; cited in Fogel, 1964, p. 17).

So to Fogel's hypothesis:

> Railroad connections between the primary and secondary markets of the nation were a necessary condition for the system of agricultural production and distribution that characterized the American economy of the last half of the nineteenth century. Moreover, the absence of such railroad connections would have forced a regional pattern of agricultural production that would have significantly restricted the development of the American economy.

To test his hypothesis Fogel takes the agricultural products shipped from the primary to the secondary markets in 1890. They moved by a combination of rail, road and water transport. Given adequate data it is possible to work out the cost of this movement. Equally it is possible to work out the cost assuming the railroad did not exist. Fogel calls the difference between these two costs 'the social saving attributable to the railroad in the inter-regional distribution of agricultural products' (p. 20).

Had road transport been the only alternative to the railway, there would be no argument, for whereas by 1890 the average cost of transport by rail was about half a cent per ton-mile, the cost by road was 17 cents per ton-mile. Fogel estimates that in 1890 some 7.7 million tons of maize and some 5 million tons of wheat entered inter-regional transportation. Assuming the difference between rail and road transport to be 16.5 cents per ton-mile, then carrying the 12.7 million tons a mere one mile would have been $2.1 million more expensive by road than by rail. Assuming that the average distance the maize and wheat were shipped was 1,000 miles, then the extra cost would be $2,100 million. Adding on the cost of road construction and maintenance as well as the extra costs involved in moving livestock, then this already astronomical figure of $2,100 million reaches $3,000 million or about 25 per cent of national income.

Had road transport been the only alternative to rail transport, the social saving derived from using the latter would have been very substantial indeed. But, of course, transport by road was not the only alternative. There was transport by water. All the primary markets were on navigable waterways.

> Of the forty-three most important secondary markets, thirty-two were located on navigable waters still in use in 1890. Seven were on waterways that had been forced into inactivity as a result of railroad competition but which could have been used in the absence of the railroad. Only four cities were without direct water connection to the midwest, and each of these was within a relatively short wagon haul of a major water artery.
>
> (Fogel, 1964, p. 24)

To illustrate the core of Fogel's argument, let us go through his case for suggesting that the transport of grain by water offered a feasible alternative, even with the amounts being shipped in 1890. We do not have space to present Fogel's *full* case, nor to assess the many assumptions he makes in presenting it. We shall not, therefore, be able to do justice either to Fogel or to his critics.

Fogel starts by presenting the actual cost of transporting wheat and corn in 1890 (Table 1). Note that not all grain was shipped by rail in that year. Some also went solely by water and some by a combination of rail and water.

Table 1   Estimate of the average actual rate

Type of transportation	(1) Rate per ton-mile (cents)	(2) Wheat and corn (tons)	(3) Col. 1 × Col. 2 (US $)
All water	0.186	1,254,000	2,332.44
Water and rail	0.229	2,423,000	5,548.67
All rail	0.523	9,073,000	47,451.79
Sum of columns		12,750,000	55,332.90
Average actual rate in cents per ton-mile (sum of col. 3 ÷ sum of col. 2)			0.434 cents

Source: Fogel, 1964, p. 39 (slightly modified).

To produce Table 1 Fogel took the average of the actual rates being charged on the Chicago to New York route in 1890. 'Casual examination of the available data' suggested that these were 'approximately the same' as those elsewhere, wherever grain was shipped in appreciable quantities (p. 38).

Of the 12,750,000 tons of grain shipped in 1890, Fogel has apportioned that going by water only, rail only, or a combination of the two. Applying the rates to these quantities, he has arrived at the cost of shipping the actual amounts moved (by each mode) for one mile (column 3). He finds that to ship his 12,750,000 tons costs $55,332.90. By dividing the former figure into the latter, Fogel gets an average actual cost per ton-mile of 0.434 cents.

Table 2   Actual transport costs and hypothetical water-only transport costs for grain in 1890, compared

	Actual transport	Water only
Quantity shopped (tons)	12,750,000	12,750,000
Average distance (miles)	1,044	1,574
Average cost ($)	0.00434	0.00139
Total cost ($)	57,769,740	27,895,215

Source: derived from Fogel, 1964, Table 2.5, p. 42.

A glance at Table 2 shows the difference between the hypothetical cost of shipping 12,750,000 tons of grain in 1890 by water only and the actual costs of shipping it. Note that to ship the grain by water transport only involved almost 50 per cent more miles (1,574 as against 1,044) being travelled. However, as the water rate per ton-mile was so much cheaper than the actual rate (remember this is an average of the three modes of transport *actually* used – see Table 1), the 'social saving' to be gained by using water transport only would have amounted to $29,874,525 (i.e. $57,769,740 – $27,895,215).

Fogel does a similar set of calculations to show that the social saving on the transport of meat would have been $8,456,000. Thus it would *seem* that the total saving on the inter-regional distribution of the two prime agricultural commodities entering this trade (grain and meat) would have amounted to some $38,000,000.

However, all is not what it seems. To transport these products by water only involved some further costs not borne by – or already accounted for in – the actual costs of their carriage.* Fogel isolates five of these costs:

* The eagle-eyed among you will have spotted that in Table 2 the average water cost was given as 0.139 cents, whereas in Table 1 it was 0.186 cents, a difference of 0.047 cents. The reason is that the latter included trans-shipment and insurance charges, while the former did not.

1   *Cargo losses:* these were higher on water transport than on rail. Fogel estimates that had water transport only been available, costs would have been $6,000,000 higher for this alone.

2   *Trans-shipment costs:* moving cargo from one type of transport to another (e.g. from lake steamer to canal barge) involved costs. The great advantage of the railway was that, once the grain or meat had been placed in a wagon, it need not be touched until its ultimate destination. Fogel estimates that using water transport only for the grain and meat entering inter-regional trade would have involved two trans-shipments at a cost of 50 cents each, making a total extra charge of $16,000,000.

3   *Supplementary wagon haulage:* About 10 per cent of the grain and meat entering inter-regional trade went to cities that were not on water routes. Fogel estimates that as these were on average 90 miles

from the nearest water point, the cost of moving the 1.57 million tons involved at 16.5 cents per ton-mile would have amounted to $23,000,000.

4   *Costs involved through water transport being slower and through it being unavailable for five months a year due to ice:* to estimate the additional costs involved under this head, Fogel comes up with a surrogate measure. Assuming that water transport takes a month longer than the combination of rail and water transport actually employed, and assuming that no commodities can be shipped for five months each year, then merchants would have to hold bigger stocks. As he points out, if merchants can replace the goods they sell the instant they sell them, they will hold no stocks (or inventories as Fogel calls them). Few merchants of any commodity, however, are in this happy position. So far as the grain and meat entering inter-regional trade are concerned, it would appear that the merchants in the areas receiving these commodities would have to hold 50 per cent more stocks if water transport only was used (because for five months they could not receive any and even when they could there was the delay caused by the one month lag). To hold additional stocks involves two additional costs. First, there is the interest on the money borrowed to buy the additional stocks (estimated by Fogel in this instance at $18,000,000 a year) and, second, the additional storage charges, again estimated by Fogel at $30,000,000 a year. The total extra costs under this head amounted to $48,000,000.

5   *Neglected capital costs:* the costs of water transport do not include the full capital cost of building, maintaining and improving waterways, since these were frequently borne by the government and therefore funded out of taxes rather than tolls. (There is a partial analogy here with roads in this country today.) Fogel puts these 'neglected capital costs', or more precisely the interest charges on them, at $18,000,000 a year.

Totalling up the additional costs under these five heads, we reach a figure of $111,000,000. Set against this is the saving of $38,000,000 arising from the difference in shipping grain and meat solely by water rather than – as actually happened – a combination of rail and water. Thus it would appear that, if Fogel's many assumptions are judged acceptable, national income in 1890 would have been diminished by $73,000,000. Since national income in that year was $12,000,000,000, this amounts to 0.6 per cent. Put another way, this meant that the 'absence of the inter-regional railroad would have retarded the development of the economy by about three months' (p. 47, fn 58).

If one accepts Fogel's finding – or for that matter even if one doesn't, believing that he has grossly underestimated the costs of transport without the railroad – the social saving would appear to be so small (and therefore even gross underestimates by Fogel were unlikely to make much difference to the outcome) as to make one wonder why there had been such a massive shift into the use of railroads. Much of the answer lies in the great difference made to shippers' profits of only a comparatively small shift in transport rates. Fogel demonstrates this by citing

> ... the hypothetical case of a Chicago wheat shipper who made
> a profit of ten per cent on the Chicago price of wheat or nine

cents per bushel on a price of ninety cents. If the cost of shipment, all factors considered, were the same by both water and
rail, the shipper would be indifferent as to which form he
used. Suppose now that technological advances made it possible for the shipper to get his bushel to market for two cents
less than before. How strong an inducement to switch from
water to rail transport would such a differential generate? By
reducing his costs two cents per bushel, the shipper could
increase his profit by twenty-two per cent.

This would be a powerful incentive indeed to shift all his shipments to
rail. Yet the social saving involved would have been a mere $3.3 million.

Later on in his book Fogel considers intra-regional transport. Of his
argument there we mention but one element, namely that in the absence
of railroads it was highly likely both road and water transport systems
would have been extended and improved. He notes, for instance, that
'not only the fundamental internal-combustion engine theory, but even
that of the diesel engine' had been published as early as 1824. Even if
one thinks this too much a flight of the imagination, Fogel's second point
– that the addition of only 37 canals and feeders, amounting in all to
5,022 miles, would have reduced the value of agricultural land 'falling
beyond the boundary of feasible commercial production in 1890 ... from
twenty-four per cent to seven per cent of the national total' – seems a
much more likely outcome. Such an expansion of the waterways – in the
absence of railroads – seems yet the more likely if one bears in mind that
the terrain through which the new canals would have had to be constructed was more favourable than that over which the existing system was
constructed.

One other aspect of Fogel's case will be considered here, namely
that during the years designated by Rostow as the 'take-off period' in the
USA (i.e. 1843–60), the railways played only a minor role in the demand
for iron and could not, therefore, have played the 'decisive' role alleged
by Rostow. Fogel shows that in the years 1840–60 'crude iron used in the
domestic production of rails averaged less than twelve per cent of total
output'. Adding all the other iron used by railroads raised this percentage to no more than seventeen. It is true that in the years 1855–60
the railroads' share rose to 25.4 per cent. Despite this Fogel notes two
additional points. First, in the period 1845–9 the leap in US iron production was as much triggered off by nails as by rails. Indeed in 1849 'the
domestic production of nails probably exceeded that of rails by over 100
per cent'. Second, from 1840–60 only 40 per cent of the rails required by
the United States were supplied by the domestic industry; the rest came
from England.

Hawke's argument

The application of Fogel's ideas to the English scene was carried out by
G.R. Hawke in his book, *Railways and Economic Growth in England and
Wales 1840–1870*, published in 1970. Hawke carried out similar exercises
to those of Fogel and, in the main, came up with the same kind of findings. True, Hawke believed that without railways the national income of
England and Wales in 1865 would have been 10 per cent or so lower than
it was: a figure double that found by Fogel for the USA in 1890. Never-

theless this was still a comparatively low figure relative to the impression one would get from much contemporary comment. Disaggregating this figure of 10 per cent reveals that the social saving derived from railways was strikingly small in some sectors of the economy. For instance, by 1865 the social saving derived from freight carried by rail was only of the order of 2.1 per cent (Hawke, 1970, p. 90). The social saving on the carriage of wheat between counties was of the order of 0.03 to 0.08 per cent of the UK national income in 1865. The level of social saving on the carriage of minerals proved also to be small (pp. 180–1). Although the production of iron for railways proved more important in England than in the USA, Hawke concludes that 'railways were not essential to the existence of an iron industry and were not significant in the development of steel before 1870' (p. 245).

Two aspects of Hawke's argument deserve comment here: the first because it demonstrates what the social saving argument is all about and what *it isn't*; the second because it shows how the results of any particular calculation of social saving may vary depending upon the initial assumptions.

As to the first aspect, Hawke notes (pp. 79–80) that the social saving resulting from the carriage of freight by the railways was negligible in the 1840s. This was so in spite of the fact that the introduction of railways had brought a sharp fall in transport costs, for the canals had to reduce their charges significantly. But canal companies were monopolists, and a sizeable proportion of their charges was made up of a monopoly rent. For example, before the railway began to compete with the Leeds and Liverpool canal, the latter's net income was five to six times its costs (p. 84). 'Any saving in transport costs resulting from the introduction of railways includes both a saving in real resources and a *redistribution* of monopoly profits' (p.80, emphasis added). Thus the effect of the advent of the railways on transport costs was not the same as their effect on national income.

The second aspect of Hawke's work deserving attention for its general significance concerns the calculation of the social saving on the carriage of passengers by rail. Hawke says there are two ways of calculating this. The first is to compare the cost of rail travel to that of coach travel, making the assumption that first class by rail was the equivalent of travelling inside the coach, whilst second and third class was the equivalent of travelling on the outside of the coach. Using these assumptions, Hawke calculates that 'the alternative cost of the 1865 [traffic] flows would be £25.5 million, and the social saving £13.1 million or 1.6 per cent of the UK national income of 1865' (p. 44). However, if one compares first class travel by rail with 'posting' at two shillings a mile, second class travel with inside coach and third class travel with outside coach travel, 'this implies an alternative cost of £60.3 million and a saving of £47.9 million or 5.8 per cent of the 1865 UK national income' (p. 44).

Conclusion

The above discussion of the work of Fogel and Hawke has necessarily been brief and hence rather stark. Nevertheless, I hope that quite apart from the main conclusions of their work, you should have derived some additional insights into the benefits of comparative studies. Two such benefits may be mentioned briefly. The first is that the technique of social saving demonstrates the significance of comparing what actually happened with what might have happened. Only when that is done is a sense of perspective imparted to the object of one's study. Second, we have seen that the application of a technique first worked out on one set of data to another data set – I refer, of course, to Hawke's using Fogel's methods to examine English railways – not only tests the value of the technique but also sets the original findings into a context, so permitting a judgement as to their uniqueness or generality. We could perhaps make a third point of a comparative nature: namely, the often stark contrast between literary (or qualitative) and quantitative evidence. It would be idle to suggest that the contrast between qualitative and quantitative evidence is always straightforward. But as a general rule contemporary opinion should be treated with caution. To cite Fogel yet again: 'Authoritative opinions of the past, on most quantitative matters which concern economic historians, are crude approximations derived from poor data on the basis of inadequate analytical tools' (Fogel, 1964, p. 245). If you do not think he should have the last word, see his debate with Geoffrey Elton (Fogel and Elton, 1983).

References

Cohen, M.R. (1959) *Reason and Nature: An Essay on the Meaning of Scientific Method*, Glencoe, Free Press.

Dillon, S. (1891) 'The West and the Railroads', *North American Review*, CLII.

Fogel, R.W. (1964) *Railroads and American Economic Growth: Essays in Econometric History*, Baltimore, Johns Hopkins University Press.

Fogel, R.W. and G.R. Elton (1983) *Which Road to the Past? Two Views of Scientific and Traditional History*, New Haven, Yale University Press.

Hawke, G.R. (1970) *Railways and Economic Growth in England and Wales 1840–1870*, Oxford, Clarendon Press.

Rostow, W.W. (1960) *The Stages of Economic Growth*, Cambridge University Press.

Soule, G. (1952) *Economic Forces in American History*, New York, William Sloane.

Appendix

The measurement of 'total output'

The most obvious difficulty is that the output of an entire economy spans a vast range of different goods and services whose quantities cannot be added up directly in terms of their physical units. It makes no sense to add bushels of wheat to metres of cloth, tons of steel, litres of milk, and so on; instead, a common unit must by found in terms of which all output quantities can be expressed. This common measure is provided by *money*. If the number of units of each commodity is multiplied by its price per unit (for example, ten million loaves at 50p a loaf, two million metres of cloth at £5 a metre, and so on) the result is a set of money amounts (£5 million and £10 million respectively in the case of the loaves and cloth just mentioned) which can be added together to give the money value of total output.

There are some disadvantages in this, as will be seen later. But there is also a very strong argument in favour of using money values in this way. The object of producing commodities, after all, is to satisfy human wants, and the contribution of any particular commodity to total output ought therefore to be rated according to the amount of such satisfaction it provides.

There is no way of directly measuring degrees of satisfaction, but failing this, the prices people are willing to pay for the various goods and services can be taken as a rough guide – at any rate in the sense that if they are prepared to spend £1 on a unit of a particular commodity, they can be assumed to expect twice as much satisfaction from it as they would get from a unit of another commodity priced at 50p, and half as much as that from one priced at £2. When the physical quantities of the various commodities are multiplied by their respective prices, they are therefore being 'weighted' according to their relative ability to satisfy wants; for example, if the number of physical units of commodity A produced in a given time period is the same as the number of units of B, but A is priced at £1 and B at 50p, the output of A will count for twice as much as that of B in terms of its contribution to the production of the economy as a whole.

The validity of this approach, however, depends on the existence of markets in which buyers are free to choose how much or little they will buy, so that the prices they pay can be assumed to reflect their preferences. It runs into difficulties where commodities are *not* bought and sold in markets. The leading case is that of public services such as defence, police protection and general administration. These must count as 'output' since they satisfy wants and call for the use of scarce resources, but they have no market prices because they are supplied free of immediate charge. The solution is to value them 'at cost', e.g. to take the total amount of civil servants' salaries, the cost of upkeep of government buildings, etc., and regard the total expense as a measure of the value of the administrative services rendered to the community. Another group of cases involves 'self-provided' goods and services, such as the potatoes eaten by a farmer who has grown them or the accommodation enjoyed by the occupant of a dwelling-house who is also its owner. Here, the commodities never come on to the market, since they are directly consumed by their producers. It is, however, possible to value them by using the prices of similar ones which *are* sold through markets: for example, the value of the services rendered by an owner-occupied dwelling can be assumed equal to the rents paid by non-owning tenants for houses of the same size and amenities; the potatoes consumed by the grower can be valued by 'imputing' to them the price which prevails in the market where the rest of the potato crop is bought and sold. The real difficulty arises when the *entire* output of some commodity is directly consumed by its producers, as food is in an economy where subsistence agriculture is practised, since there will then be no market price which can be 'imputed'. In such cases, the value set on the output will have to be an arbitrary estimate, or else the commodity will simply have to be left out of the reckoning altogether.

When the production of every commodity has been valued in money terms in one or other of the ways indicated above, the next problem is to avoid the 'double counting' which may arise from the fact that some of the economy's products are used in making others. Suppose, for example, that wheat worth £10 million is grown during a given year, and that this is milled into flour worth £15 million, which in turn is baked into loaves of bread which sell for £20 million. If these figures were added together, giving a 'total output' figure of £45 million, it would mean that the value of the flour was being counted twice (once in its own right and a second time as part of the value of the loaves into which it has been made); in the same way, the value of the wheat would be counted three times over. The correct 'total output' figure is, in fact, £20 million – that is, the value of the end product into which the others have been absorbed in the course of production. Another way of putting it would be to say that the bakers have added value worth £5 million to the flour worth £15 million produced by the millers; the millers, for their part, have added £5 million to the value of the grain worth £10 million produced by the farmers; while the farmers' output is the wheat worth £10 million they have grown. If these successive amounts of *value added* are totalled, the value of the combined output of bakers, millers and farmers is seen to be £20 million.

On this principle, each industry's contribution to total output is defined as the gross value of its production (i.e. the number of physical units multiplied by the price per unit) *minus* the value of inputs received from other industries – which include not only tangible goods, like the steel supplied to the car industry by the iron and steel industry, but also services such as the transport supplied by the railways. As long as no industry or activity is left out of the reckoning, the sum of all these *values added* must be the total output of the economy as a whole.

The Gross National Product (GNP)

The term used for the principal measure of total output is the *Gross National Product* (conventionally abbreviated to GNP). The word 'gross' means that no deduction has been made to allow for 'capital consumption' (or 'depreciation'), i.e. the wearing out of capital equipment which occurs in the course of production. It would, of course, be more logical to treat this as an input into each industry's production process, and to deduct it from total output when the 'value added' is being calculated; if this were done, the grand total of 'values added' would be *Net National Product* (or NNP). But the actual measurement of capital consumption is difficult, and though today an official estimate is made (it is normally about 9 per cent of GNP), it is subject to a considerable margin of error; the GNP figure is therefore retained as being more reliable than that of NNP.

The word 'national' also requires some explanation. Surprising as it may seem, the GNP is *not* the total output produced within the borders of a particular country; in fact, total production in this geographical sense is called *Gross Domestic Product* (or GDP) to distinguish it from GNP. This is because some of the output taking place within a country is produced by foreign-owned resources, as indicated by the outflow to other countries of profit, dividends and interest earned there; on the other hand, some of the resources owned by a country's residents are located abroad (for example, in the case of Britain in the nineteenth century, railways in the USA), and *their* output causes an *inflow* of profit, dividends and interest to that country. The difference between the two flows is 'Net Property Income from Abroad'; GNP includes this item, while GDP does not. Briefly, Gross *National* Product can be defined as the total output of the resources owned by residents of the country, wherever the resources themselves are located; while Gross *Domestic* Product is the output of all resources located within a country, wherever their owners happen to live. Like GNP, the Gross Domestic Product becomes *Net* Domestic Product (NDP) when an allowance for 'capital consumption' is deducted from it.

Both GNP and GDP are given *at factor cost,* i.e. after the deduction of indirect taxes from the market prices of the various commodities. To give an example, in 1968 the 'market price' value of tobacco bought by consumers was £1,578 million, but this figure included no less than £1,084 million of indirect taxation; the 'factor cost' of the tobacco – i.e. the amount actually retained by the makers and sellers – was thus only £494 million. A general increase in indirect taxes would increase the 'market price' valuation of GNP, causing output to seem to increase even if all physical quantities were exactly the same as before; it is to avoid mis-leading impressions of this kind that the 'factor cost' valuation is used.

National income

When the Gross National Product is valued at factor cost, it is necessarily equal in amount to the *national income.* This is defined as the total of all *factor incomes,* i.e. those received by the owners of all factors of production engaged in producing the goods and services which together make up the GNP. They include all wages and salaries (normally today about two-thirds of the total), the trading profits of companies and public enter-prises (something less than a fifth), the earnings of self-employed people like farmers, shopkeepers and small business owners (just under one-tenth), and lastly rent (about 5 per cent). All the incomes just mentioned are gross of direct taxation – that is, no deduction has been made for income tax, surtax, corporation tax or National Insurance contributions. The figure for companies' trading profits can be subdivided into divi-dends paid to shareholders, interest paid to bondholders and other creditors, and the undistributed profits which remain in the companies' hands after these payments have been made.

For any given industry or enterprise, these factor incomes corre-spond to the 'value added', which (on the definition given earlier) is the difference between the value of its output and that of its inputs from other enterprises. Thus, a company which manufactures 1,000 units of its product per month, for sale at £10 a unit, will have a total output per month worth £10,000; if its inputs of materials, transport services, etc. cost £6,000 in all, it will be left with £4,000 with which to pay the wages of its workers, meet the interest on outstanding loans, pay rent on its prem-ises, and set aside profit from which dividends can be paid. Thus, 'value added' must be equal to the total of factor incomes paid out; and since the sum of 'values added' throughout the economy is the Gross National Product, while the sum of factor incomes is the national income, it fol-lows that GNP and national income are always identical in value.

If no deduction is made from the profits of enterprises to allow for the replacement of worn-out equipment (i.e. capital consumption), national income is 'gross' in the same way as GNP was said to be; if such a deduction is made, it is 'net'. Normally, when the term 'national income' is used without prefix, it is understood to be 'net'. The identity demonstrated in the last paragraph will, of course, only hold when both magnitudes are 'net' or when both are 'gross'. That is:

NNP = national income (or NNI)

GNP = national income plus capital consumption (or GNI).

The deduction of 'net income from abroad' from national income turns it into *domestic income* ('gross' or 'net' according to whether capital consumption is deducted or not), just as it did in the case of GNP; and, of course, Gross Domestic Income (GDI) = GDP, while NDI = NDP.

Among the types of income listed earlier as constituents of the national income, one group was noticeably absent – namely, those received by retirement pensioners, widows, and other beneficiaries of social security such as the unemployed and the sick. They were omitted because they are *not factor* incomes, i.e. remuneration for the services of any of the factors of production; national income is, by definition, the sum of factor incomes. Pensions, sickness benefit, etc. are 'transfer incomes' in the sense that they involve a redistribution of factor incomes through taxation; they are provided out of the wages, profits, etc. earned in the process of producing the goods and services which make up the GNP. It would therefore be 'double-counting' to include *both* transfer incomes *and* before-tax factor incomes when calculating the national income.

All the same, there is a good deal to be said for a classification of incomes which brings transfers in. One of the main reasons for investigating incomes is to see how they are related to spending. If consumers' demand for goods and services is thought to depend on their incomes, it is necessary to take account not only of the factor incomes received by persons (wages, dividends, etc.) but also of transfer incomes, since these too are used to finance personal consumption. On the other hand, the part of personal incomes which goes to pay income tax and National Insurance contributions is *not* available to finance consumption; so the total income which is relevant to the determination of consumers' demand is *personal disposable income,* i.e. factor incomes received by individuals *plus* transfer incomes *minus* all forms of income taxation paid by individuals. Factor incomes *not* received by individuals are (a) the part of company profits which remain undistributed instead of being paid out to shareholders in dividends, and also (b) certain property income received by the government and local authorities; these amounts are 'disposable income' for companies and public authorities respectively. Total receipts from income tax, surtax, corporation tax and National Insurance contributions are a good deal larger than the amount paid out in transfer incomes; the excess receipts can be regarded as 'disposable incomes' for the government, which uses it to finance public expenditure.

(From The Open University (1971) D100 *Understanding Society: A Foundation Course,* Unit 14, The Making of the Economy, pp. 1–16.)

1.12   Capital

Introduction

Previous essays in this part have shown how Britain and the United States began to industrialize in the late eighteenth and early nineteenth centuries and have discussed the attendant population growth, expansion of the labour force and growth of agricultural production. This essay deals with an important part of that process: capital accumulation and investment. Terms like 'capital accumulation' and 'investment' are not self-explanatory, especially in the very specific senses in which they are used by economists, so the first section introduces some definitions and theoretical perspectives which you will come across in reading about the subject.

Theoretical perspectives and definitions

There are many ways of looking at the process by which a society produces its wealth and income. One is to treat the production of goods and services as a continuous circular flow, with commodities being used to create new commodities in a never-ending stream. In a very simple economy you could conceive of corn being used to feed the workforce and act as seed for the next round of harvesting of corn. In this simple world everything is simultaneously the output of one phase of the productive process and an input into the next. Though simple, such a world can be made gradually more complex – and more realistic – by multiplying the number of elements which are being considered at any time. It is a world without distinctions between capital and labour as such.

Another perspective, now commonly associated with Karl Marx but having a long pedigree before his synthesis was created, is to conceive of human labour as the source of all value and all increase in value. It is labour power acting on brute nature which creates both goods for current consumption and the means by which future consumption may be realized. This stored-up labour power is, according to Marxists, just as much the produce of labour as the reproduction of the labourer's own means of subsistence. Not only that, but any extra value beyond that needed for future production (i.e. profit) is also created by labour and belongs to the labourer, even though in a capitalist society that surplus value is extracted by the owner of the means of production through the operation of the wage contract. Labourers are paid less than the value they create and capitalists pocket the difference, claiming (spuriously according to Marxists) that the difference is the just reward for their contribution of capital to the productive process.

A third way of considering the process of production underlies all the essays in this part. If you regard it as the 'normal' or 'correct' way, then consider that it too is as much a product of certain assumptions as the other two just described. In this model there are three factors of production – land, labour and capital – each of which has a part to play and a reward to be gained in the process of production. Historically the three-factor model corresponds to the three classes of income receivers in the eighteenth century when modern political economy was born. It is a creation of a specific historical episode, but its shadow is cast over all subsequent economic analysis. In the eighteenth century, landowners received rent, workers received wages, and those who were prepared, as the saying goes, 'to adventure their capital' were entitled to interest and profit thereon. In this model, as developed by nineteenth-century economists, factors of production receive incomes which correspond to their marginal products: that is, factors are brought into the productive process up to the point at which the last unit yields an output sufficient to cover its costs. According to this theory, there is no exploitation since each factor is rewarded in respect of its contribution to the process of production.

These three perspectives are not simply abstract and somewhat esoteric concepts. At least two of them have powerfully influenced the way in which the economic history of Britain and the United States has been written. Marx and many of his successors have been concerned with the transition from a feudal to a capitalist society in Britain, the establishment of capitalist society in America, and the socio-political consequences which flowed from these processes. Accordingly, their main interest has been in what they term the 'primitive' or 'initial' accumulation of capital which started off the development of capitalism. How was it that a society in which surpluses that accrued in agricultural production were creamed off by landlords became one in which a new social group was able to obtain command over these resources for a completely novel form of production? The search for answers to this question, and an analysis of the consequences for the mass of the population affected by the change, has guided much Marxist writing on British economic history and has inspired a small number of similarly inclined American historians.

There is disagreement among these historians on the process of primitive capital accumulation. Marx himself placed great emphasis on the agrarian changes of the eighteenth century, particularly the enclosure movement in which small landholders were dispossessed and replaced on large farms by wage labourers. But he also drew attention to the accumulation of capital overseas in the British Empire in the eighteenth century; to the slave trade, later emphasized most strongly by Eric Williams in *Capitalism and Slavery* (1964); to the expansion and engrossment of the domestic trade by large merchants, some of whom became capitalist producers; and to what he termed 'the really revolutionary way', the transformation of craftsmen and artisans into petty capitalist producers employing the wage labour of others thanks to their small accumulations of capital.

Economic historians not of a Marxist persuasion have tended to react to these studies and speculations in one of two ways. Either they have ignored them as theoretically and logically unsound, being based on ideological assumptions which are unacceptable, or they have sought to undermine the empirical basis of Marxist arguments. But in doing so they have not abandoned the idea that investment and saving lie at the heart of the industrial process.

The perception that capital accumulation and investment were vital to the process of industrialization is not new. In 1776 Adam Smith, often regarded as the founder of modern economics, wrote in his *Inquiry into the Nature and Causes of the Wealth of Nations*:

> The annual produce of the land and labour of any nation can be increased in its value by no other means but by increasing either the number of productive labourers, or the productive powers of the labourers who had before been employed. The number of its productive labourers, it is evident, can never be much increased, but in consequence of an increase in capital or funds destined for maintaining them. The productive powers of the same number of labourers cannot be increased, but in consequence either of some addition and improvement to those machines and instruments which facilitate and abridge labour, or of a more proper division and distribution of employment. In either case an additional capital is almost always required.

Notice that Smith makes the point that increased capital is necessary to support a growing workforce and to increase the productivity (that is, output per head) of a fixed number of workers. Either way the society must save some of its output if it is to produce more in the future. Less jam today is necessary if we are to have more jam tomorrow.

Most subsequent economic historians have accepted Smith's emphasis on the importance of capital accumulation and investment in the process of industrialization. The development economist W. Arthur Lewis put it in a nutshell when he asserted, 'The central problem in the theory of economic development is to understand the process by which a community which was previously saving and investing four or five per cent of its national income, converts itself into an economy where voluntary saving is running at about twelve to fifteen per cent of national income or more. This is the central problem because the central fact of economic development is rapid capital accumulation' (Lewis, 1965). W.W. Rostow, whose work you have already met, postulated a take-off phase of industrialization in which, within a very short period – perhaps only a couple of decades – the rate of investment jumped from 5 to 10 per cent of national income.

Both Lewis and Rostow based their interpretations on what they saw as the historical experience of countries like Britain and the United States. In Britain, according to Rostow, the key period was 1783–1802, while in the United States take-off occurred between 1843 and 1860. The sharp rise in investment in Britain was associated with the development of steam power, the boom in canal construction, enclosure and agricultural improvement, and the expansion of the cotton, coal and iron industries. In the United States investment in railroads and the industries which supplied them absorbed the capital.

Attractive and dramatic though it is, the Lewis–Rostow notion of a sharp discontinuity in the rate of saving and investment has not met with full acceptance in either country. Phyllis Deane and H.J. Habakkuk have suggested a lesser rise in investment in this period, with the overall level only reaching 10 per cent in Britain as late as the railway age between 1830 and 1860 (Deane and Habakkuk, 1963). Americans, on the other hand, appear to have been great savers from an early stage of their history, though the rate of domestically financed investment probably did not reach Rostovian levels until the mid-nineteenth century. The qualification about 'domestically' financed investment is introduced because the USA was able to draw on British capital during the nineteenth century and did so quite extensively in the 1830s, early 1850s and from 1860 to 1875.

The most recent calculations for Britain tend to support the Lewis model, though not Rostow's insistence that there was a sudden and concentrated rise in investment. Table 1 shows that investment in Britain in the 1760s was running at about 8 per cent of Gross National Product (GNP), whereas by the 1790s it had risen to 14 per cent, at which level it stayed until the 1850s with the exception of the wartime decade 1801–10. Robert Gallman's data for the United States puts gross capital formation at 15 per cent of GNP in the 1830s, rising to nearly 30 per cent after the American Civil War (Gallman, 1966). These studies confirm the scale of the rise in investment accompanying industrialization, though important questions about the causes and effects of this rise remain unanswered.

Table 1   Total investment Great Britain, 1760–1860 (£ million per year, decade average, at 1851–60 prices)

	Fixed capital formation	Stock building	Foreign investment	Total investment	Total as % of GNP
1761–70	6.5	1.0	0.5	8.0	8
1771–80	7.0	2.0	1.0	10.0	10
1781–90	11.0	2.0	1.5	14.5	13
1791–1800	14.5	3.0	1.5	14.5	14
1801–10	16.5	1.0	2.0	15.5	10
1811–20	20.5	2.0	5.0	27.5	14
1821–30	28.5	4.0	7.5	40.0	14
1831–40	38.5	3.5	4.5	46.5	13
1841–50	49.5	5.0	6.5	61.0	13
1851–60	58.0	3.5	20.0	81.5	13

Source: Feinstein, 1981, p. 131.

To make further progress with this topic, we need definitions of some of the terms which have been used. 'Capital', as used by neoclassical economists (the third perspective described above, pp. 158–9), refers to the stock of goods which are used in the process of production and which themselves have been produced. 'Fixed capital' covers the machinery, factories, transport facilities and equipment used in producing goods and services, while 'circulating' or 'working capital' includes the power to drive the machines and the raw materials consumed or transformed in the process of production. Sometimes labour is referred to as 'human capital' and the wages paid to the worker are considered as 'circulating capital', but more commonly labour is treated as a separate factor of production along with land and capital.

The process of investment, which is at the heart of economic development as we have already seen, also needs a few definitions. If you put yourself in the shoes of a capitalist, then obviously you could increase the value of your money by simply lending it to a bank – provided, that is, the rate of interest paid exceeded the rate of inflation. If prices are rising by 10 per cent a year, you require an interest rate of more than 10 per cent if your capital stock is to increase. So if you decide to risk your capital in the production of goods, you will expect to make a rate of return which will be greater than the current rate of interest being offered by the banks. If you do not get such a return, then economists would describe your investment as inefficient, since you could have got more by leaving your cash in the bank. Any return greater than the rate of interest can be characterized as 'productive' investment, while the term 'efficient' investment may be used to denote the highest possible return on the investment which you made. The act of investment – that is, of turning cash into productive resources – is often referred to as 'capital formation', while the resources thus created may be termed a 'stock' of capital – a stock which may consist of fixed and circulating capital as already defined.

The wealth of the population of a country or a group of people within a country is the total of all potentially productive assets or claims on resources held, while the income of those people consists of the flow of sums received by them in the form of wages, rents, interest or dividends and so on. Within a closed economy – that is, one in which there is no foreign trade or foreign investment – the total income accruing to all the population is equivalent to the total amount of expenditure and saving by these people and to the total output of the society (since it is the output which generates all the income received and the expenditure on it by all groups in society). What this means is that the national income of a country is defined as being equal to its Gross Domestic Product.* In practice, when one comes to measure these identities errors creep in, but in principle they are the same. The rate of investment in a country is often expressed as a proportion of national income, so when we note Rostow and Lewis's insistence that during industrialization investment must rise from 5 to 10 per cent or over, then they are relating that rate of investment to the national income of the country concerned.

* Gross National Product includes overseas earnings. 'National income is defined to include not only the income which arises from production within the economy, but also income which accrues to domestic residents from activities carried on abroad. If these overseas earnings are excluded we have Gross Domestic Product' (Bannock, Baxter and Rees, 1984, p. 314).

Armed with these definitions, we can now examine more closely the process of saving (or capital accumulation) and investment (or capital formation) in Britain and the United States in the eighteenth and nineteenth centuries. The questions we start with are concerned with the pattern of saving in the two countries and the ways in which savings were transformed into investments. How was this investment financed and by whom? What burden, if any, was placed on the workers by the diversion of a higher proportion of the nation's resources to investment instead of current consumption? Were either of the countries able to raise this investment from domestic sources, or did they have to borrow overseas? Could the existing means of mobilizing capital cope with the increased demand, or did new institutions have to be created? What contribution did this investment make to the growth of the British and American economies?

Sources of saving and the mobilization of capital

The United States and Britain were not like many of the so-called underdeveloped countries of today. Both were relatively rich countries, though their incomes and wealth were unevenly distributed. In the United States in 1860, 10 per cent of families held over 70 per cent of the country's wealth. In Britain the top 20 per cent of income receivers obtained over

60 per cent of the total income. This means that both societies had the potential to finance industrialization, provided resources could be transferred from those who held wealth to those who wished to use it productively: in other words, from savers to investors. The problem for both countries, then, was not an absolute shortage of capital but how to mobilize it for efficient investment. The only exception to this generalization might be the United States for brief periods in the 1830s and 1850s, when domestic sources of capital were insufficient to sustain the rapid expansion of the economy, particularly the construction of the massive network of canals, roads and railways built in these years. In this case, borrowing from the United Kingdom on a large scale made up for the shortage of domestic capital in the United States. For most of the time, most of the capital needed was raised from domestic sources, though Marxists in particular have stressed the contribution of Britain's empire and foreign trade.

There are several possible sources of domestic saving in an economy. The government, farmers or agricultural landlords, other private individuals or households, and business firms can and do save part of their incomes. It is generally agreed that in the United States and United Kingdom governments were less important as savers or investors than in many countries which have industrialized since then. Nevertheless, government saving and investment was not negligible in either country during the early stages of industrialization. It has been calculated that two-thirds of all transport investment in the United States before the Civil War was undertaken by federal and local government. Much of the saving to finance this came not from tax revenue but from government borrowing at home and abroad, which means that the savings were being made by individuals, while the governments were simply acting as a means of mobilization of these funds. In Britain government borrowing and direct investment in the economy were associated very largely with wars, of which there were many in the eighteenth and early nineteenth centuries. Some of this military investment had indirect economic consequences of much wider significance, as when the technique for cannon-boring developed by John Wilkinson was later used to produce accurate cylinders for Boulton and Watt steam engines. Naval dockyards were an important source of technological change in woodworking and machine making. But, in general, British and American governments very seldom used any savings they made for direct investment in business firms. Perhaps the nearest they came was the award of prizes for invention or grants to individuals who had made technical developments. Indirectly by tariff protection they could increase the profitability of domestic firms, and we will see in a moment that this was an important source of saving for investment.

If government saving is not the answer, where did savings take place in the British and American economies in the eighteenth and nineteenth centuries? In Britain agricultural production was organized in such a way that landowners obtained substantial revenues from their often extensive properties. Rents were kept under review and raised in line with increases in agricultural output or prices. Some enterprising landlords used these revenues for direct industrial investment themselves. The Duke of Bridgewater, who built the Bridgewater canal linking coal mines on his estate to the urban market in Manchester in 1761, is one famous

* If you had a bill of
exchange you could take it to
a bank or agent who would
offer you a sum of money for
it, less than the face value, to
allow for the time before the
bank or agent could claim the
full sum from the originator
of the bill. The amount of the
discount would depend on the
rate of interest obtaining in
the market at the time.

example. As Peter Mathias notes, 'Lists of trustees of navigation (that is, canal) companies and investors read like catalogues of the county families' (Mathias, 1969, p. 177). Perhaps more commonly, the revenue from landed estates or tenant farmers when crops were sold after harvest was placed in local banks, who then might have used the resources for investment or transferred them to their London agents. The latter often provided the discount facilities* for merchants or manufacturers seeking to finance stocks of raw materials or pay the wages of their employees.

In the United States agriculture was organized very differently with a much higher proportion of owner-occupiers, particularly in the North and West, while in the South plantation cropping of cotton and tobacco was predominant (see Essay 1.10, '"King Cotton" in Britain and America'). Per capita income estimates in the North and West became available from the 1880s onwards, and they suggest much higher than average incomes which persisted beyond World War I in these areas. Now we cannot be sure that westerners were better off before the Civil War, since the spread of the railroad probably had a marked effect on farm incomes. Nevertheless, it is probably fair to guess that farmers in the North and West had a capacity for saving which contributed to the growth of the American capital stock, either through their purchases of agricultural equipment or indirectly through the banking system. In the South most wealth and income accrued to slave-owning landlords, and though many of the individuals concerned ran up spectacular debts, recent studies tend to confirm that slavery was a profitable institution before the Civil War, in no danger of imminent collapse through its own inefficiency.

Other, non-agricultural households contributed significantly to saving in Britain and America. In both countries there was a well-developed commercial middle class long before the sharp upsurge of industry in the late eighteenth and early nineteenth centuries. This was not unique to these countries, of course, for Holland and many of the smaller states of the Rhineland, for example, could point to similar social groups. It did mean that many relatively small accumulations of wealth were available and that those in control of them were on the look-out for profitable areas of investment. Nor should it be thought that all these accumulations were in the hands of merchants. Many an early industrialist was saved from bankruptcy by the intervention of widows, relatives or lawyers acting for themselves or for families who had surplus capital and some personal interest, as much as an economic interest, in the development of a firm. In aggregate, domestic savings of this kind have contributed a very substantial proportion of the national totals.

Much foreign capital came from the immigrants to the United States, a proportion of whom brought relatively substantial sums, though the majority were quite poor. The other capital assets the immigrants brought were the education and skills that they had obtained prior to migration, which the United States therefore did not have to supply and finance. Nevertheless, the bulk of capital required for US economic development was domestic in origin.

This leaves business itself as a source of saving. Today we are used to industrial firms requiring huge amounts of capital for investment, with multinationals having larger turnovers than the GNP of some small countries. The scale of investment in industry did rise in Britain and America. Recent studies tend to support the general correctness of Lewis's assertion about the rise in the rate of saving and investment associated with industrialization, though not Rostow's insistence that the rise was compressed into a period as short as a couple of decades.

Investment and industrialization

If we agree that industrialization required an increase in the rate of investment, then it is important to be clear where this investment went. Perhaps surprisingly, the bulk of it did not go into factories, machinery or prime movers like steam engines. Much more capital was required for transport improvement, agricultural investment, housing, shipbuilding and the financing of industrial stocks than for machinery and equipment. One calculation puts gross capital formation in Britain around 1770 at about £9.4 million, of which less than a million consisted of machinery and millwork (buildings, steam engines, water wheels, industrial plant other than machinery). By 1830–5 capital formation had risen to £40 million a year, but even then machinery and millwork account for £8 million. In the United States in the late nineteenth century some 60 per cent of gross capital formation consisted of building and construction, while changes in stocks of goods and raw materials accounted for another 15 per cent, leaving less than 25 per cent for durable capital equipment throughout the economy.

What this means is that industry (narrowly defined) did not require a large share of the new investment which was taking place in the economies. What was true of industry as a whole was true of the typical firm as well. Of course, there were industrial giants like Boulton and Watt, makers of steam engines, or the Amoskeag Cotton Mills in Manchester, New Hampshire, but these were very untypical firms. The majority of industrial enterprises were small and their capital requirements were modest. Indeed studies of the cotton industry in Britain, the pioneer of modern industrialization, show that as late as the 1840s (when Engels was writing about 'the ever increasing concentration of capital in fewer and fewer hands') the average firm in Lancashire remained small and used relatively little capital equipment. What it did use was as likely to be hired or rented as owned outright.

In both Britain and the United States the very early stages of industrial development did not require raising unprecedented amounts of capital. Nevertheless financing industry was not without its problems. There was no national capital market where entrepreneurs could go to sell shares or raise loans for their investment. Until the 1850s in Britain, limited liability companies could only come into being after a tedious process of obtaining either a royal charter or a special Act of Parliament. Partnerships were limited to six people, and investors in such enterprises were liable, as the saying goes, 'to the last shilling and the last acre'. In other words, even though you might invest only a hundred pounds in a company, if it went bankrupt then the whole of your assets could be called upon to meet its debts. Not surprisingly, lending money to strangers for industrial investment was uncommon. In America limited liability was available in New York as early as 1813, in Connecticut by 1817, in Massachusetts by 1830 and in New Hampshire by 1837, but general freedom of incorporation with limited liability came much later.

So how did businesses go about raising the finances they needed? The most common way of getting started was the transfer of funds from some existing trade or activity into manufacturing. Merchants who bought cloth from weavers might decide to take over the process of manufacture themselves by contracting directly with individual weavers in their own homes, by bringing the weavers together under one roof in order to exert closer control and supervision, or by employing weavers as wage labourers working in a factory in which the machinery, building and power would be owned or rented by the capitalist. We think of these as typical of the development of modern industry, but in fact they were relatively rare until well into the nineteenth century in much of British industry. Obviously the cotton industry had gone furthest down this road by then, and in the United States, too, cotton pioneered the new factory system in New England. Here, too, a decisive event was the shift of merchant capital into the industry in the 1820s, when it became evident that American overseas trade was not yielding the high level of profits which it had provided during the time the British were occupied in wars with France. As a consequence much larger firms came into being in the New England textile industry at Lowell in Massachusetts, Saco in Maine and Manchester in New Hampshire.

This illustrates another common way of raising the initial finance to begin industrial production. A group of people, perhaps from different backgrounds, might get together to form a partnership with each contributing varying amounts of capital and expertise to the joint project. Such partnerships might well involve members of the same family or kin groups or, very often, co-religionists. Contacts through church or chapel provided the knowledge, the trust and the social sanctions which reduced the risks inherent in lending money under the system we have described. Among factory owners and industrialists in the early stages of Britain's Industrial Revolution, there seem to be a disproportionately high number of Quakers, for example. Max Weber, the early twentieth-century German sociologist, was deeply impressed by the way in which religious affiliation provided the social cement, the contacts and the commercial morality necessary to underpin financial transactions in both Britain and America when he studied the development of capitalism in the two countries.

Sometimes by frugality, luck or acumen an artisan or tradesman might increase the scale of his activities and become a capitalist himself, perhaps 'employing' his family as workers at the beginning but then taking on wage labourers. In many industries movement between being a master and being an employee was quite common. In the brass trades of Birmingham, for example, it was still happening until late in the nineteenth century. For some industrial activities, as we have seen, initial capital requirements were modest and much could be rented rather than purchased. In Scotland it has often been argued that the 'cash credit' system – an early form of guaranteed overdraft by the banks – enabled many a 'lad o' pairts' (young fellow with skill and initiative) to get started. Similarly, American literature is full of the rags to riches stories of the heroes who began with nothing and built up industrial empires. We have to ask ourselves how typical this process was. Are a few authenticated examples just the tip of the iceberg or important as creating a myth that escape from wage labour was possible for the masses? Before long, industrial development had raised the scale of capital required for successful competition and made it, at the very least, extremely difficult for the newcomer to break into industrial activity on the basis of talent alone rather than financial backing. As the historian of the early stages of cotton manufacturing in New England put it, 'Large fortunes were indeed made in the cotton business but they were made from large beginnings' (Ware, 1931).

Agriculture was an important source of capital for industrialization in Britain and America, but in both countries much agricultural capital was 'ploughed back' into the land itself, not literally but figuratively. In the 1760s it seems that British farmers and landlords were spending about 6 per cent of their income on improving their land, but at the height of the Napoleonic Wars when food prices had risen sharply and agricultural profits with them, the proportion rose to 16 per cent. Much of this spending was on enclosure of land, new techniques and land reclamation when the land area in Britain under crops reached its greatest extent ever. During the post-war depression agricultural investment fell off, but it recovered in the 1840s, assisted by government loans for drainage associated with the repeal of the Corn Laws in 1846. The subsequent age of 'high farming' was based on high levels of agricultural investment in new methods, crops, livestock and chemical fertilizers. Nevertheless, the share of agriculture in total investment fell steadily, even though the absolute amount grew. This was simply the consequence of much more rapid expansion of industrial and transport investment.

In America the story of agricultural investment is of extensive growth as the land area of the country expanded and the public domain was sold off. Fierce debates have raged ever since about who gained from the land sales and whether speculators made exorbitant profits. Fortunately, we can ignore them and concentrate on investment in the land once it came into the hands of farmers or plantation owners. In the North, family farms quickly ran into labour supply problems – the cost of hiring labour for peak periods such as harvesting became higher than that of employing machinery. Hence, particularly during the 1850s, there was widespread adoption of the McCormick and other reapers. This form of investment – in machinery rather than seeds, fertilizers or farming methods – was to be very characteristic of American agriculture in the nineteenth century. It had two incidental but significant advantages. It used the mechanical skills which were common among American workers rather than more specialist knowledge of chemical and biological processes; it also created enormous demand for the agricultural supply industry, enabling it to adopt systems of interchangeable parts and standardization pioneered by armament manufacturers like Samuel Colt.

In a later essay in Book 2 you will return to the broader issues of labour supply and its influence on patterns of technological change; here we must content ourselves with the observation that agricultural investment, though declining relative to direct industrial investment, nevertheless played a part in the growth of the British and American economies. In neither country was agricultural investment a major competitor for industrial funds, and it was possible to accommodate the growth of both. This might be contrasted with the stark choice faced by the Russians in the 1920s when the investment needs of agriculture and industry were in conflict.

Of all the areas of investment in the early stages of industrialization, two caused particular difficulties for both the British and American economies: transport and domestic housing. The nature of the problems differed. Transport required large amounts of fixed investment in construction, whether it was for canals, roads, turnpikes or railways. Much of this investment had to be long term before returns came in, and banks were not keen to lock up their capital in transport undertakings. Often the scale was so massive that private interests, even if banded together in groups, were unwilling to take the risks involved. For this reason, as was mentioned earlier, state governments in America embarked on canal construction. The state of New York built the very successful Erie Canal linking the Hudson River with the Great Lakes at a cost of $7 million. 'Clinton's Big Ditch', as the canal was called after Governor De Witt Clinton, was unique. Revenue from tolls on the canal paid the interest charges on the capital borrowed even before it was completed, land values in New York State doubled, and New York established its supremacy over Philadelphia as a port and focus for commerce. Pennsylvania responded by investing over $100 million in public works, and by 1844 over 150 corporations in the state had both publicly appointed and private directors. Almost three-quarters of all canal investment was financed by public authorities, but most of the 3,700 miles constructed by 1850 were at best marginally profitable. By 1837 several states were in severe financial difficulty as a result of their transport investment and were forced to default on their borrowings.

Despite their experiences, states became equally heavily involved in railroad financing. Municipal authorities also lent heavily to railroads, and federal authorities contributed by making land grants to railroad companies, who could then sell the land or take out mortgages on it to raise funds for construction. Tariff reductions on iron also helped railroad companies during the years from 1830 to 1843.

By contrast, in Britain the bulk of the capital required for transport development was obtained from private sources. Special Acts of Parliament were necessary for setting up turnpike trusts and canal and railway companies, and these were expensive. But no state aid was forthcoming, except in the case of strategic road building in the Scottish Highlands (after the 1745 Jacobite uprising) and the Caledonian Canal. The Holyhead road and the Brighton military canal and subsidies to mail-carrying steamship companies virtually exhaust the direct investment by the state in British transport improvement. So private companies had to raise their own finances by direct appeals to the public – hence the desire to associate aristocratic names with their prospectuses. Even so, there were great problems when companies tried to move beyond their locality to attract funds. Gradually, especially in the 1830s and 1840s, a national capital market began to emerge and railway stocks were the pioneering form of investment. Blind capital seeking its return began to supplement the personal forms of investment characteristic of the early stage of industrialization.

As regards housing, though the scale of domestic housing investment was on a par with that of railways in Great Britain (in the peak years of 1841–60, £11.5 million a year were being invested in railways and £11.0 million in residential building), it presented a different aspect. Indeed, it seems that the rise in railway investment as a share of total investment was at the expense of new housing. The building industry in Britain did not experience technical innovations; it remained a highly labour-intensive, small-scale operation, though individuals like Thomas Cubitt did build up large labour forces. But housing did not yield a high enough return, at rents working-class families could afford, to attract the sort of investment mechanisms and technical progress which revolutionized the transport networks of Britain and the United States. Rapid population growth and geographic mobility exacerbated the difficulties for the new urban centres, and it was long after the classical phase of industrialization was over before either society came to terms with mobilization of finance for working-class housing, with America relying on high wages and private industry while municipal housing was the British 'solution'.

Banking and industrial growth

Economic historians have always disagreed about the role and importance of banks and banking systems in the process of industrialization. Some have emphasized the creative powers of banks and pointed to examples of banking initiative in the development of new industries, the reorganization of existing industries, and the expansion of credit throughout the economy. Others have argued that while early industrializing countries could manage without great banking initiatives, latecomers needing larger amounts of capital required a more active role by the banks. Germany and Russia are two examples of late developers in which banks were more dynamic than they were in Britain and America. However, perhaps the majority have read the historical record differently, and see banks and banking systems as largely dependent on the demands within the economy for credit in various forms. Banks respond to expressed needs; they rarely lead the way. Moreover, such critics say, countries have industrialized with very different banking systems, so it is unlikely that one type is definitely superior from the point of view of industrial needs.

There is no doubt that the formal banking systems of Britain and the United States were very different. The Bank of England was set up as a banker for the government in 1694, though it only gradually began to behave in most respects like a modern central bank. That is, it acted not only as bank for the government, but also as lender of last resort to private banks and financial institutions and as regulator or controller of the note issue, the currency of the country. In the United States there were two brief experiments with national banks between 1791 and 1811 and between 1816 and 1836. Neither developed into a single national controller of credit, largely because of jealousy of the individual states. As late as 1852 banking was completely illegal in seven states. In a couple of others it was a state monopoly, while New York had very liberal banking laws which were copied by around a dozen states by 1862.

In Britain a developed banking network existed in the eighteenth century, though it underwent changes following the many financial crises and panics which occurred. Apart from the Bank of England, there were several private banks based in London whose main links were with trade and commerce, with urban financial activities or with the needs of the landed aristocracy. Then there were a large number of country banks whose credit networks covered trade and agriculture in the provinces.

They often used London banks as their agents and sources of support during financial crises. These interconnected networks transferred funds from areas of the country like the south and west, where surpluses were accruing in agriculture, to the north where there was a growing demand for industrial capital. These banks were circumscribed by the fact that the Bank of England had a monopoly of joint-stock banking in England,* though not in Scotland where larger joint-stock banks grew up in the eighteenth century. By 1810 it has been estimated that there were over 700 country banks scattered throughout the country of varying degrees of reliability. Some of them were very difficult to distinguish from merchants and manufacturers. At this stage of industrialization, specialization in a single activity was less common than it later became.

* *The Bank of England's charter gave it the sole right to conduct joint-stock banking in England. The other banks were therefore partnerships, limited by law to six persons, all personally liable for the debts of the bank. Hence the scale on which they could operate was restricted.*

American banking was, if anything, much more fragmented and unstable. There were over 1,000 banks in 1840 and half as many again by 1860 – some, it was said, 'located so far into the woods that even a wildcat could not find them' to exchange their banknotes for gold, hence the expression 'wildcat banks'. United States banknotes were trusted in inverse proportion to the distance from the bank of issue, and it was said that dirty notes with many holes in them were preferable to clean ones, because the former had obviously been handled and accepted very often while the new ones were untried! In crises, banks often refused to pay out the full value of their notes in precious metals; at such times paper currency was devalued and trade – both domestic and international – suffered.

As argued above, the fixed capital needs for industry remained modest, while large sums were required for social infrastructure. Within industry, mining required proportionately much more fixed capital than textiles. Also the balance between the supply and demand for credit did not remain fixed over time for the economy as a whole, for industries or for individual firms. Sometimes manufacturers had to give long periods of credit to obtain sales. At other times they could finance their activities out of credit, as for example in the woollen industry in the eighteenth century, because the product was in high demand. Truck and tokens enabled them to obtain credit from their labour force (see below). From the 1820s cotton traders like McConnel and Kennedy did not have to offer credit to obtain sales, as demand for cotton goods grew and bills of exchange came into wider use as a means of tapping external credit.

In both countries banks dealt in bills of exchange, and it was through this medium that they provided much circulating capital for industry. When someone sold goods, he would draw a bill of exchange which would then be signed by the buyer signifying his acceptance of it and agreement to pay the value of the goods on a certain day. This bill of exchange could be taken by the seller to a bank, which would pay him its value minus a discount calculated on the basis of the rate of interest and the length of time before the bill fell due. These bills of exchange became a form of trading currency, and specialist bill brokers grew up whose income derived from their skill in discounting. One firm alone, Richardsons in London, had a turnover of over £20 million in bills by 1823.

Manufacturers and traders used bills of exchange to obtain the resources to pay wages and purchase new stocks of materials, and much trade credit was obtained by issuing long-dated bills – that is, ones you did not have to pay for some time. Simple refusal to meet debts until the last possible moment was another way in which businesses increased the amount of resources they had at their command. (Others were payment of low wages at long intervals and the use of truck shops or company stores to ensure that the cash paid out circulated back to the employer. Much of the blame for this is attributable to governments who did not increase the supply of money sufficiently.) Banks in Britain and America were, on the whole, quite happy to accommodate manufacturers with circulating capital, but they were reluctant to lend large sums for fixed capital investment. The reason is simple. You can usually realize the value of a bill of exchange fairly readily, but it may be impossible to sell a cotton mill or its machinery or its steam engine during a trade depression. Despite their caution, many banks in Britain and America, including the Bank of England itself, found themselves with bad debts through lending sums to industrialists which were put into fixed capital investment.

So what contribution did the different banking systems of Britain and the United States make to industrial growth in the two countries? It appears that neither system seriously inhibited industrial expansion; indeed the frequent panics and crises may be a good indication that the banks were responding only too well and too enthusiastically to the demands of industry. Because the scale of fixed capital for industry proper was relatively small and could be met very largely from retained profits, the contribution of banks to industrial growth may have been relatively peripheral in any case. It was only when major public utilities like canals and railways were involved that massive capital sums were required, and this led in turn to the development of specialized stock exchanges to supplement activities. On the other hand, there are several well-documented cases of considerable bank loans to individual firms in both Britain and the United States which came at critical stages in the history of the firms involved. The Carron Ironworks in Scotland borrowed over £13,000 for fixed capital and managed to convert another £40,000 worth of bills of exchange into part of its long-term debt. But then the firm which did not get the financial support it required from the banks may leave little or no trace on the record, so it is never possible to be certain that the banking system did meet the needs of the firm or the economy.

The effects of capital accumulation and investment

Compared with many countries attempting to industrialize, Britain and the United States did not face insuperable difficulties in saving or in mobilizing funds for investment. Certainly, there were obstacles of the kind which confront pioneers, but these were overcome because both countries were relatively well endowed with resources, skills and a flexibility of approach which allowed and encouraged new methods of mobilizing these resources. At no time was the industrialization of Britain or the United States seriously retarded by shortages of capital. Potential problems in the United States in the 1830s and 1850s were effectively met by foreign borrowing.

This does not mean that the process of growth was smooth or uncontested, or that financial crises did not occur, causing deep and lasting social distress. But, on the whole, these were not associated with an absolute shortage of capital – often the reverse. Even at the height of the Napoleonic Wars, when government expenditure was absorbing 15 per cent of Gross National Product, investment at home was able to be maintained and the per capita consumption of the people was not reduced. It is likely that receivers of rents and profits benefited disproportionately at this time, so that industrial workers, facing rapidly rising food prices, may have suffered a sharp fall in their living standards. Nevertheless, if this is the extreme case, then it can be asserted that, on the whole, the rise in the rate of investment over the whole period of industrialization did not depress the consumption of the people because the expansion of output matched the rise in the rate of investment.

Finally, we can ask how much of the increase in per capita output can be attributed to the rise in the rate of investment. The answer can be given in a very simple or a very complex way. By measuring the growth of the capital stock and the labour supply and comparing this with the growth of output, we can find out how much of the increase in the last of these was the result of increased inputs and how much was due to more efficient use of inputs – that is, better techniques. In Britain for the period 1760 to 1860, Feinstein has calculated that 22 per cent of the increase in productivity (that is, output per worker) can be accounted for by increased capital per worker, while 78 per cent – more than three-quarters – came from better and more efficient use of new methods (Feinstein, 1981, pp. 139–40). Similar calculations for the United States yield comparable results.

But what does this mean? Some might say that the three-quarters of the increase in labour productivity which cannot be explained by higher inputs of capital is just an indication of our ignorance of the causes of economic growth. There may also be errors in our assumptions and measurements. We may not have clearly specified the separate sources of growth, such as changes in the quality of labour as a result of better education and training, for example. Finally, the better techniques, sometimes referred to as 'technical progress', often involve the embodiment of progress in new capital equipment, changed forms of organization to enable it to operate efficiently, and a mechanism to ensure that savings are channelled to those who are making the investment. Separating the statistical increase in the amount of capital involved may be only the beginning of a just assessment of the contribution of capital to economic growth and industrialization.

References and further reading

Atack, J. and Passell, P. (1994) *A New Economic View of American History from Colonial Times to 1940*, 2nd edn, New York.

Bannock, G., Baxter, R.E. and Rees, R. (1984) *Dictionary of Economics*, 3rd edn, Penguin.

Bodenhorn, H. (1993) 'Capital Mobility and Financial Integration in Antebullum America', *Journal of Economic History*, vol. 52, no. 3.

Collins, M. (1991) *Banks and Industrial Finance in Britain, 1800–1939*, Macmillan.

Daunton, M.J. (1995) 'Capital and Credit: Financing Industrialisation' in *Progress and Poverty: An Economic and Social History of Britain*, Oxford University Press.

Deane, P. and Habakkuk, H.J. (1963) 'The Take-Off In Britain' in W.W. Rostow (ed.) *The Economics of Take-off into Sustained Growth*, London, International Economic Association.

Engerman, S.L. and Gallman R.E. (eds) (1996) *Cambridge Economic History of the United States, Volume 1: The Colonial Era*, Cambridge University Press.

Feinstein, C.H. (1981) 'Capital Accumulation and the Industrial Revolution' in R. Floud and D.N. McCloskey (eds) *The Economic History of Britain since 1700, Volume 1: 1700–1860*, Cambridge University Press.

Gallman, R. (1966) 'Gross National Product in the United States, 1824–1909', in D.S. Brady (ed.) *Output, Employment and Productivity in the United States after 1800*, New York, National Bureau of Economic Research.

Goldsmith, R.W. (1955) *A Study of Saving in the United States*, Princeton University Press.

Hudson, P. (1986) *The Genesis of Industrial Capital: A Study of the West Riding Wool Textile Industry, c.1750–1850*, Cambridge University Press.

Lewis, W.A. (1965) *The Theory of Economic Growth*, 8th edn, Allen and Unwin.

Mathias, P. (1969) *The First Industrial Nation*, Methuen.

Shaw, R.E. (1990) *Canals for a Nation: The Canal Era in the United States, 1790–1860*, Lexington, University of Kentucky Press.

Ware, C.F. (1931) *The Early New England Cotton Manufacture*, Boston and New York, Houghton Mifflin.

Weiss, T. and Schaefer, D. (1994) *American Economic Development in Historical Perspective*, Stanford University Press.

Whaples, R. and Betts, D.C. (1994) *Historical Perspectives on the American Economy: Readings in American Economic History*, New York.

Williams, E. (1964) *Capitalism and Slavery*, Deutsch.

1.13   War and economic progress in Britain and America: the economic effects of the French wars, 1793–1815, and the Civil War, 1861–5

War and long-term economic growth

For both Britain and the United States extremely costly wars accompanied decisive phases of their long-term advance towards industrial societies. Over five years of civil war, 1861–5, the Union and Confederate governments utilized real resources equivalent to 1.2 times the income of the USA for 1861, while the amount spent by the British government from 1793 to 1815 to secure victory over the French came to around five times the nation's total income for 1801.

For almost a decade before the outbreak of war, the British economy grew at rates never before witnessed. World trade boomed in the 1780s when exports recovered a momentum lost for over two decades after 1760, and production continued to advance for almost a decade after the outbreak of war in 1793. Perhaps upswings in the British economy from 1783 to 1802 and in the United States from 1839 to 1859 represented long cycles of accelerated growth which might have persisted in the absence of war. At least two other hypotheses on connections between war and long-run progress should, however, be entertained. First, and because there are sound historical reasons to expect upswings to give way to downswings, both wars possibly had only a marginal impact. Second, perhaps war sustained even higher rates of economic growth. The task of the historian – which is to analyse and, where possible, to measure the impact of war on *long-run* economic progress – is not easy because the problem involves speculation about a plausible pace and pattern of economic growth without war. Facts are difficult enough to establish without discussing what *might* have happened. Nevertheless, counter-factual reasoning is implicit in the question: to investigate the effects of war presupposes some hypotheses about the plausible growth paths of America and Britain untroubled by civil and international strife.

There is no mistaking the *immediate* impact of war on the growth rates of American and British per capita incomes. During the war years these rates declined below pre-war trends and then accelerated over the post-war period. Dislocation and destruction contingent upon war reduces the capacity of economies to maintain steady growth in the production of goods and services, and phases of rapid recovery often succeed the termination of hostilities. Alas, it is far more difficult to gauge gains and losses for several decades after the war. Something can be measured. For example, military action destroys and damages the capacity of labour and productive assets to produce future output. Given information on the expected life of workers and capital, it may be possible to estimate the values of streams of future output lost through warfare.

The gloomy data now available for these two wars have indicated that destruction and damage to people and property by the Civil War tended to be more serious. Losses of manpower from death and wounds formed a smaller proportion of Britain's rapidly growing supplies of labour. Economists are, moreover, inclined to observe that the Englishmen killed or maimed on active service in the French wars came overwhelmingly from among the unskilled: those whose potential contribution to economic growth was the least valuable and most easily replaced. And while the Civil War raged on American territory, enemy forces hardly set foot on British soil. Their depredations were confined to the colonies and to ships on the high seas, and did not equal the property confiscated by British forces from France and her allies.

Imputation and measurement of the effects of war are so difficult to handle that historians prefer to make the simple (but useful) assumption that, without war, countries would continue to grow at some specified pre-war rate of advance. They can then measure differences between consumption per head, advancing hypothetically through time at the pre-war rate, and actual consumption achieved over war and post-war periods. Their calculations do not 'measure' the losses or gains attributable to war, but simply offer discussable orders of magnitude.

Their estimates suggest that during the war years the living standards of the English and Americans declined by 16 to 20 per cent below normal, and it took just over a decade of 'recovery and reconstruction' to restore consumption to *predicted* levels. Measured in this way, the 'Yankee' burden imputable to the Civil War disappeared by 1878. But for the South the immediate and long-term costs of the conflict stand way above anything experienced by their antagonists. The Confederacy, which contained 27 per cent of America's population and received 20 per cent of its national income, carried 65 per cent of the costs (short and long term) of the Civil War. For white southerners alone, the economic costs of war represented an enormous and persistent loss of real income. No wonder the Civil War is still regarded as a major catastrophe for the South.

These calculations of the burden of war, we must recall, rest on the critical assumption that without war economic growth in America and Britain would have proceeded at pre-war rates. Such numbers are useful. They help us think concretely about otherwise vague notions about the costs of war. They structure our arguments around illuminating attempts to refine and qualify disputable estimates. They also cajole us towards two general conclusions: first, war exercised a limited influence upon the economies of Britain and the northern United States; second, the Civil War severely restrained economic progress in the South. But major historical assumptions underlying such calculations need to be analysed. For the northern states and for Britain, historians will need to be convinced that war neither stimulated nor retarded long-term capital formation, industrial production or agricultural development, nor really altered institutions and policies closely connected with economic growth over the nineteenth century. Several historians have claimed that the high growth rate achieved by the South from 1839 to 1859 was not sustainable.

The South

The high cost of war

Although the southern economy did not stagnate, it suffered a catastrophe in the 1860s and persistent retardation compared to the rest of
America thereafter. During the war the region's living standards plum-
meted, and as late as 1914 standards remained about 50 per cent below
the level that might have been reached *if* consumption had continued to
grow at the rate observed for two decades before secession. Behind these
statements lies a 'counter-factual' South untouched by warfare where
slavery, plantations and other institutions survived and international
demand for cotton continued to expand at the rates enjoyed by southern
agriculture for decades before secession.

Just to expose the historical premises behind estimates of its burden
is to raise almost all relevant arguments about the long-run impact of war
on the South. How serious was damage from warfare, fought largely on
southern territory? How long could slave plantations have survived? What
effects on economic growth might be imputed to their demise and to the
emancipation of slaves? Finally, was world demand for cotton likely to
grow at a constant rate to 1914? My third question implicitly separates the
legacy of slavery from the legacy of war – a separation which raises insolu-
ble problems. Historians might agree that slavery had to end some time
before the twentieth century, but when and how becomes crucial for any
assessment of a war which did, in fact, bring about its abolition in 1866.
My fourth question distinguishes the impact of war from the growth of
international demand for cotton. Manufacturing industries normally
expand in familiar ways: phases of rapid expansion tend to be succeeded
by deceleration when their markets become saturated or when they have
exploited the available potentialities of cost-reducing innovations. Cotton
textiles certainly developed along this familiar growth path. By the 1860s
and after 70 years of expansion, the growth rate of British and European
cotton industries decelerated when their potential for further improvements in productivity diminished. World demand for the South's leading
cash crop was, it appears, destined to slow up. The cotton boom which
had persisted unabated from 1802 to 1860 (and had carried per capita
incomes in the old South close to northern standards) was not sustainable.

Warfare

Federal troops certainly destroyed farm buildings, fences and equipment
and decimated livestock. Tales of devastation (exemplified by Sherman's
infamous march through Georgia) are graphic testimony to the horrors
of war. Recent research is not inclined, however, to attribute significant
long-term effects to the destruction of capital. Farm inputs and social over-
head capital (particularly railroads) seem to have been repaired soon
after the war. Livestock populations took decades to replenish, but given
the sharp reduction in slave labour supplies available for the cultivation
of cash crops, no overall shortage of mules and horses emerged to reduce
the productivity of farmers. Modern economic evidence contradicts the
myth of a prostrate South with its recovery impeded by shortages of land
and capital, and workstock (equipment, animals, etc.) damaged or

destroyed by military action. Of course, the *immediate* impact of warfare can only be described as serious, but the diminished capacity of the South for sustained growth must be attributed mainly to the demise of slavery.

Emancipation

Speculation on the emancipation of slaves by peaceful agreement seems fruitless, but immediate and long-term costs of their freedom flowed from the defeat of the South. For slave owners the point is obvious because they lost (without compensation) a property right worth nearly $3 billion, and before the war southern whites had expropriated up to half the output produced by their slaves. Although the direct impact of emancipation in 1866 affected not more than 40 per cent of all white families resident in the South, the 'multiplier effects' generated by reduced expenditures of slaveholders spread the effects of abolition among a majority of white southerners.

Not all whites suffered. Small farmers presumably welcomed the demise of larger and more efficient slave plantations. We must also be clear that the transfer of a property right is not equivalent to a loss of productive capital. Emancipation simply accorded slaves legal rights to the full fruits of their own labour. Since their skills and capacity for work remained unimpaired, that represented a massive transfer of income from slave owners to freed men and women and not an immediate loss of wealth and income for southern society as a whole. Nevertheless, this reallocation of potential earning power to ex-slaves did not imply that the black workforce of the post-war South continued to labour nearly as productively as it had under slavery.

Land tenure and agricultural credit in the post-war South

Black people certainly gained from emancipation. Their incomes and working conditions improved markedly compared with slavery. Nevertheless the post-war settlement which provided ex-slaves with 'nothing' but freedom also depressed their productivity below pre-war levels. After the Civil War the American government did nothing to reform the South's system of property rights and institutions for the allocation of productive resources. That failure deprived blacks (and poor whites) from obtaining access to cultivable land, workstock, implements, credit and other inputs (even public education) on terms which might have increased their incomes. Post-war construction not only left blacks in a position of deprivation compared to whites, but also restrained the capacity of the southern economy for growth.

Slaves owned no property and possessed few skills when abolition turned them onto the market to compete with whites (who were bitter from their loss of human wealth and who soon gained control of institutions for legal repression). Perhaps it might appear ahistorical to expect a state, and one which had just fought a costly war to maintain the Union, to do more for ex-slaves. After all, the United States offered nothing but freedom to its poor white immigrants. Nevertheless, critics of the peace settlement see it as a missed opportunity to compensate black people for the income expropriated from them under slavery by transferring rights to land as well as labour to freed men and women. Congress discussed land redistribution, but the idea was quickly abandoned by the president. Instead, a new tenure system emerged as a functional solution to the presence of an immobile but rapidly growing population of black (but also poor white) landless labourers, without access to credit or means to acquire even rudimentary skills in farm management. Out of numerous local and particular bargains between this 'free' proletariat and those who not only owned cultivable land but also possessed other indispensable means to carry on commercial agriculture – such as farm implements, workstock, seed, provisions and credit – there evolved a variety of agreements which constituted the reconstructed institutions of southern agriculture. That system exhibited features which distinguished it sharply from the family farms dominant in other regions of the United States. Out of the old plantations, southern landowners created thousands of small-scale farms which they rented to ex-slaves (and poor whites) for the most part under sharecropping contracts. That 'free enterprise' solution certainly provided employment for a mass of landless black workers, and maximized returns for those who leased land and capital to them. But sharecropping operated to restrain the development of larger and more capital-intensive farms. Only that progression could really lift the incomes of this largely black agrarian proletariat above the lowest rungs of the economic ladder. Perhaps the foremost disadvantage of sharecropping was that it catered for the natural desires of the young to marry early and cultivate their own holdings. Under-equipped farms gave them every incentive to procreate and maximize the size of family workforces. Finally, their status as black people located at the bottom of the social scale rendered it difficult for them to obtain access to loans or working credit on any but unfavourable terms. They borrowed at exorbitant rates of interest. They procured the food and farm inputs essential to carry their families through the seasons on credit from white storekeepers, who took advantage of their political and market power to mark up prices to a point which seems to constitute extortion. The system almost certainly encouraged excessive and ultimately unprofitable specialization on the export of cotton.

Civil War and the northern economy

Gains from war

In contrast to the historiography of a prostrate South, there is a tradition of emphasizing the gains the North derived from victory in 1865. That tradition emanates from historians disposed to perceive events as glamorous and tragic as the Civil War as a 'watershed' in the economic life of the nation. For economic development so many influences are at work that all claims made for the beneficent effects of war on structural change must be specified and their contribution to the growth rate measured. Above all, the appraisal of war must be conducted within a framework which compares its costs and benefits with other policy options available at the time. For example, any scheme to fully compensate white southerners for the emancipation of slaves would have cost northern taxpayers far less than the war. Alternatively (alas, with hindsight), it is difficult to perceive how permanent secession of Slave States from the Union might have damaged the North. Although the economic implications of an independent Confederacy are difficult to adumbrate, there can be no presumption that the Union, which survived a costly attempt to break it up, constituted an optimal polity for long-run economic progress. Southerners who supported secession would certainly agree. Trade and other economic relations between the North and an 'independent South' would certainly have survived secession (think of Canada and the US). Northern businessmen looking back at the enormous bills shouldered to maintain a United States and considering the damage military action and the abrupt abolition of slavery inflicted on their markets in the South may well have wondered about alternative polices. As time went on (and federal taxes collected from citizens of the 'affluent' North helped to sustain living standards in a 'depressed' South), any *material* gains from prosecuting the Civil War receded in the perceptions of Americans into the realms of the problematical – until, that is, generations later historians reminded Americans that the 'triumph of capitalism' owed something tangible to the victory of the North.

Industry and agriculture

That reminder from historians neglected to set the Civil War in a long-run context and failed to quantify its costs and benefits for industry and agriculture. For example, a majority of statistical indicators mark out the years 1861–5 as a period of retardation compared either with the 1850s or with the post-war decades. While the woollen industry enjoyed prosperity from military orders, cotton textiles slumped for want of raw material. Boots and shoes made in Massachusetts lost markets in the South. Iron utilized to manufacture small arms amounted to only a tiny fraction of iron embodied in railroad lines laid down from 1856 to 1860; railroad investment declined sharply during the war years. So did residential construction, another consumer of basic iron. Thus, although pig iron production held up, this major industry experienced nothing like its rate of increase from 1866 to 1880. Apart from woollens and watches, it is difficult to detect any *industry-wide* examples of accelerated growth from 1860 to 1865. Indeed in so far as purchases by the Union army and navy substituted for normal civilian consumption of processed food, clothing, buildings and other manufactured goods, it is difficult to see how the reallocation of income from taxpayers to the armed forces could expand aggregate demand for industrial goods.

Furthermore, there seem to be few organizational or technical improvements which might be associated directly with the Civil War. Pressure from a gun company led Joseph Brown to develop the universal milling machine in 1862. Military demand prompted McKay's improvement to the machine for stitching soles to the uppers of boots. In general, the Civil War generated few innovations, even in weaponry. Basically, it distracted scientists and technologists from pursuit of more utilitarian objectives.

Although agricultural advance had begun earlier and its origins must be found in the abundant supplies of land, immigrant labour, capital and transportation available to the rural economy (plus access to expanding European markets), the war did stimulate northern and western farming. Urban food prices jumped about 70 per cent above pre-war levels. Inflation encouraged farmers to shift more rapidly into commercial agriculture, while wartime labour shortages prompted them to mechanize. The output of farm implements and machinery increased by 110 per cent from 1848 to 1859, by 140 per cent from 1859 to 1869, and by 95 per cent from 1869 to 1879.

Financial and fiscal policies

Greater encouragement to investment and production probably flowed from the methods used by the Union government to fund the war effort. Inflationary finance augmented the profits of private business as their wage bills lagged behind rising prices. But not for long and in no measure could 'windfall' profits from wartime inflation make up for the massive diversion of funds away from private investment into the coffers of the army. Government demands for loanable funds undoubtedly stimulated the propensity to save and invest among Americans. Those same demands promoted the spread and efficiency of banks and other financial intermediaries to collect and allocate savings. Congressional regulation of banks promulgated in 1863–4 encouraged flows of funds from the rural economy into the urban and industrial sectors. Since there seems to be no good case to posit significant spin-offs from the activities of the state in the capital market of the United States, the largest long-term gain from financial policy must be found in the consistent efforts made for more than two decades after the war to redeem a national debt accumulated to hold the Union together. That policy transferred income from taxpayers to bond holders and affected interest rates. Its effects are difficult to measure, and the most recent exercise in quantitative history suggests it may have added up to 2 per cent to national income for 1890 – hardly compensation for the destruction and neglect of the capital stock for five years in the 1860s.

One of the enduring consequences of the Civil War was to raise and maintain the level of protection against manufactured imports into the United States. American tariff history is summarized as high and rising duties from 1816 to 1832, succeeded by a series of reductions which brought down the average rate on dutiable imports from around 62 per cent in 1830 to 20 per cent in 1860. Tariffs imposed to finance military expenditure and to offset excises imposed on domestically produced commodities for the same purpose pushed the rate to nearly 50 per cent in wartime. It remained in the 40 to 50 per cent range for the rest of the century. Victory for the North reversed a tendency towards free trade from 1832 to 1860 which had been strongly supported by the South. Thereafter successive Republican administrations favoured protection and rarely hesitated to impute the successful development of particular sectors of manufacturing to their policy. There is, however, no evidence that northern industry required the levels of protection it enjoyed from 1860 to 1914 or that the distributive effects of tariffs (which transferred income from American consumers to industrialists and their employees) really 'jacked up' rates of saving investment. Furthermore, there can be no presumption that protection promoted an allocation of resources which in the long run fostered higher levels of per capita income – even for the northern states.

War and the British economy, 1793–1815

Estimating the cost

The modern consensus (based on hindsight) tends to regard the French wars as an interlude in the irreversible progress of the Industrial Revolution. War was not powerful enough to arrest, merely to slow up, the long-term growth of the economy. Unfortunately the rate of steady growth that might be predicted for a quarter of a century after 1792 is disputable. Historians have questioned the capacity of an economy prone to cyclical depression to sustain growth at the rate observed from 1783 to 1792. Their point is well taken because the marked acceleration in growth rates observed for that decade might be depicted as recovery from the American War of Independence, destined to peter out as the economy ran into diminishing returns from population pressure.

Historical evidence supports the view that by 1783 the technology required for expansion in several industries (especially textiles, metals and steam power) had become commercially viable. Advances in transportation and agriculture could also proceed within well-defined technological and economic frontiers. What seems to have been required for steady growth was a favourable economic environment of the kind stimulated by investment and the recovery of trade in the 1780s. Over that decade exports and private capital formation accelerated rapidly to replace the 'wasteful' military expenditures of 1776–83 as sources of demand for domestically produced goods and services. Nevertheless, three problems had emerged as potential impediments to sustained expansion in demand: population pressure, the upswing in food and raw material prices, and possible restraints on the expansion of money and credit to fund private investment expenditure.

Unless historians are prepared to argue that conflict with France interrupted a potential acceleration or deceleration in the pre-war rate of growth of income per capita, it is possible to offer a plausible calculation to suggest its long-term consequences were slight. Consumption standards declined well below predicted levels during the war years. But only ten years after Waterloo, actual levels of consumption were about the same as what might have been predicted if the wars had never happened. At that point, the cost of war disappears. Once again the historical assumptions behind these discussable numbers must be debated in detail.

Financial and fiscal policy

Before the war the state spent around £7 million a year to provide for the defence of the realm and its civil government. By 1813–17 expenditure (in real terms) on Britain's war effort came to five times that sum. Yes, the British navy and the army succeeded from time to time in expropriating foreign ships, weapons, food, forage and other property, but that represented a negligible proportion of the resources used to defeat France. And the same comment applies to the loans made by foreigners towards the war effort. But a far more serious qualification to the obvious deduction that the French wars must, therefore, have operated to depress British consumption standards and investment emerges from a Keynesian-inspired view that the eighteenth-century economy required higher and continuous injections of government expenditure to maintain full employment. If this hypothesis proves correct, *some* share of military expenditure 1793–1817 was financed by taxes levied upon incomes and money borrowed from savings created by the rise of expenditure stimulated by war. The prosecution of war, by raising the overall level of demand for goods, services and loans, undoubtedly absorbed manpower and resources which might have been unemployed. In this sense and to some unmeasurable extent, the war paid for itself. This ostensibly paradoxical hypothesis not only can be backed from statistics of the numbers of unemployed maintained by poor relief in wartime, but finds still stronger support from the rather limited rise in the rate of interest on a vastly expanded national debt. The interest rate moved from just below 4 per cent before the war to just under 5 per cent during the conflict, despite inflation and a continuous rise in private investment from just over £11 million a year from 1781 to 1790, to £17 million (in real terms) from 1801 to 1810. Although the rate at which private capital accumulated slowed down compared to the 1780s (and to the three decades which followed Waterloo), the wartime achievement appears as something remarkable. How did a society spending so much money on war manage to maintain such a high rate of private capital investment?

Part of the answer must be that war against revolutionary France for 'the defence of property' elicited a patriotic response from those classes persuaded to lend higher proportions of their incomes to an aristocratic government mobilizing military forces to defend their social positions. They certainly had a great deal at stake. The ownership of property of all kinds (but particularly land) was highly concentrated. Over the second half of the eighteenth century its distribution had probably grown even more unequal. Among the affluent, considerable potential for savings and impersonal investment may have remained latent, and required only the stimulus provided by war and a modest rise in interest rates to attract funds into consols, exchequer bills, annuities and other paper securities sold by the Treasury. Ministers did everything to arouse patriotism and to maintain confidence. Apart from minor panics in 1797 and 1805, investors kept faith that the British constitution (with its national debt) would survive conflict with France and that the Royal Navy would continue to protect their wealth from enemy invasion.

Meanwhile (and this is the major argument) William Pitt and his successors at the Exchequer pursued tax and monetary policies well designed to maintain levels of private capital formation and to facilitate loans to the state at one and the same time. The strategy pursued by the government to finance this war imposed an immediate and major share of the burden onto the consumption standards of the population at large and encouraged private capital formation to go ahead. Investment was reduced slightly but by no means 'crowded out' by government demand for loanable funds. But private consumption fell sharply, from over 82 per cent of national expenditure from 1788 to 1792, to around 72 per cent from 1793 to 1812, and was depressed right down to 64 per cent during the closing stages of the conflict. Government 'squeezed' consumption in two ways: obviously by heavy taxes and indirectly through an inflationary monetary policy.

For previous wars in the eighteenth century, governments borrowed the money required for additions to military expenditure and imposed taxes simply to pay interest on the debt thereby created. The 'burden' of these wars fell largely upon future generations of taxpayers, and wartime borrowing operated to crowd out private investment. Pitt's departure from this traditional strategy imposed a much larger share of the cost of war upon his own generation, and by deliberately restricting the sums borrowed by the state, he left more funds available for private investment. Furthermore, a high proportion of the additional taxation levied was utilized to pay interest on the national debt, which still accumulated rapidly from £290 million to £862 million. Between 1793 and 1815 the government raised nearly £607 million as extra (or war) taxes and transferred £236 million to its creditors as interest payments and a further £176 million as sinking fund repayments of debt. Transfers from taxpayers at large to the government's creditors can be depicted as the reallocation of income from social groups with lower propensities to save and invest to a more affluent rentier class with higher propensities to reinvest in paper securities.

During the years 1797 to 1819 the rapid growth of the banking system and the extension of its functions as purveyors of loans and credit to the state and to private business alike were greatly assisted by the monetary policy pursued by governments after 1797. Up to that year (indeed during all previous years in the eighteenth century), supplies of bank credit available to the government and the rest of the British economy had been constrained by the Bank of England's obligation to redeem its notes and other obligations in gold on demand (known as convertibility). That legal requirement had effectively restrained the growth of the money supply within flexible but nevertheless defined limits.

In 1797 (after nearly two years of procrastination), the cabinet refused to accede to the bank's attempt to restrict credit to the government on the grounds that its gold reserve was insufficient to meet potential demands for the redemption of outstanding notes. Pitt simply suspended that legal obligation and thus secured the bank's unequivocable financial support for the war effort. While successive cabinets left its directors free to regulate supplies of credit to the private sector, ministers issued no guidelines on how the bank should manage the money supply in wartime. Their advice and actions showed the cabinet to be consistently in favour of a liberal extension of credit to support the demands of the private sector for funds, and to be unperturbed by warnings from the opposition about the consequences of an inflationary expansion in supply of money.

For a government anxious to borrow as easily and cheaply as possible, the suspension of convertibility held clear advantages. For industry and agriculture the gains from a flexible supply of cheap bank loans were no less obvious. London and country banks could expand credit secure in the knowledge that the Bank of England would impose no sharp contraction in the money supply as long as war lasted. Within these 'liberal' financial conditions, the scope and profitability for banking and other financial institutions improved. Dealings in an ever-growing volume of public securities constituted a secure and profitable basis for the expansion of the entire financial system. That development, together with the liberal monetary policy which underpinned it, are clearly important factors behind the remarkably high levels of private investment during the war years. But for social groups (like the majority of workers) whose incomes lagged behind rising prices, the monetary policy pursued after

1797 represented yet another form of 'taxation' on their standard of living.

Agriculture and industry

For well over a century agriculture had become steadily more productive. Signs of renewed and more rapid growth became apparent in the 1780s as a response to demands from a growing population (moving towards towns and industrial employment). As food and raw material prices rose, landowners began to invest more in improvements to their property, and from a depressed level the pace of enclosure picked up again after 1785. These tendencies intensified during the years 1793 to 1815, regarded by contemporaries and historians alike as a period of prosperity for agriculture despite runs of poor seasons and high taxes.

Several circumstances contingent upon war contributed to its development. Agricultural prices advanced at an unprecedented rate, and certainly more rapidly than the prices of industrial goods and services. That marked shift in the terms of trade between agriculture and other sectors of the economy added to the incomes of landowners and farmers. They could purchase not only more manufactured consumption goods (textiles) but also farm inputs (metal goods, bricks, coal, etc.) at falling real prices to them. For several English counties labourers' wage rates lagged behind prices of primary produce for most years of the war – again exemplifying the tendency of wartime inflation to transfer income from wages towards profits and rents. Investment in enclosure, land drainage, buildings and rural roads was also assisted by easy credit and by a lag in the costs of these forms of capital formation behind rising grain and beef prices.

Agriculture responded positively to these incentives. Its output went up. Gross annual investment expenditures from 1791 to 1820 rose well above levels maintained before the war and over the post-Waterloo decades of agricultural depression. Parliament gave sanction to enclose nearly three million acres of land between 1793 and 1815, roughly one-half million acres more than had been enclosed for six decades before hostilities began. About one-third of this land represented acres previously uncultivated. During the war landowners consolidated land into large farms, drained and fertilized infertile land, asserted their legal rights to scrub and waste and common land on the fringes of villages, and extended the margin of cultivation. Except for disastrous seasons like 1801 and 1811, agriculture produced just about enough to feed the country's rapidly growing population.

The years from 1793 to 1815 appear as an interlude in the long-term growth of agriculture when the stimulus of rapidly rising prices impelled a somewhat conservative sector of the British economy to push out the frontier of cultivation and increase the rate of growth of production. Once up onto a higher production curve, landowners and farmers reacted to the declining prices of the post-war era politically and economically. Politically they mobilized parliamentary pressure to reduce their tax burdens and, apart from the tariffs on imported wheat, supported liberal tendencies towards a *laissez-faire* state. Economically they innovated and through reductions in costs attempted to retain the prosperity enjoyed during the wars with France. In retrospect that war might be presented as a fortunate stimulus which helped to avoid the tendency of a sluggish agricultural sector to run into diminishing returns and thereby slow up the long-term progress of an urban industrial economy.

The effects of war on industry are less clear cut. For seventeen years preceding the conflict with France, industry had developed in periods of war and recovery from war with the American colonists and their allies. After 1793 not only did factors unconnected with military policy (such as population growth and the diffusion of improved technology) continue to influence the rate and pattern of industrial development, but the imputable impact of war varied widely from one industry to another. Finally, the data on output and investment required for precise analysis hardly exists.

For nearly a quarter of a century after 1793 industrialists seem to have been less constrained than we might expect by the fiscal and monetary policies pursued by the government to prosecute war. Their workforce (particularly supplies of skilled labour) was not seriously denuded by the recruitment of adult males into the forces of the Crown. In some industries (building materials, iron, metal products, hosiery and woollens and leather) there is evidence of a wartime wage lag which may have redistributed income from workers to their employers. War affected each industry in certain specific ways. First, the government levied taxes upon its inputs and outputs, or the chancellor taxed products which were competitive with, or complementary to, a particular manufactured commodity. Second, some industries welcomed military orders, but that stimulus may have reduced supplies and increased prices for other industries. For example, basic iron delivered to gunfounders could be 'at the expense' of nailmakers. Finally, interruptions to imports could both stimulate and restrain domestic output. Obstacles to exports invariably depressed an industry's production.

On average the rate of growth for industrial production proceeded more rapidly during the 1780s and 1820s than it did during the war years, but the gap between the pre-war and wartime growth rate does not seem large. Comparisons at this level of aggregation tell us very little, however, about the impact of war itself. All I can feasibly do is to distinguish industries where available evidence suggests that the balance of influences flowing from wartime taxation, military expenditures and dislocations to foreign markets generated some positive stimulus to production, from industries where similar effects appear negative or at best neutral. Any real answer to this question lies in largely unwritten histories of major British industries.

Just a handful of industries may have been hurt by taxes imposed to finance the war. Building and construction, malt, brewing, spirits, salt and firms processing tropical foodstuffs (particularly sugar) suffered from taxes and/or interruptions to supplies of imported raw materials. Shipbuilding, iron and armaments enjoyed stimulus from military demand. Several major industries (including iron, metallurgical products, woollens, linens, candles, soap, leather, etc.) experienced limited additions to the taxes they paid, as well as rising costs of imported raw materials. It cannot be maintained that the growth of such industries as cotton, silk and paper was seriously held back by taxes or by higher costs of imported goods. Despite a frenetic search for revenue, fiscal policy (designed to avoid burdening manufacturing industry with taxes on raw materials) continued to allow iron, coal, salt, stone, soap and other items used by manufacturing enterprise (together with internal transportation) to remain relatively free from duties.

Apart from coal and lead, industries could escape taxation on the output they exported. As levies on commodities delivered for domestic consumption rose in wartime, incentives to sell outside the home market increased, and for several industries (particularly for salt, glass, paper, cotton and silk) the share of output sold abroad went up. Encouragement to exports and discouragement to industrial imports (long built into taxation policy) intensified under pressure of the long wars with France and did not relax until long after Waterloo. Protection for all varieties of textiles, metallurgy, glass and industries processing domestic grain and animal products (brewing, spirits, candles and soap) rose during these years. British industry hardly needed heightened levels of protection, which persisted for some four decades after 1793. But revenue requirements certainly had the effect of diminishing sales of some residual imports of industrial commodities on the home market, and thereby made some addition to the profits and investible surplus which accrued to Britain's industrialists.

Tariffs compensated for the wartime income tax. Before 1799 profits from industrial and commercial enterprise escaped from taxes almost entirely. Levies assessed on the property of more affluent groups in British society fell upon the ownership of land, houses, carriages, horses and the employment of servants. Only to a limited degree did such taxes touch industrial or commercial profits. During the war when progressive taxes levied upon the expenditure patterns of landed gentlemen (horses, carriages, servants, dogs, armorial bearings) increased rapidly, Parliament also agreed to a comprehensive income tax. In 1799 Pitt's innovation brought merchants and industrialists into a tax net which they had previously evaded. But administrative difficulties in taxing profits (compared to rents from real property or interest paid on the national debt) indicates they probably contributed less than an 'equitable' share of this new tax. The income tax (levied at a flat rate) did not seriously erode their capacity to reinvest in transport, industry, trade and other growing sectors of the economy. In 1816 commercial, industrial and landed interests united and forced Liverpool's administration to repeal this hated tax.

Although the government's 'squeeze' on private consumption depressed demand for industrial goods, such macro effects are not easy to analyse. Taxes and loans detracted from household expenditures on manufactured goods, but that negative influence could have been offset by increased government demand for industrial commodities. Until historians construct a complete breakdown of military expenditures from 1793 to 1815, it is impossible to say where in the economy *the balance* of the budgetary process might reside. Meanwhile, there can be no presumption that money taxed or borrowed from British citizens and then spent by the army and navy really augmented total demand for industrial goods. International conflicts in the eighteenth century were not nearly so capital or technology intensive as modern warfare. Weapons remained simple. Ships (and ordnance) constitute the only really expensive capital goods utilized by military forces of the day. Armies walked on their feet and fought on their stomachs. To keep them in the field or at sea, what soldiers and sailors required above all was food, together with a modicum of durable warm clothing. Probably most of the money spent by the armed services went on victuals and clothing. If that is the case, then agriculture may have played a larger role than industry in sustaining the forces of the Crown against the French Revolution. Two centuries ago war did not presage any substantial reallocation of demand towards industry or require any massive redeployment of capital and labour into the manufacturing of goods for the armed services. Where that occurred on any scale (namely in iron, shipbuilding and small arms), the capacity and skills created became redundant or excessive for several years after the war. Depression then afflicted these industries until their long-term development readjusted to normal demands from a peacetime economy.

Foreign trade

Historians agree that the significance of exports for the British economy rose markedly from 1783 to 1802, when the ratio of exports to national income doubled to reach 18 per cent. Over the last two decades of the century something like a quarter of the addition to national output and 40 per cent of the increment to industrial production took the form of commodity exports. Thereafter exports declined, falling to 11 per cent of national income by 1841. 1802 appears as a turning point because for two decades before the short-lived Peace of Amiens exports grew at the exceptional rate of 6 per cent a year. For the rest of the war (indeed until 1826) their growth rate declined to a mere 2.5 per cent a year.

Obviously high rates achieved from 1783 to 1793 represent something of a rebound from the American War of Independence, perhaps from a far longer depression in British trade stretching back to the 1760s. But why should an export boom persist for nine years after the outbreak of war with France? A major part of the answer must be that most of the increment to exports from 1793 to 1802 travelled to the Americas, outside the main theatre of warfare in Europe. Nevertheless, exports to Europe were maintained despite the forcible closure of the markets of France, Spain, Italy and the Netherlands to British goods. Some of these sales substituted for supplies from Europe's own industries dislocated by warfare. Some had been stimulated by demands from foreign armies and navies – even by purchases originating with the forces of France and her co-belligerents. Some part of £22 million of the subsidies transferred by the British government to its allies to field troops against the French found their way back via expenditures on exports, especially woollens and arms.

Perhaps the important factor sustaining European demand for British goods flowed from the exclusion of French, Dutch, Spanish and other hostile ships from international commerce. During the war against revolutionary France, British forces captured French and Dutch colonies in the Caribbean and the Indies. French colonial trade had already suffered seriously from the slave revolt on the plantations of San Domingo in 1791. When the Royal Navy interfered with enemy trade on all sea lanes, an increasing share of the world's carrying trade in slaves, sugar, coffee, spices, raw cotton, tea, dyestuffs, drugs and other colonial produce passed into the hands of British shipping and mercantile interests. London and other British ports also assumed far greater responsibility for the finance and insurance of Europe's imports even when carried in neutral (largely American) ships. Services supplied by British ships, banks, mercantile houses and insurance companies for international trade expanded rapidly as a consequence of war on the high seas. Superior naval power restrained the rise in transaction costs and risks for Britain's commercial and shipping interests well below wartime increases in costs and risks experienced by their European competitors. Profits from international commerce rose and became available as loans to the state and for private investment in the domestic economy. This developing network of British mercantile enterprise promoted the sale of domestic industrial products in Europe and the Americas. The years from 1793 to 1815 marked the final phase for British commerce of a long transition to an apex of undisputed dominance over shipping, banking, insurance and distribution services for the international economy. That transition rested ultimately on sea power but, sustained by liberal monetary policy from 1797 to 1819, had incalculable spin-offs for the development of Britain's ports, financial institutions, economic policies and, above all, export industries.

Up to the Peace of Amiens in 1802–3, war positively assisted in the growth of British exports. But its role must not be exaggerated because technical progress in the spinning sector of cotton textiles (together with the declining cost of raw cotton) represented the *major* impetus behind the upswing in British exports over the long boom from 1783 to 1802. Cotton's share of total exports moved from 6 per cent in 1784–6 to 42 per cent by 1815. Over the first decade of war when cotton exports grew at 17.3 per cent a year, they contributed about 70 per cent of the total addition to exports. That astonishing rise emanated from the cheapness and superiority of British cottons compared to woollens, linens and silks. Everywhere (Britain, Europe and America) substitution of cotton for other materials proceeded rapidly despite the war.

As the pioneer industry and site of new technology, British cotton textiles possessed obvious attractions. But the war reinforced and helped to maintain its advantages on world markets for a longer period than peacetime conditions might have allowed. To begin with, obstacles to trade constrained the diffusion of British machinery to the textile industries of France, Saxony, Switzerland, Catalonia and the Netherlands. Furthermore, when the Royal Navy interrupted supplies of raw cotton, European merchants purchased more readily procurable imports of British fabrics and yarn. After 1815 Europe's cotton industries adapted to Britain's early start, first by weaving imported yarn into cloth and then by establishing mechanized spinning mills. That sequence of post-war import substitution (assisted by tariffs) might well have occurred earlier (certainly in Europe, perhaps in the United States) but for the circumstances of an abnormally long conflict with France which stimulated British merchants and entrepreneurs to invest and to capture an 'inflated' share of the world's cotton textile production. Something akin to this process also occurred in woollens and metallurgy.

Protracted warfare from 1793 to 1815 interrupted and dislocated international trade among the economies of western Europe and the United States. In peaceful years the normal operation of commerce ensured that quasi-monopolistic gains from the deployment of advanced technology in textiles, metallurgy or any other industry did not accrue for long periods to any one national economy. War, together with its aftermath of dislocation, lengthened the time taken by competitive industrial regions of western Europe to catch up with best practice methods of production and to accommodate to Britain's comparative advantages by adjusting their economies to a new international division of labour. By 1792 British industry, shipping, mercantile and financial institutions already possessed a lead over foreign rivals, and the economy stood poised to gain an increasing share of international trade in manufactured goods and commercial services. International conflict particularly over the years 1806–14 (when Napoleon attempted unsuccessfully to close European markets to British exports and services and when the British government entered into conflict with the United States over the rights of neutral shipping) certainly imparted risk, instability and dislocation to the domestic economy. War is never an optimal environment for the development of international commerce, but the short-term costs imposed on British exports must be balanced against visible gains from the seizure of enemy colonies, the capture of the carrying trade, unification with Ireland, and the opening of Latin America to direct trade. Finally, in longer-term perspective, historians will wish to explore the point that war inflicted relatively more damage and costs on the economies of rivals and to consider the idea that naval power provided Britain with an opportunity to seize a greater share of world trade in manufactured goods and commercial services than her undoubted comparative advantages really warranted. Once in position, British industry and commerce built upon the advantages of a lead in the international economy for which they should give some modicum of thanks to the French Revolution.

Conclusion

Counter-factual speculation seems inseparable from discussions of the economic effects of wars. Their immediate impact is possible to gauge, but their long-term consequences are so difficult to specify and measure that historians prefer to assume war usually interrupts economic advance which would have continued at some specified pre-war rate. That assumption needs to be qualified by historical research into periods before, during and after wars. Nevertheless, estimates generated by that assumption prompted us to argue that for the northern states of America and for Britain, if war retarded economic growth while it lasted, neither conflict had a significant impact on long-run development. Losses of capital and manpower seem tragic but not serious. Both British and federal governments pursued financial and fiscal strategies designed to minimize constraints on private investment. On balance, their policies may even have raised long-term rates of saving by regressive taxes and income transfers, by promoting the habit of buying paper securities, and by improving financial institutions. War provided incentives to improve and expand agriculture. On the whole, war hampered the progress of industry. The examples of technical progress and diffusion associated with military procurement seem trivial compared with the constraints, higher taxes and obstacles placed in the way of normal sales at home and abroad. But the British economy almost certainly gained a 'disproportionate' share of the international markets in textiles, metallurgy and commercial services because its vanquished competitors suffered real setbacks in wartime.

Neither North nor South engaged in civil war to achieve economic gains. Even white southerners fought basically to defend a valuable property right in slaves. As a result of defeat, their region (particularly the Deep South) suffered decades of economic deprivation which flowed from the destruction wrought by warfare, from the abrupt abolition of plantation slavery, and from the neglect of the federal government to reconstitute the agrarian institutions of the old South upon a more efficient basis. There can be no question that the failure of the American political system to bring about a peaceful and efficient transition from a slave to a free economy in eleven states of the Union imposed substantial losses on the people of the South for decades after the end of the Civil War. Citizens of the North also suffered a marked decline in their standard of living for nearly two decades after the attack on Fort Sumter. Of course, the war enhanced the power of the North to enact federal legislation in the interests of the Union. Several laws passed during and in the aftermath of the war (related to banks, the public domain, tariffs and contract labour) apparently favoured the interests of an 'industrializing' North over an 'agrarian' South. That dichotomy of interest was never clear cut. Given time and shifts in political power, Congress may well have enacted similar legislation with or without the surrender of the South. Furthermore, the significance of laws and institutions favourable to the 'triumph of capitalism' should not be exaggerated. Even at its height, the power of the South cannot be represented as a shackle on the industrial progress of other regions. Similar agnosticism is surely the most reasonable response to other posited economic advantages derived by the North from the Civil War. On examination they turn out to be a small recompense – a tiny offset towards the huge economic burden borne to free slaves and to hold the Union together. War is never an advantage for economic progress. Sometimes its effects are not as costly as others.

Further reading

Andreano, R. (ed.) (1967) *The Economic Impact of the American Civil War,* Cambridge, Mass., Scheukman Co. Pub.

Ashton, T.S. (1959) *Economic Fluctuations in England, 1700–1800,* Oxford University Press.

Davis, R. (1979) *The Industrial Revolution and British Overseas Trade,* Leicester University Press.

Dickinson, H.T. (ed.) (1989) *Britain and the French Revolution, 1789–1815,* Macmillan.

Digby, A. *et al.* (eds) (1992) *New Directions in Economic and Social History,* vol. 2, Macmillan.

Emsley, C. (1979) *British Society and the French Wars,* Macmillan.

Floud, R. and McCloskey, D. (eds) (1994) *The Economic History of Britain since 1700,* 2nd edn, 3 vols, Cambridge University Press.

Fogel, W. and Engerman, S. (1974) *Time on the Cross,* Boston, Little, Brown & Co, .

Gayer, A.D. *et al.* (1953) *The Growth and Fluctuations of the British Economy, 1790–1850,* Oxford University Press.

O'Brien, P.K. (1988) *The Economic Effects of the American Civil War*, Macmillan.

Ransom, R. and Sutch, R. (1977) *One Kind of Freedom: The Economic Consequences of Emancipation*, Cambridge University Press.

Walton, G. and Shepherd, R. (eds) (1981) *Market Institutions: Economic Progress in the New South*, New York, Academic Press.

Wright, G. (1978) *The Political Economy of the Cotton South*, New York, Norton.

Index

Acknowledgements

Grateful acknowledgement is made to the following sources for tables in this book:

Essay 1.10, *Table 5*, from F. Crouzet, *Explorations in Economic History*, 1980, Economic History Association; Essay 1.11, *Tables 1 and 2*, from R.W. Fogel, *Railroads and American Economic Growth: Essays in Economic History*, 1964, John Hopkins University Press; Essay 1.10, *Table 3*, from R. Davis, *The Industrial Revolution and British Overseas Trade*, 1979, Leicester University Press; Essay 1.10, *Table 2*, from D.C. North, *Growth and Welfare in the American Past: A New Economic History*, 1974, 2nd edn, Prentice-Hall, Inc.; Essay 1.10, *Table 1*, from S.D. Chapman, *The Cotton Industry in the Industrial Revolution*, 1972, Macmillan, London and Basingstoke.